A Will and a Way

Columbia Studies of Social Gerontology and Aging

COLUMBIA STUDIES OF SOCIAL GERONTOLOGY AND AGING
Abraham Monk, General Editor

A WILL AND A WAY

What the United States Can Learn from Canada about Caring for the Elderly

Robert L. Kane
and
Rosalie A. Kane

Columbia University Press
New York

Library of Congress Cataloging in Publication Data

Kane, Robert Lewis, 1940–
A will and a way

(Columbia studies of social gerontology and aging)
Includes index
1. Old age assistance—Canada. 2. Old age assistance
—Canada—Costs. 3. Aged—Home care—Canada.
4. Long-term care facilities—Canada. 5. Health
insurance—Canada. I. Kane, Rosalie A. II. Title.
III. Series.
HV1475.A24 1985   362.6'0971   85-16616
ISBN 0-231-06136-6 (alk. paper)
ISBN 0-231-06137-4 (pa.)

Printed in the United States of America

Columbia University Press
New York and Guildford, Surrey

This book is Smyth-sewn and printed on permanent
and durable acid-free paper.

Acknowledgments

THIS monograph owes its existence to the many people in Canada who shared their information and opinions with us. We are enormously indebted to them all.

For information about Ontario, we thank Diane Anderson, Bill Baine, Ted Ball, Ray Berry, Heather Boon, Bruce Buchanan, Paul Donoghue, Yale Drazon, Marcia Farquar, Les Fazekas, Michael Gain, Paul Gould, Glenn Heagle, Suzanne Herring, David Kennedy, Michaela Kirby, Gordon Kumagai, Penny Palmer, Walter Lumsden, Steve Newroth, Betty Nicholson, Jack Sargeant, Glen Simpson, Gordon Skelhorne, Jerry Villa, Malcolm Walker, and Bob Youtz, all of the Department of Health. We also acknowledge Lawrence Crawford, Janet Rowney, and Dorothy Singer, Department of Community and Social Services; Cromwell Sparling, Ministry of Municipal Affairs; Charles Barnes, Brenda Elias, Maureen Quigley, Ed Segalman, and Dale Taylor, Metropolitan Toronto; Marie Davidson, Jean McIntyre, and Joyce Cayhill, Placement Coordinators from Ottawa, Brockville, and Hamilton, respectively; Judy Campbell, Marie Lund, and Jean Lorimer, from the Home Care Programs in Ottawa, Toronto, and Brockville, respectively; Alan Warren and Barbara Schulman, Ottawa-Carleton District Health Council; Cope Schwenger, University of Toronto; Ron Bayne and Mark Magenheim, McMaster University; Jacques Krasny, Extendicare; John Maynard, Ontario Nursing Home Association; Nicholas Manherz, Ontario Association of Homes for the Aged; Maggie Fietz, Ontario Association of Homemakers Agencies; Patricia Bragan-Spindel and Edward Mitchell, Concerned Friends of Ontario Citizens in Care Facilities; Chris Stewart, Ontario Advisory Council on Senior Citizens; Don dal Bianco, Rest Home Association of Ontario; Peter Simcoe, Ontario Red Cross; and Mrs. Butler, Victorian Order of Nurses. (All affiliations pertain to the time of our last contact; some may have changed subsequently.) Thanks also to Ben Hutzel, Rose Levitan, and Robert Smolkin.

For information about Manitoba, we are indebted to David Pascoe, Kay Thomson, and Evelyn Shapiro, Manitoba Health Services Commission; Sol Schubert and Jim Zaperelli, Manitoba Housing and Renewal; Betty Havens, Provincial Gerontologist; and Neena Chappell and Nora Lou Roos, University of Manitoba. For information about the Continuing Care Program, we thank Enid Thompson, Director, Office of Continuing Care, Trudie Bernard, Lynne Fineman, Yvonne Hrynkiw, Peter Klassen, Sue MacKenzie, Phyllis Olson, Anne Reider, and Isobel Salvail, all Regional Continuing Care Coordinators, and Margaret Mackling of the Victorian Order of Nurses. We also thank geriatric specialists Jack MacDonell and Colin Powell, and Roland Bazinet, administrator of the Fred Douglas Lodge.

For information about British Columbia, we thank Ludo Bailey, Elizabeth Bristowe, Robert Buchanan, Ray Goodacre, Edward Halfrich, Myrna Hall, Myrna Halsall, Barbara Kaminsky, Doris MacKay, Eva MacKay, Diane Ouston, Jerry Reichert, Phil Scott, Don Thompson, and Murette Williams, all associated with the British Columbia Ministry of Health at some time during the course of our study. From the Vancouver Health Department, we thank Tom Cairney, Elaine Campbell, Lillian Hiltz, Sandra MacKenzie, Thelma Moholland, Sally Shivers, Michael Sorochan, David Stott, and Jerome Walter. Other key British Columbia informants included Annette Stark, University of British Columbia; Gloria Gutman, Simon Fraser University; Jane Rosetta, Vancouver Department of Human Resources; Pat Tidball, Pharmacare; Greg Boorman and his staff at the Boundary Long-Term Care Program; Lynn Beattie and Wayne Wright, University of British Columbia Medical Center; David Wooldridge, Royal Jubilee Hospital, Victoria; Edna Galbraith, British Columbia Pri-Care Association; Johannes Van Den Hooven, British Columbia Long-Term Care Association; Francis Brunelle, British Columbia Health Association; Norman Rigby, British Columbia Medical Association; Virginia Langdon, Social Planning and Review Council of British Columbia, and Jonathan and Christine Wisenthal.

From a national perspective, many people supplied us with invaluable help. We thank M. McNaught, P. Michaelson, N. N. Papove, Mrs. Prasada, G. B. Rosenfeld, L. W. Rehmer, all of Health and Welfare Canada; Susan Fletcher and Leroy Stone, Statistics Canada; Mireille Badour and Lola Wilson, Office of Aging; A.

Margery Boyce, Department of Veterans Affairs; Sylvia Goldblatt, Canada Housing and Mortgage; and Francine Beauregard, National Advisory Council on Aging.

In addition to those mentioned by name, many others spoke with us on the telephone, often at length, and described long-term care operations at local levels. Many people sent us materials on the strength of a phone call. These contributions are deeply appreciated.

From The Rand Corporation, we are indebted to research assistants Sharon Arnold and Sandra Riegler, as well as Janice Jones and Jessie Cho, who typed the manuscript through its various iterations.

We owe special thanks to those who carefully examined and commented on earlier drafts of the manuscript. Art Daniels, Paul Gould, Myrna Hall, Betty Havens, Barbara Kaminsky, David Kennedy, Betty Nicholson, Margaret Redston, L. W. Rehmer, Cope Schwenger, Michael Sorochan, Enid Thompson, Kay Thomson, and Marilyn Willis all reviewed the manuscript and made helpful detailed comments from the perspective of knowledgeable Canadians. Professor Emeritus Robert Morris of Brandeis University reviewed the manuscript in detail from a United States perspective. All of these people enhanced the accuracy of the book, but we take responsibility for any lingering errors.

Finally, our deep thanks to the Henry J. Kaiser Family Foundation and to Dr. Bernard Nelson, project officer, for their financial support of the study. Had the Foundation not been convinced it was worthwhile to examine long-term care in Canada, this book would not have been written.

Robert L. Kane
Rosalie A. Kane

Contents

Figures

Tables

A Will and a Way

CHAPTER 1
Why Study Long-Term Care in Canada?

MOST Canadian provinces offer long-term care benefits that are considerably more generous than those offered in the United States. From the perspective of federal and state policy in the United States, the very existence of these Canadian benefits and programs raises compelling questions. How do Canadian provinces afford universal long-term care entitlements? Who really uses them and how do the benefits fit in with other health and social services? How satisfied are consumers and providers? And, above all, what can we learn from the Canadian experience that would help us develop reasonable public long-term care policies in the United States?

This monograph describes the evolution of long-term care in three provinces: Ontario, Manitoba, and British Columbia. The universally insured long-term care programs launched there pinpoint useful lessons for the United States. At a time when American policymakers are reeling under the actual and anticipated costs of the limited public long-term care benefits currently provided, examining the operational programs in Canada is useful. Information about such programs complements the insights that can be gained from demonstration programs in the United States. Although the latter provide crucial data, the artificiality of a demonstration leaves lingering questions about the effects on consumers, providers, and costs if the demonstrated program were to be translated into public policy. With appropriate care to avoid overexuberant extrapolations, we can derive such information from studying operational programs to the north.

What Is Meant by Long-Term Care?

Over the last decade, long-term care has figured prominently in the professional literature and the popular press. Nevertheless, the term eludes definition. When long-term care is studied in one country to draw lessons for another, the definitional problem is magnified.

The Health Care Financing Administration has defined long-term care as "a range of medical and supportive services for individuals who have lost some capacity for self-care due to a chronic illness or condition and who are expected to need care for an extended period" (U.S. DHHS. HCFA 1983:3). The California Long-Term Care Act of 1982 defined it as

> a coordinated continuum of preventive, diagnostic, therapeutic, reha-bilitative, supportive, and maintenance services that address the health, social, and personal care needs of individuals who have re-stricted self-care capabilities. . . [The programs should] promote physical, social, and psychological independence in the least restricted environment.

Such definitions suggest that long-term care includes all traditional health services *plus* extra health-related services that address prob-lems of incapacity. In approaches that embrace such a wide range of medical and social services and even housing, long-term care seems to refer to a population served—i.e., anything done for the chronically functionally impaired—rather than define an array of ser-vices. Operationally, however, long-term care in the United States (and in most countries) is differentiated from other components of the continuum, and refers to specific services designed to fill in blanks for the chronically impaired. In that vein, long-term care has tended to refer to sustained personal care and health-related ser-vices.

Two loosely defined service systems—acute hospital care and pri-mary medical care—although separately funded, intersect with long-term care to provide the comprehensive package of services embodied in most definitions. Yet another system of care—mental health care—is also programmatically differentiated from long-term care, but the boundaries are blurred. Any study of long-term care arrangements must consider reverberations in all sectors that pro-vide service to functionally impaired persons. At the same time, it is counterproductive to denote every health and social service received by an old person as long-term care. This invites a two-class system of acute and primary health care: one for the frail elderly and one for everyone else. On the other hand, it is certainly possible that more effective as well as efficient ways can be developed to get acute medical care to persons already receiving long-term care; in that sense, some separate service streams may be indicated.

For practical purposes, long-term care in the United States has meant two types of services: the nursing home, and its so-called alternatives. All care delivered in a nursing home is considered long-term care, with the possible exception of physicians' direct services to the resident. (In the United States, nursing home care is heavily subsidized by Medicaid, whereas physician services to residents are covered under Medicare.) In the United States, long-term care has also come to connote an array of services that could be developed in the community to serve the nursing home eligible populations—that is, people with restricted self-care capacity. Because the nursing home sector receives the bulk of public long-term care funding, the hope of reducing nursing home use has been a major motivation for establishing and funding community-based programs. This second group of long-term care programs is therefore often characterized as "alternatives to nursing homes." Clearly, however, community-based long-term care has a potential constituency separate from those destined for nursing homes, just as high-quality nursing home care also has a legitimate social purpose despite the availability of community care.

"Alternative" long-term care programs range across health, social service, and even housing. Nursing and housekeeping are core services offered under the nursing home roof, and thus home health and homemaker agencies become major community-based long-term care providers (apart, of course, from an individual's own family and friends). The diverse assortment of other programs that could be called long-term care includes day care, senior multipurpose centers, home-delivered and congregate meal programs, home renovations, protective social services, congregate housing, telephone reassurance service, and transportation. Long-term care even includes case management programs that allocate, coordinate, and/or monitor all the other resources. Services can be mixed and matched to compensate for functional impairment—there is no single formula for community-based long-term care. Community care is, by its nature, more flexible than institutionally based care.

Counterparts to most American institutional and noninstitutional long-term care services are found in Canada. For our study, we took long-term care to mean health, social, and personal care services for elderly persons with restricted self-care capabilities; these services include those designed to diagnose and correct the functional problem, to help people compensate for functional deficits, or to permit maximum feasible independence and dignity despite the functional problems. We especially sought to describe Canadian counterparts to nursing homes, home health programs, other community "alternatives," and case management services.

Rationale for Study

Armed with a definition of long-term care, we return to the reason for the study reported here. *With some interprovince variation, residents of Ontario, British Columbia, and Manitoba have a nonmeans-tested entitlement for long-term care in nursing homes (or the Canadian equivalent residential facility). In British Columbia and Manitoba (and, to a lesser extent, in Ontario) long-term care services at home are also insured or provided by government agencies.* Our purpose was to describe and analyze the ongoing experience of three provinces in implementing their long-term care benefits. We wanted to know how many people used the benefits and how the users were characterized. We wanted to know the costs of the programs and how they were contained. We were interested in how adding nursing home benefits affected the use and costs of other segments of the delivery system—e.g., hospital—and similarly, how expanded home care programs affected nursing home use. We were interested in arrangements to stimulate the desired supply of appropriate services and to monitor their quality. We also wanted to understand the problems that were encountered in the evolution of long-term care programs from the perspectives of provincial policymakers, long-term care providers, and citizens.

Present Long-Term Care in the United States

Our specific questions were prompted by current dilemmas in the United States. These are highlighted by a quick review of how long-term care benefits are organized in the United States, and some of the demonstration efforts that test potential policy reforms. In contrast to the Canadian situation, the insured benefits for long-term care in the United States are sharply limited. The only nonmeans-tested benefits are a circumscribed nursing home care and home health care benefit under Medicare, the health insurance program for the elderly. Medicare long-term care benefits were designed to cover brief convalescent periods in connection with episodes of acute hospitalization rather than to meet prolonged dependency needs. Under Medicare, nursing home care is covered only for "skilled services" and only for 100 days. "Custodial care" is specifically excluded. Similarly, home health care is covered only for skilled services for the homebound, and is further circumscribed by requirements for rehabilitative potential and intermittency of service need. Homemaking is barely covered at all. Elderly persons with long-term care needs that fail to qualify them for reimbursement under Medicare must fend for themselves unless or until their income and assets are depleted to those allowable under Medicaid, the health care financing program for the poor. Medicaid *will* pay for nursing home care for those who are eligible on the basis of financial need, and, depending on the state, it may pay for home health services.

Under Title XX of the Social Security Act (the block-grant Social Service amendments), in-home supportive services may be provided to low-income, vulnerable, older persons. The scope of these programs varies greatly from state to state. Finally, a small amount of in-home services is provided under Title III of the Older Americans Act, which also provides congregate meals and limited day care. Older Americans Act programs, by law, are available regardless of ability to pay but they meet only a small portion of need.

Table 1.1 shows the distribution of public expenditures for selected long-term care programs in the United States in 1978. As it dramatically indicates, most public long-term care dollars went to nursing homes, and most of those were accounted for by Medicaid, the health care program for the indigent. Despite the $7.2 billion

Table 1.1
Public Expenditures for Selected Long-Term Care
Services in 1978
(In $ million)

Program	Nursing Homes	Home Care	Meals	Transportation	Day Care
Medicare	396	548			
Medicaid	7,246	160			
Title XX		481	22	71	
Older Americans Act					
Veterans Administration	218		247	19	34

SOURCE: Adapted from U.S. DHHS, 1981, p. 67.
NOTE: These data are older than one would like, a reflection of the lag-time in gathering summary financial information even from unpublished sources.

that Medicaid spent on nursing home care in 1978, however, all public sources of payment for nursing homes combined amounted to only about half the bill. The remainder was paid by the consumer, with less than 2 percent of that amount covered by private insurance. In contrast, the public expense for *home care* was only a minute proportion of the public investment in nursing home care. Although the dollar amounts have increased, these patterns have persisted into the 1980s.

Home care expenditures are rising rapidly in the wake of changes in hospital financing. Under the impetus of prospective payment, hospitals are strongly motivated to discharge patients. Medicare-financed home health agencies are growing in size and number, with particular growth noted among proprietary firms. In addition, legislation implemented in 1982 permits state Medicaid programs to apply for waivers to offer community-based long-term care services to Medicaid recipients eligible for nursing home placement, provided that the cost of those services does not exceed 75 percent of the cost of nursing home care. Experience with these waivers is currently being evaluated; the benefit, of course, is available only to the Medicaid recipient, and states are moving cautiously into waiver programs because the costs are hard to predict.

The relatively small amounts of public money expended on home care are dwarfed by the private expenditures devoted to care of the

frail elderly at home. The latter amount is difficult to estimate, however, because community-based service is purchased privately from
a large array of providers, including self-employed people, or is
given by unpaid relatives.

At this juncture, United States policymakers face a dilemma. On
the one hand, older persons and their families are dissatisfied with
long-term care for a variety of reasons: high out-of-pocket costs,
low availability of community-based services at any price, and poor
quality of care and life in nursing homes. On the other hand,
despite limitations on benefits, and financial and other hardships for
nursing home users, the astronomical *public* costs of nursing home
care threaten continuance of the system. Furthermore, relentless
demography foretells the expansion of the population over age 75
that is at greatest risk for long-term care! Planners are thus reluctant
to recommend widespread expansion into community-based benefits that might reduce the unpaid care presently provided by family
and friends.

Federal and state authorities are well aware of problems in the
quality of the nursing homes on which so much money is spent.
Indeed, the cost of inspecting the industry in a systematic and
rigorous way and following through with corrective action has been
judged prohibitive. The nursing home industry claims (with some
justification) that meager reimbursement rates militate against major
improvements. The inspection system is widely recognized as both
expensive and insufficient. In 1983 the Institute of Medicine began
a Congressionally mandated study of nursing home regulation. Its
report is expected in July 1985.

Although many nursing homes are thought to be inadequate,
most are full. Underwriting the development of new beds and bearing some of the costs of improved quality would further escalate
expenses. Before marketplace forces could drive poorer nursing
homes out of business, the supply of high-quality homes and community alternatives would need to be increased enormously, and
potential customers (either through their own buying power or with
the help of case managers purchasing on their behalf) would need
better ways to make discriminating decisions at the time of purchase.

Long-Term Care Demonstrations in the United States

To offset that bleak picture, various demonstration projects have experimented with expanded services and/or expanded eligibility criteria for public funding. Such demonstrations have been conducted under waivers of the regular requirements of the Medicare or, more usually, the Medicaid program. Evaluators are studying the cost-effectiveness of various expanded benefits with two general kinds of questions: (1) do the new programs prevent or postpone institutional care and lead to a more appropriate mix of patients being treated in nursing homes? and (2) do the new programs reduce aggregate costs? Some of the demonstrations resemble the programs of Canadian provinces in that an assessment of functional ability as well as, or instead of, a means test is used to determine eligibility for service.

Long-term care demonstrations have been and will continue to be a vital source of information for policy. However, generalizability of their findings is limited by the very nature of demonstrations. Necessarily, they are time-limited and serve a circumscribed population. Early demonstrations in long-term care were plagued by problems in start-up and in enlisting a caseload (Greenberg, Doth, and Austin 1981). Results tended to be equivocal because less than rigorous experimental methods were used to select comparison groups. Sometimes community-based programs look like effective alternatives to nursing homes at first blush, but are later found to be serving a less frail population than those who enter nursing homes (Kane and Kane 1980). Weissert's analysis of a major demonstration under Medicare concluded that homemaking and day care services were additions to, rather than substitutes for, nursing home care (Weissert et al. 1980a, 1980b). In turn, the Weissert study has been criticized on the grounds that the programs established for the demonstration were atypically expensive and not integrated enough into the service system to be selected by the experimental group.

Certainly, no demonstration in the United States has been able to seize total control of access to long-term care services. For example, the ACCESS program in Rochester, New York, has mandated that Medicaid recipients be filtered through a case-management service and has been able to show reduction in nursing home use for that population (Eggert, Bowlyow, and Nichols 1980). But private-pay patients are under no obligation to accept recommendations, and they have not been much influenced by the ACCESS program (Williams 1983).

Perhaps the most ambitious long-term care demonstration, which builds on all its predecessors, is the Long-Term Care Channeling Demonstration (Baxter et al. 1983). Operating in defined communities in ten states, it is using a randomized selection method to test the effects of case management and expanded services on nursing home use, long-term care costs, and other parameters. Despite the constraints of using a circumscribed demonstration project to extrapolate to an operational system, the Channeling Demonstration should generate copious useful information.

Within the rather different constraints of generalizing from one setting to another, we can learn a great deal about operational long-term care programs from the Canadian experiences, which will complement the lessons derived from American demonstrations, including the Channeling Demonstration. The present uneasy adherence to acknowledgedly unsatisfactory policies in the United States makes the timing opportune.

To summarize the current problem in the United States neither consumers nor public payors like what they are getting for their expensive long-term care dollar, yet various reform measures seem to risk even greater runaway costs. Studying long-term care in Canada is particularly timely because the three provinces under scrutiny have made nursing home and home care benefits available without means-testing and with minimal consumer cost-sharing. Those two features are almost heretical in the United States political climate of the early 1980s, yet arguably they may be part of the strategy to hold *down* costs. For this to be possible, however, the provincial governments needed to develop specific strategies to allocate these resources, to encourage their appropriate quality, and to control costs in programs with high natural demand. Communities in the United States on the threshold of long-term care reform can benefit from that experience.

A Note on Terminology

The terminology for long-term care programs in Canada sometimes differs from our own. Even the key term "nursing home" may be used differently or not at all. In Manitoba the term "personal care home" is used instead to refer to all levels of a long-term care facility; in Ontario, three types of residential settings—nursing homes, homes for the aged, and chronic hospitals—shelter persons who in the United States might be in nursing homes. Our test for inclusion as a long-term care program was whether a given program met needs that in the United States would make the person eligible for, or at risk of, nursing home care. Of equal interest was how services such as hospital care, primary medical care, mental health, and even housing affected and were affected by long-term care services.

Table 1.2 offers Canadian analogues to United States terminology. The next chapter discusses the further complexity that arises when we consider levels of institutional care. There, comparing the provinces raises some difficulties because identical language is used different ways. For example, Manitoba uses the term "Personal Care Home" as an umbrella under which four levels of care are

Table 1.2
Analogues to United States Terminology
in the Three Canadian Provinces

United States Terminology	Ontario	Manitoba	British Columbia
Nursing Home LTC facility	Home for the Aged Nursing Home Chronic Hospital[a]	Hostel Personal Care Home Extended Care Unit[a]	Nursing Home Extended Care Unit[a]
Home Health Home Care	Acute Home Care Chronic Home Care Home Support	Continuing Care	Long-Term Care Home Nursing Home Care
Case manager	Home care coordinator Home care case manager Placement coordinator	Care coordinator	Assessor Case manager

[a]We recognize that some states (e.g., Maryland, Massachusetts, and New York) maintain chronic hospitals as entities distinct from Skilled Nursing Facilities. However, the Chronic hospitals in Ontario and the Extended Care Units in British Columbia and Manitoba house virtually all who cannot transfer and therefore serve many people who would be at the high level of the care continuum in SNFs in the United States.

identified. In contrast, British Columbia uses Personal Care (abbreviated P.C.) to connote the lightest, almost residential level of a five-level institutional system.

Population Aging in Canada

Canada confronts a substantial population over 65, now approaching 10 percent. This is a somewhat slower rate of population aging than in the United States (attributed to proportionately heavier immigration of young adults throughout the twentieth century and a slightly stronger baby boom in Canada). However, by the year 2000, when nearly 12 percent of the population will be over 65, the age structure of Canadian society will closely approximate that in the United States. Figure 1.1 illustrates age pyramids for both countries in 1980 and 2000, showing the close similarity in the latter configurations.

As in the United States, the oldest segments of the population over 65 are growing the fastest. Stone and Fletcher (1981) project an annual growth rate of 3 percent per year for the population *over 80* in the next two decades, compared to an annual growth rate of 2 percent for the entire population over 65. The proportion of persons over 80 increases this way until about 2005, at which time members of the baby boom cohorts reach 65 and enter the official "elderly" category. As in the United States, population aging in Canada is uneven, both among and within provinces.

The demographic moral for both countries is that the ranks of those who need health services in general and long-term care in particular will continue to grow. The resources available for such programs depend partly on the ratio of workers to nonproductive members of society. Several kinds of dependency ratios have been calculated to make those predictions in both Canada and the United States. The most common formulas are population-dependency ratios; the youth dependency ratio is calculated by the ratio of youth to adults under 65; the aged dependency ratio is the ratio of persons over 65 to working-age adults; and the total dependency ratio is the sum of the two dependent groups as a proportion of the working age group. (Some variation is created by the assumptions about the age at which youth enter the labor force.) By this crude

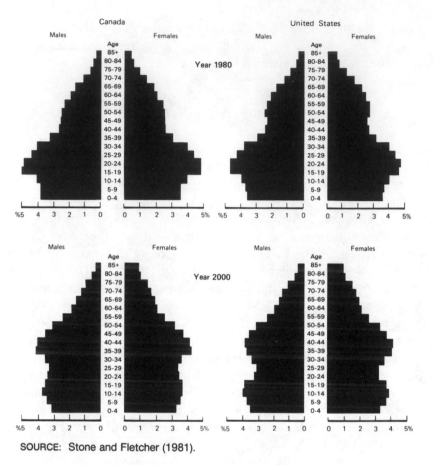

SOURCE: Stone and Fletcher (1981).

Figure 1.1. Age pyramids in Canada and the United States, 1980,
and projections for year 2000.

indicator, the aged dependency ratio in Canada has steadily increased since the turn of the century, moving from 10/100 in 1901 to an expected 31/100 in 2051. However, the total dependency ratio shows a different picture. In 1901, again in Canada, there were 99 dependent children and older persons for every 100 persons of working age, but only 72 such persons in 1981. This proportion remains fairly constant through 2051, never reaching the high level that characterized 1961 (as a result of the baby boom effect). Table 1.3 shows these ratios. The United States calculates the ratios somewhat differently from Canada because children 18 and 19 are placed in the denominator with the workers rather than in the numerators with the dependent. Therefore, the United States ratios are somewhat more favorable, although in both countries the aged dependency ratio rises steadily through the middle of the next century.

Commentators and policymakers in the United States often cite the growth in the aged dependency ratio as an ominous portent for future health and social services. The 1982 report of the Senate Special Committee on Aging (United States Senate 1983:10) anticipates a dramatic increase in the need for services and argues that the aged dependency ratio is more important than the youth dependency ratio because "it is primarily publicly funded programs that serve retirees." In contrast, Canadian commentators usually focus on the total dependency ratio, note the decrease in the ratio of children, and assume that public expenditures in areas such as schools and youth services will be reduced. Typical is the conclusion of Denton and Spencer (1980:25) that "future increases in the older population of the order indicated in our projections would certainly not impose an unmanageable burden on the economy or the population of working age." Canadian officials seem to be less alarmed by dependency statistics that terrify their American counterparts; perhaps this attitude partly explains why universal long-term care programs have been launched in Canada but not in the United States.

Table 1.3

Dependency Ratios in Canada and the United States, 1900-2051

	Canada			United States[a]			
Year	Youth Dependency Ratio[b]	Aged Dependency Ratio[c]	Total Dependency Ratio[d]	Year	Youth Dependency Ratio	Aged Dependency Ratio	Total Dependency Ratio
1901	.89	.10	.99	1900	.76	.07	.83
1921	.84	.09	.93	1920	.68	.08	.76
1941	.67	.12	.79	1940	.52	.11	.63
1961	.83	.15	.98	1960	.46	.18	.64
1981	.56	.16	.72	1980	.46	.19	.65
1991	.52	.18	.70	1990	.42	.21	.63
2001	.50	.20	.70	2000	.41	.21	.62
2021	.46	.27	.73	2025	.38	.33	.71
2031	.47	.33	.80				
2041	.46	.31	.77				
2051	.47	.31	.78	2050	.37	.38	.75

SOURCES: Canadian data from Denton and Spencer 1980; United States data from U.S. Senate 1983.

[a] In the United States data, child dependents are 0 to 17 years and the working population is 18 to 64 in calculation of ratios.

[b] The youth dependency ratio in Canada is the ratio of persons 0 to 19 years to those 20 to 64.

[c] The aged dependency ratio in Canada is the ratio of persons age 65+ to those aged 20 to 64; in the United States it is the ratio of persons aged 65+ to those aged 18-64.

[d] The total dependency ratio is the ratio of the sum of the child and aged dependent groups to those over ages 20 to 65.

Scope of the Study

Health care in Canada is a *provincial* responsibility, with each of the ten provinces running its own health care programs. Some general conditions (discussed in chapter 2) need to be met before provinces can tap into federal cost-sharing. Otherwise, the provincial governments make their own decisions about the nature of the benefits and the organization of services. Therefore, we keyed our general programmatic descriptions to the provincial level. However, governmental levels above and below were of definite interest. The general federal policies created incentives or disincentives for particular provincial decisions. Similarly, the types of implementation decisions made by municipal or city governments within the three provinces gave local variation to provincial long-term care programs.

Because our resources prohibited studying all ten provinces, we deliberately concentrated on Manitoba, British Columbia, and Ontario, which we selected as representing (1) provinces with a substantial older population and a heavy investment in long-term care, and (2) points on a spectrum in a controlled, community-based, long-term care effort. Manitoba and British Columbia have systems with considerable control over use of services and with substantial home care components. From provincial sources there, we had the opportunity to trace provincial experience with insured long-term care benefits over time. (Manitoba, with the longest systematic experience, afforded the greatest promise.) Ontario, the most populous province, represents a less well-coordinated approach to long-term care, but insured nursing home care has been in place for more than a decade. At the time we began the study, Ontario had a well-developed acute home care benefit and an underdeveloped chronic home care benefit. Ontario also afforded us information about an insured nursing home benefit in a delivery system with substantial numbers of proprietary nursing homes.

The three provinces contain slightly more than half the country's population over age 65, and account for about one-third of the Canadian land mass (see figure 1.2).

The rationale for our choice of provinces for study is clarified by noting those not chosen. Table 1.4 ranges the ten provinces on characteristics related to our choice. Quebec, next to Ontario the most populous province, is currently developing an interesting

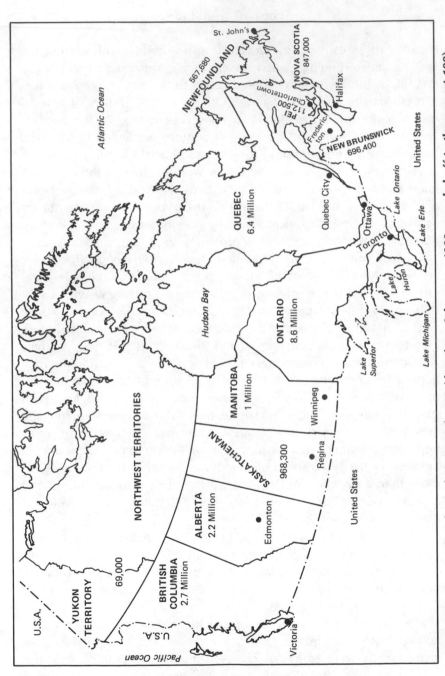

Figure 1.2. Provincial population as of 1981 (data from Schwenger 1983, rounded off to the nearest 100) and location of capital cities.

Table 1.4

Comparison of Provinces on Selected Characteristics in 1981

Province	Population	Percentage of Canada's Population	Population Age 65+	Percentage Over Age 65 in Province	Percentage of Canada's Population Age 65+	Percentage of Land Area	Long-Term Care Features
Study Provinces							
Ontario	8,625,110	35.4	868,185	10.1	36.7	9.7	Nursing home care insured Medically oriented home care program insured
Manitoba	1,026,245	4.2	121,820	11.9	5.2	5.9	Nursing home care insured Home care insured Case management
British Columbia	2,744,470	11.3	298,175	10.9	12.6	10.1	Nursing home care insured Home care insured Case management
Non-Study Provinces							
Newfoundland	567,680	2.3	43,780	7.7	1.9	4.0	Nursing home care not insured
Prince Edward Island	112,510	0.5	14,895	12.2	0.6	0.1	Nursing home care not insured
Nova Scotia	847,445	3.5	92,555	10.9	3.9	0.6	Nursing home care not insured
New Brunswick	696,405	2.9	70,555	10.1	3.0	0.8	Nursing home care not insured
Quebec	6,438,400	26.4	569,380	8.8	24.1	14.7	Nursing home care insured Home care and case management developing as insured programs
Saskatchewan	968,310	4.0	116,170	12.0	4.9	6.2	Nursing home care insured Home care developed as insured program
Alberta	2,237,725	9.2	163,395	7.3	6.9	7.0	Nursing home care insured Home care developing as insured program
Territories	68,890	0.3	2,035	3	0.01	41.0	Not applicable. Territorial governments too atypical
CANADA	24,343,180	100	2,360,975	9.7	100	100	

approach to long-term care. We excluded Quebec, a French-speaking province, from major attention partly because of the newness of the program and partly because unique political and cultural factors make extrapolations from that province difficult. Quebec is also a "younger" than median province, with only 8.8 percent over 65. The four Atlantic provinces, each with a population under one million, had not yet begun to insure nursing home care as a universal benefit at the time we began the study. Although some have substantial proportions of elderly, they were both too small and too underdeveloped in long-term care to be ideal candidates. Similarly, Alberta and Saskatchewan were slower in developing home care services than were Manitoba and British Columbia (although Saskatchewan led the provinces in providing insured hospital care and, later, insured physician services). Furthermore, only 7.3 percent of Alberta's population is over 65.

Canada as a Source of Extrapolations

Canada is probably the best foreign country from which to draw extrapolations to the United States. For this reason, health services researchers have already made extensive use of the Canadian example to draw conclusions about national health insurance (Hatcher 1981; Soderstrom 1978; Andreopoulos 1975). Below we catalogue the advantages of using Canada as a northern laboratory for our study of long-term care. We also list some key differences between the two countries that must be considered in drawing inferences for policy.

Advantages of Studying Long-Term Care in Canada

- As in the United States, power in Canada is divided between provincial and federal governments, and a major theme is the appropriate purview of each government for raising taxes, spending money, and establishing policy.
- Block grants from the federal government to provincial governments have been at the heart of Canadian long-term care funding. Block granting is a topical issue for health and human services in the United States today.

- The United States and Canada are culturally and geographically akin. Despite some obvious differences, the two countries resemble each other more than they do any other country. Both encompass vast territory and have mobile populations. Their citizens are socialized by similar (and often identical) media. Their economic systems and interests are intertwined, and both are currently experiencing worrisome unemployment.
- Although the United States has ten times the population of Canada, their age distributions and predicted demographic shifts over the next fifty years are comparable.
- Canada affords the opportunity to examine the delivery of long-term care in large cities (e.g., Toronto and Vancouver), where the challenge mirrors the difficulties faced in metropolitan areas in the United States.
- A fee-for-service system of medical care is the dominant mode of physician reimbursement in both Canada and the United States. In both countries, physicians move freely between hospital and community practice.
- In the main, Canadian hospitals are not operated by governmental authorities. The predominant model is the acute, nonprofit, community hospital.
- For-profit long-term care facilities and home-health agencies exist in Canada and have been incorporated into the plan for public long-term care benefits. Any long-term care reform in the United States will similarly need to incorporate large and powerful proprietary nursing home and home care industries.
- The ten provinces provide examples of different decisions. The mix of providers and the benefit packages differ, as does the amount of control within the system.
- Canada has amassed operational experience with technologies of great interest in the United States, including homemaking services, comprehensive assessments, day care, case management, and hospital geriatric evaluation units.
- Finally, despite perennial concerns about costs, the long-term care system in Canada seems to work. A comprehensive universal benefit has been offered without swamping the resources. It behooves us to understand how that was done.

Differences

The two countries also differ:

- Canada is an easier federal system to manage because there are fewer players. With a smaller population divided among only ten provinces and two territories, intergovernmental communications are less cumbersome and more personal.
- Canada's smaller population means a less cumbersome health care system. Fewer major hospitals, medical schools, and agencies have to interact.
- Senior civil servants tend to remain in place in the federal and provincial governments, even when the political party in power changes. In Canada, the cabinet ministers (analogous to the cabinet members of presidents and governors in the United States) are elected office-holders from the party in power. But the civil service immediately below the minister enjoys comparative stability. This permits long-range planning and also improves the institutional memory of government agencies. (Normally, this is an advantage for coherent policy development, although a few Canadian commentators contend that longevity in office can invite program stagnation.)
- The national ethos differs. We were reminded several times during our site visits that the preamble to the Declaration of Independence in the United States sets forth "life, liberty, and the pursuit of happiness" as primary goals. In contrast, the British North America Act (the original Canadian constitutional document) cites "peace, order, and good government" as a goal for the union of the provinces.
- Canadian long-term care programs are built on a foundation of universal hospital and medical care insurance. The question is whether the United States could develop a similar long-term care system without substantial Medicare reforms.
- Canada's defense expenditures are not as burdensome.
- Litigation over health and social welfare programs (and indeed all litigation) is rare in Canada. Therefore, community programs have had the flexibility to evolve an array of services without winding up in court to defend their allocations to individuals.

- Canadian cities are safer than those in the United States. Programs for older people at home can be predicated on the idea that frail elders are unlikely to be victimized.
- Most universities in Canada are land-grant colleges and all have subsidized tuition. Thus Canadians with college-aged children are less burdened with expenses and, presumably, are therefore more able to assist parents.

Guiding Themes

The three provincial long-term care programs evolved and changed even as we studied them, complicating our descriptive task. We tried, nevertheless, to capture essential details and to gather opinions on how well programs work in practice. Recognizing that the programs are dynamic, we probed the reasons for administrative decisions and changes. In addition, we sought quantitative data on the use and costs of long-term care. Below are the themes that guided our inquiry.

Relationship Between Long-Term and Hospital Care

Long-term care has been compartmentalized in the United States, as it has, to some extent, in most industrialized countries. Yet persons needing the sustained personal care and health-related social services that constitute long-term care will also need timely and appropriate hospital services. The two services are not always in harmony. The hospital/nursing home relationship in particular can easily degenerate into a mutual but hostile dependence. Hospitals complain that nursing homes refuse to accept the difficult cases, thus causing long delays in hospital for the hard-to-place patient. Similarly, they complain that some nursing homes "dump" difficult patients on the hospital on the slightest provocation. Nursing homes complain that hospital discharge planners send patients to them with no information—or worse, misleading information. And, under pressure of time, hospital employees have incentives to arrange institutional care rather than home care for persons who meet the very general nursing home eligibility criteria.

Long-term care programs—particularly community-based programs—are often expected to show effects in reduced hospitalization for the long-term care patient. The logic of this expectation has not been fully explored, nor is it clear what the average hospitalization rates *should* be for a frail population of octogenarians.

When hospital beds are full, the pressure to discharge the elderly patient to a nursing home is intense. In regions where hospital beds are empty, an interest in creating chronic units is often expressed. Meanwhile, few hospitals have developed programs to meet the specific needs of the elderly patient, who may well deteriorate in the hospital. And current public policy permits a nursing home bed to be saved only for a few days for a resident who needs to spend time in the hospital.

We therefore explored the relationship between long-term care and acute care in the three provinces, keeping these general issues in mind. We were interested in the movement of patients between the programs, the backup of long-term care patients in hospitals, the preferred method of treating the terminally ill, the communication patterns, and the problems encountered.

Relationship Between Long-Term and Primary Medical Care

The physician usually provides the link between patient and hospital. For long-term care patients living in nursing homes, that link too often is broken. A physician is needed to diagnose and treat acute ailments and to manage chronic conditions so that patients can function as well as they are able. Primary care could be delivered in nursing homes in various ways. For example, residents could be expected to continue using their own physicians; the nursing home could contract for physicians' services; the nursing home could hire a chief of medical staff to supervise the quality of medical care for all residents; nonphysician personnel such as nurses, geriatric nurse practitioners, and pharmacists could participate directly in primary health care. All these approaches have been tried in various combinations in the United States.

Several issues arise. Whatever system evolves for primary care in nursing homes, it should ensure competent diagnostic, curative, and rehabilitation service; it should offer incentives to competent providers to practice in nursing homes, and it should allow nursing home residents a reasonable opportunity for satisfactory relationships with their primary health care providers. Although nursing home patients in the United States are covered by Medicare, they usually do not directly engage their physicians; therefore, it is easily forgotten who the consumer is and whose Medicare benefit is being expended for physician services. We were interested to see how the three provinces dealt with this problem of delivering competent and proactive medical care to nursing home residents.

A separate issue in the relationship between primary medical care and long-term care involves the physician in the role of certifier and care planner. In the United States, the doctor has the legal responsibility to determine whether a patient is eligible for skilled nursing care—or rehabilitation service, or day hospital, or a host of health-related services. The physician also advises the patient and family about whether the necessary "skilled" care could be provided at home. This places a burden on the physician to be aware of resources, to withstand pressures of anxious relatives, and to work with members of other disciplines who can evaluate such factors as the suitability of home and neighborhood, the ambulation potential of the patient, or the potential for assistive devices. Physicians in the United States have been loath to make referrals to home health programs. We were interested in how the provinces had worked out the roles of primary care physicians and other health care professions in the initial recommendations for long-term care. We also wondered how well informed the community physician was about the gamut of long-term care alternatives.

Relationship Between Health and Social Programs

Long-term care is on the boundary of health care and social services. In fact, long-term care addresses indivisible social and health care needs with pragmatic services. These services may be medical (e.g., administering medications or medical regimens, giving physical or occupational therapy, doing health education); they may involve health-related personal care (e.g., bathing assistance, toileting assis tance); they may involve household tasks (e.g., cooking, cleaning, laundry); and they may involve social assistance (e.g., companionship, reassurance, shopping, writing letters). Both health and social services tend to be engaged in delivering long-term care, and the respective mandates often reflect historical decisions rather than logical division of labor. Sometimes rather arbitrary distinctions are made between personnel designated as home health aides and those designated as homemakers or chore workers, even to the point that two paraprofessionals (each with his or her own supervisor) can come into the same home to deliver unskilled services that could have been done by one person. Sometimes homes for the aged under social welfare auspices seem markedly similar to nursing homes under health auspices. We explored the balance struck between health and social authorities in the three provinces and the mechanisms to enhance communication, eliminate duplication, and keep long-term care from being inappropriately medicalized while ensuring necessary medical input.

Utilization Trends

Long-term care is an amorphous service with an imprecise constituency of potential users. Many frail elderly spouses care for each other at home, and other family members are also heavily involved in such care. The question arises about how heavily a nonmeans-tested benefit for nursing home care would be used. Presently, high costs and the need to spend to the poverty level before receiving Medicaid reimbursement act as a deterrent to using nursing home care. We are also interested in how heavily a home care and homemaking benefit would be used, especially as that benefit is publicized over time. Therefore, we set out to chart the demand for a variety of long-term care services initially and as the programs in the three provinces evolved.

We also attempted to chart the use of other health care services by older persons, particularly hospital services and physician visits. By charting trends before and after the introduction of the long-term care benefits, we hoped to be able to address the issue of the relationship between use of long-term care service and use of other health care services.

Costs of Care Trends

The costs of service components are closely related to the utilization patterns. Rising costs occur for more reasons than the growth in numbers of users; costs are also influenced by the intensity and the price of service. Home care costs are influenced, therefore, by the degree of professionalism of personnel, the numbers of service hours typically authorized, administrative overhead, travel costs and, of course, the wage scales of providers. Nursing home and hospital costs are also influenced by staffing patterns and wages. The extent to which hospitals and nursing homes are unionized may also account for accelerating costs. We attempted to trace the costs of long-term care and other health care services over time and, as much as possible, describe the reasons for increase.

Individual Patterns of Care

Examining utilization and cost of long-term care and other services in the aggregate shows changing patterns. However, we were also interested in the way individuals used services. Such information is hard to come by. At the least, it requires that the individual user be uniquely and consistently identified in multiple information systems. Longitudinal data are needed to explore the subject more fully.

Information about patterns of individual care can shed insight into the following kinds of questions:

1. Does a person use more home care over time? What are the characteristics of those whose home care use stabilizes at a low level? At a high level? How long do various types of persons tend to receive home care?
2. Are home care users more or less likely to enter institutional care than those who did not receive home care? What are the characteristics of those who use both systems?
3. What kind of movement occurs between levels of institutional care? Do people inexorably proceed from lighter to heavier levels of care? Is there ever movement in the opposite direction? Do those who use home care tend to enter institutions at heavier care levels? Because Manitoba and British Columbia have systems with multiple levels of care, we hoped to be able to observe those trends.

4. What is the average length of stay in nursing homes for vari-
    ous kinds of residents? Do patterns emerge that differentiate
    long-stay and short-stay residents?
5. What patterns can be described for the use of other health
    care services—acute hospital, physician services—of people
    who use home-based or institutionally based long-term care?

In the United States, this kind of information is elusive. Utilization
records usually treat readmissions to nursing homes after intervening
hospitalizations or transfers from one home to another as new cases.
Other long-term care services delivered by state social service agencies or area agencies on aging are not easily traced to individual
recipients. And a wide range of home-based services have simply
been unavailable for the typical person at risk for long-term care.
The provincial programs in this study were characterized by universal entitlement to a rather wide array of benefits. Therefore, we
were particularly interested in knowing as much as possible about
the way individuals cumulatively use these benefits.

Supply Trends

Changes in the supply of long-term care services over time was
another theme for our study. Here we were interested in numbers
and distributions of programs.

The supply of nursing home beds always seems to equal demand:
Nursing homes always being full, the number of residents equals the
number of beds. This situation inspires efforts to control the supply
and rationalize the distribution of licensed nursing home beds to
keep use down. Some have even speculated that the only way to
promote home care in the United States is to artificially restrain the
growth of nursing homes. However, the same logic prevails on the
hospital front, and efforts to restrain the growth of hospital beds
may inflate the demand for nursing home beds. We were
interested in this dynamic in the Canadian provinces, especially as
nursing home care became a universally insured benefit. Because
housing is a substantial aspect of long-term care that may explain an
ability to use home-based services, we also tried to chart the availability of housing units for the elderly over the same period. We
thought it possible that the availability of purpose-built and/or

affordable housing might reduce the need for low-care residential facilities.

The inadequate supply of home care in the United States is widely deplored. Yet we have little information about the capital costs and the required lagtime to create viable home health agencies. Some authorities suggest that almost the only requirement to generate a home health agency is a ready market for the services. Others foresee problems in amassing a qualified staff, especially in regions where a labor pool may not be available. Trager (1980) has suggested that several years of capacity-building are needed for an agency to establish an efficient and creditable operation. In our study of Manitoba and British Columbia in particular, we had an opportunity to learn what was entailed in mobilizing the capacity to deliver long-term care services at home once funding for that service was available.

Auspices of Service

One facet of the supply question is the auspices under which the service is offered. Institutional facilities may be proprietary, public, or voluntary nonprofit (e.g., sectarian). We were interested in observing the distribution of facility size and ownership over time and studying how the provincial governments sought to influence that distribution. Similar questions arose about the auspices of home health service, which ranged from direct provision by health departments, through nonprofit agency provision, to proprietary agency provision.

Profit-making in health facilities and programs is a sensitive and elusive subject. Instinctively, many feel that a profitable facility is bound to cut corners on amenities and even on necessities such as food. Few data are available, however, that really measure quality of care and life in facilities of different ownerships. Nonprofit facilities may have a different and more generous operating budget and/or a different resident mix. In Canada, chain nursing home ownership has also emerged as a phenomenon comparable to that in the United States. To the extent possible, we have tried to explore the characteristics of the facilities and health care programs, with an emphasis on exploring differences between proprietary and nonprofit agencies in efficiency, responsiveness to clientele, admissions policies, prices, and range and quality of service.

Control of System

We are particularly interested in the way the long-term care benefits have been managed so that those entitled to them receive them, but overuse, misuse, and attendant runaway costs are avoided. A handful of theoretical approaches are possible: The supply of services can be constrained, with the resultant queueing serving as a rationing device; fixed budgets can be established to constrain service providers; or an assessment of need can be imposed before permitting access to service. Another less palatable way of holding down service use is to create a stigmatized or undesirable service. Although one hopes that no policymaker consciously sets out with this goal in mind, the unattractiveness of a program such as the modal United States nursing home to most potential residents and their families (and the "welfare" stigma) restrains use. If facilities are made more desirable and entitlement to their use made universal, then some control mechanisms are surely necessary.

The Manitoba and British Columbia long-term care benefits are mediated by a case management system that entails professional decisionmaking about the extent of an individual's need. The Ontario program has designed Placement Coordination Services to rationalize use of resources through voluntary involvement of users and providers.

Budgeting and rate-setting processes are also a form of control. Many hospitals and long-term care facilities received global budgets in all three provinces, and we were interested in how such a method affected costs. We were interested in what kind of incentives prompted facilities and programs to be efficient despite a global budget.

Ways to Ensure Quality

Hand in hand with ensuring appropriate use of long-term care services is the issue of monitoring and ensuring the quality of service. This task is difficult because of unclear and subjectively varying definitions of quality, a large number of programs and locations, and inadequately funded quality-control mechanisms. Often quality deficits are a matter of ignorance, and the best correction is education and program consultation rather than punitive sanction. This is especially true if the industry as a whole tends to be staffed by undertrained persons. We were interested in learning how quality control was handled in the provinces under study. Our attention extended to quality control in home health programs as well as in the institutional sector. Services delivered in individuals' homes are particularly difficult to monitor, and the clients may be particularly vulnerable to fraud, abuse, theft, and mistreatment.

Consumer Choice

Another theme is the extent of consumer choice built into the long-term care programs. Consumer choice can be examined on several levels. The older person may or may not have a choice about whether to receive care at home or in some kind of residential facility. Then, too, the individual bound for a nursing home may or may not be able to exercise preferences about the location and type of facility where he or she is to live. Building individual choice into the program may be difficult because it interferes with timely hospital discharges and efficient use of resources. Knowing that the Canadian long-term care programs try to honor personal preferences even for particular facilities, we were eager to learn the mechanics for implementing that kind of humane policy and the necessary limits to its application.

Formal and Informal Systems

One of the concerns about long-term care entitlements at home is that they may discourage voluntary efforts at long-term care. Voluntary efforts are divided into two types: the long-term care provided by relatives, especially spouses and adult children, and the long-term care provided by volunteers instead of paid employees of social and health care agencies. There is a thin line between offering services that encourage family members to undertake or continue delivering the care and offering services that supplant that care. Once the Canadian provinces began offering services at home, we were interested in exploring the effect on informal family and voluntary assistance. We were also interested in how the boundaries were established for the public component of a program and how family characteristics were or were not taken into account when service plans were authorized.

Incentives

We explored the incentives created by the long-term care programs for all parties to the transaction: hospitals, nursing homes, physicians, home care providers, long-term care users, families of long-term care users, regulators, and public officials. Most commentators recognize that perverse incentives characterize health care programs in the United States. For example, some procedures can be reimbursed only if they are performed in hospitals. Long-term care facilities are paid more for heavy care patients, and thus have a disincentive to rehabilitate residents to a more self-sufficient status. Residents, too, may have a disincentive to recover if it means a move to a less attractive and unfamiliar setting. In the United States, some federal/state cost-shared programs have more advantageous matches than others, giving states the incentive to shift clientele.

Often the incentives created by new policies are not immediately apparent. We were interested in understanding those incentives that were deliberately created to influence the mix and type of long-term care provided and those that crept into the system willynilly. For the latter, we were interested in the corrective actions made by long-term care programmers. One of the least understood areas is the incentives for the long-term care recipient and his or her family to use various forms of care. Our expectation was that the motivations would be complex and could well involve the value of a home and the desire for advantageous transfer of property among the generations. We thought it useful to garner as much information as possible about the incentives of the consumers from the initial Canadian experience.

Acceptability

Finally, the acceptability of the long-term care programs to potential users and their families, to the taxpayer (who must support the gamut of governmental programs), and to the providers is a crucial issue. We tried to explore this question through discussions with representatives of consumer, provider, administrative, and legislative groups. We were interested in whether the long-term care programs enjoyed the confidence of a large cross-section of the Canadian elderly, including those of relatively high education and income. We were interested in whether any public sentiment had been expressed about whether the investment in long-term care was too much, not enough, or just right. And we were extremely eager to explore the reactions of health care providers—especially hospitals, voluntary and proprietary nursing homes, and home health agencies—to the evolution of policies that constrained their budgets, their activities, and their choice of clientele.

The Rest of the Book

This book is organized to address the general issues raised in this introductory chapter. Chapter 2 reviews Canadian health and social service policies as the background against which the three provinces evolved their systems. Chapters 3 through 5 describe the long-term care programs in Ontario, Manitoba, and British Columbia. Chapter 6 discusses general issues concerning use and costs in all three provinces, and chapter 7 discusses issues that arose at the service delivery level in local areas. Much of the information for chapter 7 was derived from telephone interviews with case managers and home care providers in the three provinces. Chapter 8 presents our conclusions, and Chapter 9 our inferences for policy development in the United States.

A final caveat is in order. The major fieldwork for this study was done in 1982, with additional on-site and telephone work in the first part of 1983. The programs under review are still evolving. We have attempted to update information as much as possible and in some instances have acquired 1984 information. Unless specifically indicated, however, readers should assume that comments about the current situation are correct as of the summer of 1983.

REFERENCES

Andreopoulos, S., ed. 1975. *National Health Insurance: Can We Learn from Canada?* Toronto: Wiley.

Baxter, R. J., R. Applebaum, J. J. Callahan, Jr., J. B. Christianson, and S. L. Day 1983. *The Planning and Implementation of Channeling: Early Experiences of the National Long-Term-Care Demonstrations.* Np: Mathematica Policy Research.

Denton, F. and B. Spencer 1980. "Canada's Population and Labour Force: Past, Present, and Future." In V. W. Marshall, ed., *Aging in Canada: Social Perspectives.* Ontario: Fitzhenry and Whiteside.

Eggert, G. M., J. E. Bowlyow, and C. W. Nichols 1980. "Gaining Control of the Long-Term Care Systems: First Returns from the Access Experiment." *Gerontologist*, 20:356–363.

Greenberg, J. N., D. Doth, and C. Austin 1981. *Comparative Study of Long-Term Care Demonstration Projects: Lessons for Future Inquiry.* Minneapolis: University of Minnesota Center for Health Services Research.

Hatcher, G. H. 1981. *Universal Free Health Care in Canada, 1947–77.* Washington, D.C.: GPO.

Kane, R. L. and R. A. Kane 1980. "Alternatives to Institutional Care of the Elderly: Beyond the Dichotomy." *Gerontologist*, 20:249–259.

Schwenger, C. W. 1983. "National Context—Canada," a compilation of materials prepared for the Commonwealth Fund Forum, "Improving the Health of the Homebound Elderly: Best Prospects from Five English-Speaking Countries." London, England, May 23, 1983.

Soderstrom, L. 1978. *The Canadian Health System.* London: Croom Helm.

Stone, L. O. and S. Fletcher 1981. *Aspects of Population Aging in Canada.* Statistics Canada and National Advisory Council on Aging, Ottawa.

Trager, B. 1980. *Home Health Care and the National Health Policy* (Special issue of *Home Health Care Services Quarterly*). New York: Haworth Press.

U.S. Department of Health and Human Services, Social Security Administration 1976. *Compendium of National Health Expenditures Data.* Publ. No. SSA 76–11927. Washington, D.C.: GPO.

U.S. Department of Health and Human Services, Health Care Financing Administration 1981. *Long Term Care: Background and Future Directions*, HCFA Publication No. 81–20047. Washington, D.C.: GPO.

U.S. Senate 1983. Special Committee on Aging, *Developments in Aging: 1982*, vol. 1. Senate Publication No. 98–13. Washington, D.C.: GPO.

Weissert, W. G., T. T. H. Wan, B. Livieratos, and S. Katz 1980a. "Effects and Costs of Day-Care Services for the Chronically Ill: A Randomized Experiment." *Medical Care*, 18:567–583.

Weissert, W. G., T. T. H. Wan, B. Livieratos, and J. Pellegrino 1980b. "Cost-Effectiveness of Homemaker Services for the Chronically Ill." *Inquiry*, 17:230–243.

Williams, T. F. 1983. "Assessment of the Elderly in Relation to Needs for Long-Term Care: An Emerging Technology." Paper prepared for workshop on the impact of technology on long-term care, Washington, D.C., 2/16/83. Mimeo.

CHAPTER 2
Background: Health and Welfare Policy in Canada

IN 1867, when four provinces (Ontario, Quebec, New Brunswick, and Nova Scotia) confederated to become the infant Dominion of Canada, health and welfare were designated as provincial responsibilities. Provincial rights are guarded in Canada with the same zeal as states' rights are protected in the United States. The bulk of this book, therefore, deals with three illustrative *provincial* long-term care programs nested in three *provincial* health care systems. However, health and welfare programs in all provinces share common features derived from their shared federal context.

Although the Canadian government cannot dictate to provinces how much they can spend on health or social services or how they should use the money, the federal government does exert considerable leverage. Under the constitution, the federal government is empowered to levy corporate and personal income taxes. Much of this tax revenue is returned to the provinces through cost-sharing agreements that permit the provinces to exercise their constitutional responsibility for health, welfare, and educational programs. The various cost-sharing plans create incentives that encourage some kinds of provincial initiatives and discourage others. Federal cost-sharing also serves to reduce the discrepancies between social programs in richer provinces (e.g., Alberta and Ontario) and poorer provinces (e.g., the four Atlantic provinces).

The broad outlines of major cost-shared health and social welfare programs were developed in a painstaking process of federal-provincial conferences, with subsequent ratification by provincial legislatures. On several occasions, constitutional amendments were needed to allow the federal government to provide income security programs directly. (This was necessary for unemployment insurance in 1940 and old age security in 1951.) All health insurance programs remained provincial. However, even after general principles of a cost-shared program were accepted by a majority of the provinces representing a majority of the population, federal cost-sharing for the provincial health insurance programs was contingent on provincial adherence to the agreed-upon precepts.

This chapter summarizes modern health, income maintenance, social welfare, and housing policies in Canada. The emphasis is on health, but other spheres are also related to long-term care. In some instances, general federal policies help explain the directions taken by provinces in developing their long-term care programs. The chapter concludes with a brief overview of long-term care provisions in each province.

Health Policy in Canada

Two major pieces of legislation, the Hospital Insurance and Diagnostic Services Act of 1957 and the Medical Care Act of 1966, provide the basis for universal health insurance in Canada today. In addition, important legislation in 1977, the Federal-Provincial Fiscal Arrangements and Established Programs Financing Act, replaced the cost-sharing arrangements provided in the previous legislation, altered the relative financial risks taken by the two levels of government, and reallocated the federal share of money for provinces to use for long-term care. These three pieces of legislation evolved over decades of study and deliberation at federal and provincial levels. In late 1983, the federal government put forward a controversial new Health Act that clarifies and makes more stringent the conditions for its cost-sharing in the provincial health programs.

Hospital Insurance

Hospital insurance was the first area of national health insurance to be developed. It was preceded by nongovernmental voluntary prepayment plans, by government programs in some provinces (notably in Saskatchewan and British Columbia), and by a federally stimulated build-up of health facilities and personnel resources to overcome perceived shortages that arose during the depression and war years (Mennie 1982). The latter was accomplished through a National Resources Fund Program introduced in 1948. The resulting growth in bed capacity during the 1950s meant higher health costs. This in turn placed more pressure on governments to protect patients from these rising costs and hospitals from swelling deficits created by unused beds. During that time, the few universal publicly administered provincial programs seemed to combine efficiency and equitable access better than hospital programs in the provinces that used voluntary insurance coupled with government subsidies (i.e., "welfare" payments) for people unable to afford their bills.

Accordingly, the Hospital Insurance and Diagnostic Services Act, approved in 1957, paved the way for a nationwide system of provincial comprehensive hospital insurance plans in Canada. The act established the principles of a national program, the list of services to be covered, and the cost-sharing formulas to be used for provinces that decided to develop qualifying plans. By July 1960, all provinces had a hospital insurance program in place.

All inpatient services were insured. These included accommodation and meals at the ward level; nursing service; laboratory, radiological, and other diagnostic procedures; drugs and related preparations; use of the operating rooms; radiotherapy; physiotherapy; and services of all hospital employees. Outpatient services delivered by hospitals and approved cancer clinics were also covered. Rehabilitation and chronic disease hospitals were counted as hospitals for cost-sharing under the act. *Excluded* were nursing homes, tuberculosis sanatoria, and mental hospitals. Therefore, if a province decided to offer nursing home care as an insured benefit, it had to assume the complete costs, recouping federal cost-sharing only for indigent beneficiaries under the Canada Assistance Plan (described below). Major capital costs, research, ambulance, and administration of the provincial programs were also not cost-shared.

Federal principles were fourfold. The programs were to be *comprehensive* in their coverage of hospital services. Programs were to be *universal*, meaning that reasonable access to ensured service was to be guaranteed and that virtually 100 percent of the population was to be covered under "uniform terms and conditions." Benefits were to be *portable* across provinces. And finally, programs were to be *administered publicly* on a nonprofit basis. With these provisos, the federal government paid about half the actual program costs using an equalizing formula that gave greater federal funding to poorer provinces. (The federal contribution to a province for inpatient services equaled one-quarter of the national per capita cost of the authorized inpatient services plus one-quarter of the per capita costs of the authorized services in the particular province times the number of covered people in that province.) All services were virtually free to patients at the point of use.

Provinces had the flexibility to determine how to raise the revenue for their share of the costs. Sales tax and general revenues were tapped. At the beginning, most provinces also used a premium system for part of the financing, but, at this writing, only three provinces (Ontario, British Columbia, and Alberta) and the Yukon territory retain premiums. Provinces were also free to use nongovernmental intermediaries to manage the benefit payment as long as the overall programs were publicly administered. By 1977, however, all provinces had eliminated nongovernmental intermediaries for their hospital insurance.

Each province developed a budget review process to reimburse hospitals on the basis of their actual costs. Initially, a line-by-line process tended to be used to establish a prospective budget and derive an all-inclusive rate per patient day. Monthly payments were made to hospitals based on this formula, with an annual adjustment based on actual utilization and cost. Under this system, hospital costs rose rapidly in the 1960s. In the 1970s, provinces began asserting tighter budgetary controls, replacing line-by-line procedures with global budgeting, imposing limits on allowable patient days, and becoming tougher about end-of-the-year adjustments for overruns. Ontario and Quebec experimented with incentive reimbursement approaches, but, at least initially, these seemed to make little difference in cost (Mennie 1982). The prospect of keeping any savings realized failed to entice hospitals, because they recognized the likelihood that next year's budget would be reduced correspondingly. Moreover, hospital administrators were subject to staff pressures to expand technologically (Mennie 1982).

Therefore, the major way to control costs of the hospital program was to control the growth of hospital beds and of other resources allocated to the system. As Mennie acknowledges: "From the inception of health insurance development in Canada, it has been recognized that program design objectives require that the supply

and distribution of health resources inputs be controlled by governments rather than market forces." As later chapters show, the three
provinces in our study succeeded in reducing the supply of hospital
beds. However, long-term care beds occupy an anomalous position
in this approach. On the one hand, controlling the growth of long-
term care beds is a necessary strategy for controlling costs of a
universally insured long-term care program. At the same time, this
interferes with strategies for reducing expensive hospital beds by a
deliberate substitution with long-term care beds. Table 2.1 shows
those trade-offs in the first decades of hospital insurance, when
national hospital bed ratios declined and nursing-home bed ratios
rose.

Table 2.1

**Hospital and Institutional Beds in Canada,
1962-1978**

Type of Bed	Number per 1000 Population		
	1962	1972	1978
Hospital			
Acute short-term[a]	5.5	5.5	4.7
Chronic long-term[b]	0.9	1.2	1.5
Psychiatric[c]	3.0	1.9	1.1
Tuberculosis	0.6	0.1	—
Total hospital	10.0	8.7	7.3
Other institutions			
Homes for special care[d]	3.1	5.2	6.0
Mental disorders[e]	0.8	1.1	1.4
Total other	3.9	6.3	7.4

SOURCE: Mennie 1982.
[a]Includes rehabilitation.
[b]Extended care in hospital and chronic hospital.
[c]In general, hospitals and freestanding.
[d]Freestanding nursing homes and homes for aged
included.
[e]Long-term residential care for mental illness and
retardation.

Medical Insurance

Federal cost-sharing for hospital insurance freed funds for Saskatchewan to begin a program of insured medical care, which was introduced in 1962. This became a model for the Medical Care Act of 1966 (sometimes called Medicare). This act provided federal cost-sharing with provinces that developed a program to insure physician services both in and out of hospitals.

The federal principles were similar to those for the hospital insurance. The program was to be *comprehensive*, meaning that, at a minimum, all medically required physician services delivered anywhere and all surgical/dental services delivered in hospitals were to be covered. (The services of other health providers could be included at provincial option.) The program was to be *universal*, meaning that 95 percent of insurable residents needed to be covered by the provincial plan under uniform terms and conditions. The requirements for *public administration* and *portability* were also in force.

The initial formula for cost-sharing held that the federal government's share would equal half the national per capita average cost of insured medical services times the number of insured people in the province. This method benefited poorer provinces because the costs of the more expensive provincial programs were averaged into the calculation of the federal payment to all provinces.

The Medical Care Act stipulated that insured residents must have the right to free choice of physician. As in the United States, the vast majority of Canadian physicians are paid on a fee-for-service basis. The rates for physicians' services were determined by periodic negotiation between the provincial Medicare program and the provincial medical association. Provinces differed in their requirements that the participating physicians accept the provincial rates as payment in full. In one province (Quebec), beneficiaries were not reimbursed for services given by physicians who "opted out" of the Medicare program. (This rule effectively eliminates opting out.) Sometimes the physician who opted out was forbidden to bill the province directly, but the patient could collect the authorized amount from the plan to apply to the doctor's bill. In other provinces, the physician could bill the plan for the accepted fee and, upon informing the patient in advance, also bill the patient for additional charges. The Canadian government currently perceives various forms of extra billing by physicians as a barrier to universality, an issue that is discussed further below.

The Medicare program met with initial resistance from the medical profession, punctuated by well-publicized physician strikes. (The best-known battle was waged when Saskatchewan developed its unilateral provincial medical insurance plan. The provincial government's ability to withstand the physicians' strike encouraged the national program [Taylor 1978].) By April 1971, each province had implemented a medical care insurance program. Table 2.2 summarizes the implementation timetable of the two major insurance programs in each province.

Table 2.2

Dates When Provincial Hospital and Medical Care Insurance Programs Began

	Date Program Began	
Province	Hospital Insurance	Medical Care Insurance
Federal Program	July 1, 1958[a]	July 1, 1968[b]
Newfoundland	July 1, 1958	April 1, 1969
Prince Edward Island	October 1, 1959	December 1, 1970
Nova Scotia	January 1, 1959	April 1, 1969
New Brunswick	July 1, 1959	January 1, 1971
Quebec	January 1, 1961	November 1, 1970
Ontario	January 1, 1959	October 1, 1969
Manitoba	July 1, 1958	April 1, 1969
Saskatchewan	July 1, 1958	July 1, 1968
Alberta	July 1, 1958	July 1, 1969
British Columbia	July 1, 1958	July 1, 1968
Yukon	July 1, 1960	April 1, 1972
Northwest Territories	April 1, 1960	April 1, 1971

SOURCE: Soderstrom 1978.

[a]The Hospital Insurance and Diagnostic Act (*Statutes of Canada*, 1957, ch. 28) was proclaimed in April 1957.

[b]The Medical Care Act (*Statutes of Canada*, 1966, ch. 64) was proclaimed in December 1966.

Established Program Financing, 1977

By 1977, the two health insurance programs, like certain post-secondary education programs, were considered "established" in the sense that they had reached sufficient maturity and enjoyed sufficient public support that provinces would be unlikely to discontinue them. At that time, rather dramatic changes were made in the funding arrangements. Indeed, 1977 marks an important milestone for "fiscal federalism" in Canada (Parliamentary Task Force 1981). A thorough review of the revenue sources and program responsibilities of the two levels of government was undertaken at that time. The provisions of the 1977 act that affected health financing were as follows:

1.   Each province received a basic per capita block grant, amounting to half the former federal contribution in 1975. This per capita block grant escalated annually according to population and GNP increases, and was payable only if the province continued to meet basic program conditions.
2.   The federal government turned over to the provinces the revenue from 13.5 percent of personal and 1 percent of corporate income tax revenues, applying a specified equalization formula for this transfer.
3.   Each province received an additional $20 per capita as an *annual* "extended care" payment (escalated *annually* on the same basis as the basic block grant). This was to be used only for extended health services such as home nursing, ambulatory care, or nursing home care. The basic program conditions (e.g., universality, comprehensiveness, portability and public administration) did *not* apply to this second block grant. By 1981–82, the per capita contribution was $29.75 and the overall federal cost of the extended care block grants had reached $720 million.

The new funding arrangements were a political compromise designed to satisfy, at least in part, both provincial and federal concerns about the old system. Provinces had complained that the old system was excessively rigid. Because only hospital and physician services were covered, provinces had disincentives to develop less expensive ways of meeting health needs through long-term care programs or ambulatory service. For instance, if a province wished to cover inpatient long-term care prior to 1977, it either had to pay the whole bill or offer the service in a hospital and pay 50 percent of this inflated cost of the inappropriately high level of care. On the other hand, the federal government was uncomfortable about sharing in unpredictable costs by continuing a blank check for half the actual program costs. The provinces had rejected earlier offers of block granting for health plans because of the financial risks. But when the tax points were added to a general package that included postsecondary education money, the compromise was struck.

The 1977 provisions dramatically increased the incentives of the provinces to control the costs of their health programs. Contemporary analysts (e.g., Van Loon 1978) predicted that provincial efforts at regulation would increase and that conflict between fee-for-service physicians and provincial governments would escalate. Although anticipating that provinces would be fairly successful in controlling costs in the long run, Van Loon predicted that the 1977 arrangements would show little immediate effect and that the extended care block grant would have a perverse effect on overall costs. Although its intention was to allow inexpensive alternatives to hospital and physician care, it was recognized that the outpatient and long-term care services could become add-ons rather than substitutions. Moreover, the financing arrangements created a windfall for provinces at the beginning and encouraged provincial expansion despite general recognition that the adequacy of payments in meeting costs would decrease over time.

Table 2.3 shows the growth in the federal contribution for the cost of health care from $4.6 billion in 1977–78 in the first year of Established Program Financing to $9.3 billion in 1983–84.

Proposed Canada Health Act

Some cost-containment strategies that appeal to the provinces directly impinged on the four program conditions. Universality had never been well defined, and modest cost-sharing by consumers had been allowed in the past. However, in recent years, federal authorities have complained that hospital user charges and extra billing by physicians compromise the basic principles of the

Table 2.3

Federal Government Contribution
to Provinces for Health Care
(In $ million)

Year	Contribution
1977-78	4,673
1978-79	5,345
1979-80	6,094
1980-81	6,814
1981-82	7,731
1982-83	8,512
1983-84	9,354

SOURCE: *Preserving Universal Medicare*, 1983, p. 29.

program. Provinces countered by noting that the federal government stopped sharing the risks of accelerating costs in 1977 and therefore should be less doctrinaire about principles.

In 1983, the federal Department of National Health and Welfare proposed a Canada Health Act to reaffirm and define the major principles required of each provincial program for eligibility in cost-sharing. The initiative grew from concern that user charges and extra billing by physicians and, under certain conditions, premiums, were eroding principles of universal access and portability required under the law. Under the Established Programs Financing Act, the federal government has no recourse but to withdraw its entire block payment if program conditions are violated. Viewing that measure as too drastic to be practical, the new policy would deduct from a province's basic block grant an amount equivalent to the total sums collected by direct charges to the beneficiaries. (Proponents point out that, under the original system, when the federal government paid half the actual costs, any user payments had been deducted from the provincial costs that formed the basis for the federal match.)

As background for its proposal, the Ministry of Health and Welfare summarized current policies on funding sources, extra billing, and user charges for the provincial health plans (see table 2.4).

Table 2.4

Provincial Health Insurance Plans: According to Funding Source and User Charges

Province	Source of Funding	Extra Billing for Insured Services by Physicians	User Charges[a]
Newfoundland	No premiums; financed from general taxation	To extra-bill, doctor must opt out of plan and bill patient directly. Patient applies to plan for reimbursement of fee-schedule portion. Estimated annual amount of extra-billing $0.03 million	$5.00 daily charge to a maximum of $75.00 (estimated annual amount, $1 million)
Prince Edward Island	No premiums; financed from general taxation	Doctors may extra-bill and remain in plan by billing patient directly; patient then seeks reimbursement from the plan. If patients not charged more than plan schedule, doctors bill plan directly. Doctors may also opt out for all patients. Estimated annual amount of extra-billing, $0.05 million	No user charges
Nova Scotia	No premiums; financed from general taxation	Doctors may extra-bill and remain in the plan. Doctor bills plan for fee and patient for extra amount. Estimated annual amount of extra-billing, $3.4 million	No user charges
New Brunswick	No premiums; financed from general taxation	Doctors may extra-bill and remain in plan by billing patient directly; patient then seeks reimbursement from the plan. If patients not charged more than plan schedule, doctors bill plan directly. Estimated annual amount of extra-billing, $0.2 million	Daily charge for patients awaiting nursing-home placements. $6.00 user charge for outpatient services (no charges for senior citizens until November 1, 1983, when charge of $3.00 will apply)
Quebec	3% payroll tax levied on employers; also general taxation	Virtually no extra billing is permitted	Daily charge for prolonged care patients

Province	Source of Funding	Extra Billing for Insured Services by Physicians	User Charges[a]
Ontario	Premiums and general taxation; premium exemptions for welfare recipients and elderly; premium assistance for low income; temporary premium assistance in cases of financial hardship	To extra-bill, doctor must opt out of plan and bill patient directly. Patient applies to plan for reimbursement of plan-schedule portion. Estimated annual amount of extra-billing, $49 million	Daily charge for most chronic care patients
Manitoba	No premiums; financed from general taxation, including part of 1.5% payroll tax levied on employers	To extra-bill, doctor must opt out of plan and bill patient directly. Patient applies to plan for reimbursement of plan-schedule portion. Estimated annual amount of extra-billing, $0.8 million	Daily charge for patients awaiting nursing-home placement
Saskatchewan	No premiums; financed from general taxation	Doctors may extra-bill and remain in plan by billing patient directly; patient then seeks reimbursement from the plan. If patients not charged more than plan schedule, doctor bills plan directly. Estimated annual amount of extra-billing, $2.3 million	No user charges
Alberta	Premiums and general taxation; premium exceptions for elderly and very low income; premium assistance for low income	No opting in or out required. Doctors may extra-bill if patients agree beforehand. Doctor bills plan for authorized fee and patient for extra amount or may bill patient for full amount. Estimated annual amount of extra-billing, $14.5 million	$5.00 admission charge (estimated annual amount, $1.8 million). Also daily charge for chronic care patients after 120 days. Extensive increases planned but postponed. Program is optional. Few hospitals have introduced changes
British Columbia	Premiums and general taxation; premiums paid on behalf of social assistance recipients; up to 90% premium assistance for low-income earners; temporary premium assistance in cases of financial hardship	Virtually all doctors have agreed not to opt out of the plan or extra-bill. Estimated annual amount of extra-billing, $0.00	Has a sliding scale of user charges, ranging from $4.00 for emergency services to $7.50/day for a hospital bed (estimated annual amount, $28 million). Also has daily charge for chronic-care patients Extensive increases on all charges effective September 1, 1983

SOURCE: Based on "Preserving Universal Medicare," a briefing kit released by Health and Welfare Canada on July 20, 1983.

[a] Each province has unique exemptions to these charges, which have not been included in the table.

Overall Costs of Health Care in Canada

Commentators have long noticed that overall health costs in Canada under the universal health insurance programs compare favorably to health care costs in the United States. Writing in 1979, Hatcher (1981) pointed out that Canada was able to hold health care expenditures at about 7 percent of the GNP for almost a decade, whereas they approached 9.5 percent of a much larger GNP in the United States. Hatcher attributes this success to the control maintained by the provincial programs:

> In a country that retains predominantly nonprofit hospitals and private fee-for-service medical practice, costs can only be contained by a health insurance system that is virtually free to patients, is universal, and brings nearly all health expenditures under a single public authority in each State or Province. (p. v)

Figure 2.1 shows the trends in total health care spending as a percentage of the GNP under the health insurance programs, compared with costs during the same period in the United States. A steady increase is apparent as the two Canadian insurance programs were implemented, followed by a leveling-off with cost containment efforts of the early 1970s. Indeed, the increase began *before* insurance programs came into effect and were part of a deliberate strategy of federal grants to provinces to ensure an adequate baseline of hospital beds and physician manpower in *anticipation* of universal insurance.

Table 2.5 shows what these Canadian GNP percentages mean in dollars. In the decade from 1971 to 1980, overall health expenditures from all sources rose from $7.1 billion to $21.4 billion—an increase from about $330 per capita to $893. The proportion of health expenditures financed *publicly* remained steady at about 75 percent. By contrast, the average per capita health expenditures in the United States were $508 in 1975 and $1,067 in 1980. However, the proportion of the expense that is publicly borne in the United States has remained at about 40 percent since 1975. According to Maxwell's analysis (1981) of health expenditures in ten industrial nations, Canada is somewhat anomalous in its combination of public funding and private delivery. Most countries with substantial public spending for health account for much of that expenditure in government administered institutions. For example, in 1975, Sweden spent about 82 percent and the United Kingdom spent 73 percent of its health dollar in government-administered institutions; the figures for Canada and the United States were only about 21 percent and 19 percent, respectively. Canada demonstrates that a high degree of government financing need not go hand in hand with government operation of the delivery system.

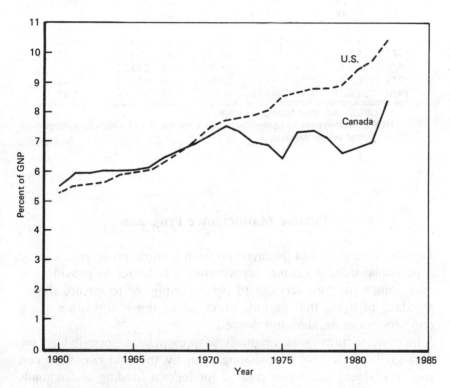

SOURCE: U.S. data from Gibson and Waldo 1982, and Mueller and Gibson 1976; Canadian data supplied by L. Rehmer, Department of Health and Welfare.

Figure 2.1. Health care expenditures as percentage of gross national product in United States and Canada, 1960-1982.

Table 2.5
Public and Total Health Expenditures in Canada, 1971–1980

Year	Overall Expenditures			Public Expenditures			Public $ as % of Total $
	Amount ($ billion)	% of GNP	Per Capita	Amount ($ billion)	% of GNP	Per Capita	
1971	7,123	7.54	329.90	5,217	5.52	241.62	73.24
1972	7,790	7.40	356.98	5,781	5.49	264.92	74.21
1973	8,721	7.06	395.11	6,454	5.22	292.40	74.01
1974	10,248	6.95	457.59	7,676	5.20	342.75	74.90
1975	12,340	7.46	542.97	9,433	5.71	415.06	76.44
1976	14,088	7.37	611.86	10,806	5.66	469.32	76.70
1977	15,395	7.37	661.29	11,711	5.61	503.04	76.07
1978	16,902	7.33	719.44	12,765	5.54	543.35	75.52
1979	18,836	7.20	794.72	10,460	4.00	441.32	55.53
1980	21,400	7.33	893.18	16,150	5.53	674.06	75.47

SOURCE: Adapted from Schwenger 1983.
NOTE: Schwenger indicates that figures for 1979 and 1980 are extrapolations based on partial data.

Income Maintenance Programs

Long-term care cannot be divorced from income programs. Indeed, a perennial debate centers on whether it is better to provide low-cost, long-term care services to older people, or to ensure them a standard of living that permits purchase of these and other goods and services as needed and desired.

Income security was originally a provincial responsibility, met through hefty federal cost-sharing. But by the mid-twentieth century, precedent had been created for federal funding and administration of unemployment insurance on the basis of the need for uniformity of benefit and efficiency of administration. Presently, other income maintenance programs have also been moved to the federal level.

Canadians who for various reasons are unable to generate sufficient income are now guaranteed a minimum income through a number of federal, provincial, and joint programs, including universal income entitlements financed by federal tax dollars; means-tested income supplements financed by federal tax dollars; contributory pension and unemployment insurance systems; and provincially administered welfare and worker's compensation programs. Provincial social assistance and social services providing assistance to persons in need are cost-shared with the federal government under Canada Assistance Plan (CAP) agreements. Social service programs that do not fulfill CAP requirements may be funded provincially or by municipal governments. Direct payments to individual Canadians include a universal Family Allowance System that has no analogue in the American Social Security system.

The programs of greatest relevance to older Canadians are the following:

- *Old Age Security (OAS)*, a federally administered universal entitlement to all Canadians who are eligible by age and Canadian residency;
- *Guaranteed Income Supplement (GIS)*, a federally administered income-tested supplement payable to OAS pensioners with little or no other income, which provides recipients with a minimum guaranteed income.
- *Spouse's Allowance*, which is payable to OAS pensioners' spouses aged 60–64 whose income is below certain levels, thus providing the couple with a minimum guaranteed income equivalent to that of a pensioner couple.
- *Canada Pension Plan (CPP)*, a federally administered compulsory contributory retirement plan financed by employer and employee contributions that applies everywhere but Quebec, and the *Quebec Pension Plan (QPP)*, an analogous plan established by that province.
- *Provincial Income Supplement Programs*.

Table 2.6 summarizes salient features of these plans and table 2.7 summarizes the coverage and cost of each federal income maintenance program. Appendix A offers more descriptive detail on each program.

Table 2.6

Income Programs for Seniors in Canada

Program	Date Begun	Eligibility	Taxable	Financing	Benefits in January 1984
Old Age Security (OAS)	1951	65+, Canadian resident (40 years as adult)	Yes	Federal	Maximum $263.78 per month; prorated for those with partial residency
Guaranteed Income Supplement (GIS)	1967	65+, Canadian resident; income tested	No	Federal	Designed to bring total income of individual to $529.38 and couple to $937.28 per month
Spouse's Allowance	1975	Pensioner's spouse or widow/widower aged 60–64; residents; part of benefit means tested	No	Federal	Basic benefit equal to OAS prorated as residency and additional means-tested benefit up to maximum OAS/GIS combination
Canada Pension Plan (or Quebec Pension Plan)	1965	All workers	Yes	Contribution of workers and employers	$387.50 maximum retirement pension per month; retirement benefit and survivor's benefit related to contributions; flat death benefit to estate also
Provincial plans in 6 provinces and 2 territories, e.g., Guaranteed Annual Income System in Ontario (GAINS), Guaranteed Annual Income (GAIN) in British Columbia, Saskatchewan Income Plan (SIP), etc.		Income tested; 65+ in most jurisdictions; 55+ in some provinces	No	Provincial	Varying small benefits that supplement OAS/GIS to a higher guaranteed income

SOURCE: Constructed from information in Canadian Governmental Report on Aging, 1982.

Table 2.7

**Scope of Canadian Federal Income Programs
(In $ billion)**

Program	Number of Beneficiaries in March 1983	Total Value of Benefits Paid 1982/83
OAS	1,174,833 (OAS only)	$7.005
GIS	1,250,852	$2.416
Spouse's Allowance	87,524	$0.221
Canada Pension Plan	1,455,953	$3.036
Quebec Pension Plan	463,490	$1.043

SOURCE: Health Information Division, Department of Health and Welfare.

Income Source and Adequacy

In 1979, approximately half the income of persons over 65 in Canada was accounted for by public sources. As table 2.8 shows, however, those at the lower end of the income scale were likely to depend entirely on public money. Women household heads over 65 were the most dependent on public sources of income. This is analogous to the situation in the United States, where about one-fifth of all elderly living alone and two-fifths of the black elderly living alone depend almost entirely (i.e., for 90 percent or more of their income) on Social Security and Supplemental Security Income, and women are more likely than men to rely on this income. In both countries, the reliance on public sources of income is greatest at the oldest age levels, where the effect of age is added to the effect of the higher proportion of females in the oldest age groups.

In 1979, the median incomes for unattached men and women aged 65 to 69 in Canada were $6,000 and about $5,000, respectively. At age 70+, the income of unattached men and women drew much closer, both at medians slightly above $4,000. By comparison, the average income for unattached adults of all ages in

Table 2.8

Percentage of Income of Elderly Canadians from Public and Nonpublic Sources in 1979

Source	Single Males[a]		Single Females[a]		Couples Both 65+	
	Income Under $3,500	All Income Levels	Income Under $3,500	All Income Levels	Income Under $5,900	All Income Levels
OAS/GIS	87.0	35.7	86.6	48.2	88.2	40.2
CPP/QPP	3.7	8.5	2.8	7.7	4.9	8.5
Other public[b]	1.2	1.7	2.4	3.1	2.4	2.6
All public	91.9	45.8	91.9	59.0	95.5	51.4
Investment	6.8	28.3	5.0	23.2	4.1	25.7
Private pensions and annuities	0.8	14.6	2.2	12.7	0.1	14.0
Earnings	0.4	11.2	0.9	5.0	0.2	8.9
All private	8.1	54.1	8.1	41.0	4.5	48.6
Total	100.0	100.0	100.0	100.0	100.0	100.0

SOURCE: Adapted from Canadian Government Report on Aging, 1982.
[a]Includes only those living on their own. Excludes those living in the families of relatives, but may include some living in families of unrelated people.
[b]Includes provincial income supplements, veterans pensions, and worker's compensation pensions.

1970 (nine years earlier) was $11,500 for men and $6,000 for women. The average family income was about $24,000 for families headed by men, a little under $10,000 for families headed by women, and about $15,000 for families headed by persons over 65 (the great majority of those household heads are men). As a point of comparison, the median income of unattached older people in the United States in 1981 was $5,750 (compared with $11,200 for all unattached adults), and the median family income of families headed by a person over 65 was $15,400 (compared with $23,950 for families in general).

In Canada, as in the United States, the income of older people in relation to younger people has improved greatly over the last decade, particularly because public pensions are indexed. In both countries, however, substantial poverty remains and is most apparent for women, people over 75, and (in the United States) blacks. The Canadian government calculates low-income thresholds using a formula that considers as poor any family that spends more than 58.8 percent of its income on shelter, food, and clothing. Table 2.9 shows the percentage of persons officially considered to be low-income in Canada in 1979 and 1980. In the United States, by comparison, poverty was established as $3,950 for a single person over 65 and $4,930 for a couple in 1980; by this less-generous standard, 24.4 percent of unattached men and 32.3 percent of unattached women over 65 were poor.

Summary

Although the approach to income maintenance in Canada includes a system of universal minimum benefits (the OAS) as well as a pension plan (analogous to Social Security in the United States) and income-tested supplements (analogous to SSI in the United States), the income picture of the old is similar in the two countries. In

Table 2.9
Proportion of Poverty in Canada for Selected Groups, 1979 and 1980

	Proportion in Poverty	
Group	1979[a]	1980[b]
All families	13.1	12.2
Families with head aged 65+	21.9	14.2
All unattached men	30.9	29.7
All unattached women	47.6	47.4
All unattached persons aged 65+	66.3	61.5

SOURCE: Schwenger 1983.

[a]Poverty levels are established according to size of community and, in 1979, ranged from $4,802 for a person in a rural area to $6,493 for a person in a city over 500,000. Thresholds for an elderly couple ranged from $6,275 to $8,567.

[b]In 1980, the level for poverty ranged from $5,289 to $7,152 for an individual and $6,912 to $9,436 for a couple.

both countries, the elderly tend to own their own homes, and therefore the asset picture looks more favorable than does the income
picture. In both countries, the elderly receive in-kind benefits that
make their incomes go further. In the United States, those in-kind
benefits for medical care and other assistance would differentially
raise the income of older people more than in Canada because all
Canadian citizens receive basic health benefits. In both countries,
however, specific programs targeted for the elderly (e.g., housing
and transportation subsidies) and tax breaks augment the income of
seniors.

In both countries, the very old, women, and those who live alone
are increasingly vulnerable because of low incomes. Therefore, we
can appropriately compare long-term care programs in Canada and
the United States without having to account for different effects
because of an income differential favoring the Canadian elderly.

Social Services

As in the United States, social services in Canada are a multifaceted
group of programs provided by philanthropic organizations and consumer groups as well as by governments. They encompass a wide
array of activities designed to enhance the functioning of individuals
and families, to prevent disadvantage and disability, to rehabilitate
to higher levels of social participation, to develop individual capaci-
ties, and to protect persons whose safety and well-being are at risk.
Construed so broadly, health, income maintenance, housing, justice,
vocational rehabilitation, and recreation services might be considered forms of social service. In this section, we particularly consider general social service functions such as are provided in the
United States under Title XX of the Social Security Act and Title III
of the Older Americans Act. These tend to be a cluster of rather
poorly defined services that include general relief, counseling programs of various types, child welfare, adult protective services, nutri-
tional programs, and a wide range of supportive programs for families and individuals.

All levels of Canadian government are involved in social service
programming. The municipal governments are most often the direct
providers of public social services, but the bulk of the costs are met

by the provinces. In turn, provinces receive approximately 50 percent cost-sharing for programs developed to serve persons in need.
As in the United States, private nonprofit organizations depend not
only on private donations but also on government contracting for
their operating funds. And in many cases, funds received from the
municipal governments or directly from the provincial governments
are cost-shared by the federal government.

Canada Assistance Plan

The main mechanism for federal cost-sharing for social services is
the Canada Assistance Plan (CAP), which became effective in 1966.
Replacing various cost-shared categorical assistance plans, CAP is a
program through which the federal government pays 50 percent of
the cost to provinces of providing social assistance to persons in
need and 50 percent of certain costs of providing welfare services to
persons who are likely to become in need if they do not receive
such services. (The provinces may in turn establish cost-sharing
arrangements with municipalities.) Social assistance includes cash
payments as well as purchase of goods.

The mechanisms for determining cost-sharability under CAP are
complex. Oversimplified, the federal government will pay 50 percent of the costs of all local and provincial programs that provide
general relief or purchase food, clothing, equipment, or any such
commodities for persons deemed to be in financial need. Services
(e.g., counseling, homemaking, day care) for persons in financial
need would also be cost-shared. Provinces do the needs-testing to
document the number of persons needing service. Under CAP, the
federal government shares in paying the program expenses (i.e., the
deficit after fees are collected) for a variety of residential programs
designed to serve persons at risk of being in need. Many of the
latter programs come in the category of "Homes for Special Care,"
which include old age homes, hostels for transients, homes for
unmarried mothers, halfway houses for the mentally ill or for
alcoholics, and a variety of similar programs. Work assistance programs, day care, and home health are also included. To qualify for
cost-sharing, the program must meet the province's standards for
programs of that type and the organization must have been listed as

eligible for cost-sharing. CAP tends to benefit most those provinces that can best afford to mount programs.

In 1976–77 and again in 1978–79, CAP transferred about $1.6 billion to the provinces, and almost $2 billion in 1981–82. (This money benefited all age groups, but over the years, the elderly came to receive less from CAP because the federal OAS/GIS and the extended health care block grant met many of their needs.) The growth of the CAP expenditures was held in check in the late 1970s largely because the Extended Care block grant instituted under the 1977 Established Programs Financing *replaced* CAP cost-sharing that had existed for persons in need who were receiving extended health care before that time. Therefore, not all the money in the per capita extended care block grant was new money.

The federal government developed elaborate guidelines to distinguish between programs and items that continued to be cost-sharable under CAP and those that were assumed to be covered by the new block grants. For example, most nursing home care and home health care became covered by the extended care grant. However, CAP shares in the costs of specific items not covered in the health programs such as comfort allowances, clothing purchases, and special equipment purchases for nursing home residents in financial need and for people in need who are receiving home care. Various homemaking programs that are strictly social in auspice and intent are still cost-sharable under CAP.

The CAP program assisted provinces in developing residential facilities for the elderly and home-support/homemaking programs *before* such programs became part of an insured long-term care benefit. The evolution of long-term care programs in our three provinces took on their particular characteristics because of municipal and private nonprofit programs that had already been established, stimulated partly by community efforts and partly by federal cost-sharing policies. As in the United States, Canadian communities in the 1970s and 1980s contain a potpourri of social agencies delivering community and residential services, and these agencies became incorporated in any provincial efforts to link health and social services into a system of long-term care.

Other Federal Programs

In addition to the CAP program, the federal government directly administers programs for aging veterans. The two major financial assistance programs for war veterans are the payment of disability pensions and payment of allowances to qualifying persons who are unable to work because of age or incapacity and have insufficient income. In 1981, a comprehensive program of social benefits was introduced to foster independent living for veterans. Building on the universal health programs that veterans received as citizens, the new Aging Veterans Program added home maintenance (grounds-keeping, home modification, meals-on-wheels, day hospital and day care) and nursing home care in the veteran's home community.

Finally, Health and Welfare Canada established its New Horizons program in 1972. This is a small grants program to local groups of senior citizens to encourage retired persons to participate in the community and to develop programs for their own benefit and support. Programs sponsored by New Horizons include educational and recreational projects as well as community service projects for the elderly such as telephone checking and information and referral projects.

Housing

Housing is, of course, a necessary condition of community long-term care and a basic component of all institutional care. Persons who cannot house themselves affordably and safely may find themselves admitted to residential facilities. Many persons over 65 in Canada own their own homes. Still others live with adult children; it has been estimated that, at the most, only a third of the noninstitutionalized elderly are renters. Renters are at greater financial vulnerability. A 1978 survey estimated that 25 percent of elderly homeowners, compared with 50 percent of elderly renters, spend more than a quarter of their income on shelter, and about one-fifth of elderly renters spent 40 percent or more of their income that way (Canadian Governmental Report on Aging 1983).

The Canada Mortgage and Housing Corporation (CMHC), established in 1946, has made low-interest loans available to provinces for the construction of low-income housing, some of which was ear-marked for the elderly. Public housing construction was phased out in 1978, but prior to that time, provinces could borrow 90 percent of the approved project capital costs at 2 percent interest. The costs of the rent subsidy and the maintenance of the buildings are shared on a 50–50 basis. Tenants are charged no more than 25 percent of their income in such housing. CMHC will cost-share rent subsidies on a 50–50 basis with the provinces even on buildings owned by private developers.

The CMHC also had a program of nonprofit housing, wherein it made loans to nonprofit societies for the construction of hostels, lodges, homes for the aged, and other such specialized congregate housing. Church groups and other nonprofit societies had an incentive to develop homes for the aged and nursing homes under these conditions. Mortgage rules permit 20 percent of the residential area to be used for common living and recreational space. Currently, CMHC is encouraging cooperative housing, where the building is owned cooperatively by the tenants. CMHC makes 2 percent mortgage money available for the developers and then shares the rent subsidies in the same way as with the nonprofit sector. By 1980, almost 138,000 rental units in public and cooperative housing had been constructed for seniors, and the federal cost of the rent subsidy was close to $160 million in 1980. Also about 46,000 hostel or other residential beds for the elderly had been built under this program by 1980.

Although CMHC plays a major role in funding social housing, private agencies, and municipal and provincial authorities are also responsible for both funding and administration. Other housing programs include a federal loan program for housing repair (Residential Rehabilitation Assistance Program) and provincial shelter allowance and tax rebate programs.

Provinces differ in the extent to which they are involved in housing programs for seniors, but all have made substantial investments. For example, Manitoba had about 7,300 public housing units for seniors in 1982–83 (10 percent of these units were designed for couples). In addition, Manitoba subsidized the rent for tenants in 3,000 other privately owned units. Ontario has developed a system of nonprofit municipal housing corporations and currently has a portfolio of about 63,000 units designed for seniors. Alberta's building program was perhaps the most ambitious. In October 1983, Alberta had about 10,900 self-contained apartments equipped to accommodate wheelchairs, and another 3,400 under construction. By October 1983, the province had built more than 7,200 beds in lodges—these were for seniors who could not or *preferred* not to maintain an independent home or apartment; 490 additional beds were under construction, and 484 self-contained cottage units were attached to the lodges. Alberta's 1982 expenditures for senior housing were $12.4 million.

The extent to which housing resources meet housing needs for the elderly in Canada is hard to determine. In almost all instances, the housing construction and shelter subsidy is considered quite separately from any services that might be provided to assist frail older persons to remain in these houses. Sheltered housing with self-contained units and accompanying services in a single package (such as is available in England) is underdeveloped. However, the location of many seniors in certain housing complexes has enabled more efficient targeting of services (e.g., home health, meals, homemaking) to those tenants.

In general, the provinces have made few conscious efforts to integrate their housing development and their long-term care planning into a coordinated strategy, even though activities in one sector clearly affect the other. For example, the federal/provincial stimulation of lodges and homes for the aged may have worked at cross-purposes with the effort to develop services for the frail elderly in their homes. And, of course, the appeal of public housing (and the lodges and homes for the aged as well) will be affected by the availability of low-rent housing in the particular city. In Winnipeg, for example, where public housing units are small, and affordable private housing is available because of a large rent subsidy program, the public housing for seniors is somewhat underutilized. On the other hand, a good supply of public housing and easy availability of home care seems to diminish the attractiveness of the lowest levels of residential care facilities. Some of these in all three provinces have vacancies, yet residential-level facilities often are structurally difficult to convert to higher levels of institutional care.

Background for Long-Term Care

Canadian provinces face populations that are aging in roughly the same proportions as in the United States, with similar accelerated growth in populations over age 65 with high dependency risks. Each province is responsible for developing a long-term care program to meet the needs of the frail elderly, and efforts along those lines were well under way before the extended care block grants of 1977 were inaugurated. Before 1977, however, public efforts were financed largely by municipalities and provinces. The federal contribution was substantial in that period, however, through two mechanisms: CAP cost-sharing for assistance and services to persons in need, and low-interest loans to nonprofit organizations for the construction of homes for special care.

When we began our study, all provinces, with the exception of the four Atlantic provinces, had a universal insurance program for nursing home care. Ontario and Manitoba began such insurance before the extended care block grants were established in 1977, whereas British Columbia's 1978 start date coincided with the infusion of new money. To clarify health policy, the federal government issued guidelines in 1973, setting forth and defining five levels of institutional care:

1. Residential
2. Extended care
3. Chronic hospital
4. Rehabilitation
5. Acute hospital

Care at levels 3 through 5 is automatically covered by provincial health insurance programs. All provinces further differentiate an extended care level (analogous to nursing homes) and a residential level for persons needing minimal health care. Not all provinces with insured nursing home benefits reach down to level 1: Manitoba and British Columbia do; Ontario does not. Also, some provinces have developed additional levels of care within the extended and residential categories. In our study, both Manitoba and British Columbia did so, whereas Ontario used only the fivefold federal classification.

Nomenclature for institutional care in each province is idiosyncratic, complicating comparisons among the provinces as well as extrapolations to the scene in the United States. Table 2.10 shows some of these distinctions. Note that Manitoba uses the term "Personal Care Home" to refer to the entire institutional program, whereas British Columbia uses the term "Personal Care" to refer to its lightest level of institutional care. The term "extended care" is used in Ontario to refer to care received by people deemed eligible for the extended health benefit; these people live either in Homes for the Aged (which also have a large residential component) or Nursing Homes. But Manitoba and British Columbia use "extended care" to refer to a heavy level of care, equivalent to level 3 in the Canadian government's formulation. Such extended care units are usually found in hospitals and are equivalent to Chronic Hospitals in Ontario, which are either freestanding or attached to acute care hospitals. In British Columbia, the term "private hospital" is used to refer to for-profit nursing homes that house the heaviest level of patients—i.e., extended care by British Columbia's terminology and chronic care by the federal terminology. In the United States, some of the persons who fall into level 1 (residential care) in Canada would be found eligible for the ICF level of nursing home, whereas others would be in Board and Care Homes. The Canadian level 2 would house people at the ICF or SNF level in the United States, whereas anyone at level 3 would probably qualify for SNF in the United States as inability to transfer is a rough prerequisite for level 3.

Noninstitutional long-term care programs (e.g., home nursing, homemaking, meals) have been available in many Canadian communities, especially in urban areas, for many years. They are provided by a variety of public, nonprofit, and proprietary organizations and financed by fees as well as public dollars. Each province faced the task of combining existing and new services into a coherent, widely accessible community long-term care program and determining the extent to which such services should be universally provided to the frail elderly.

The next three chapters examine how Ontario, Manitoba, and British Columbia met these challenges.

Table 2.10

Terms Used in Manitoba, British Columbia, and Ontario
for Levels of Care

Canadian Levels	Manitoba[a]	British Columbia[b]	Ontario[c]	United States Analogues by Resident Mix
Level 1 (Residential)	Personal Care Home, Level 1 (Hostels)	Personal Care Boarding Homes	Homes for the Aged Rest Homes Boarding Homes	Board and Care ICF (lower levels)
Level 2 (Extended)	Personal Care Home, Level 2 Personal Care Home, Level 3	Intermediate Care, 1-IC1 Intermediate Care, 2-IC2 Intermediate Care, 3-IC3	Homes for the Aged (Extended Care) Nursing Homes Satellite Homes	ICF SNF
Level 3 (Chronic)	Personal Care Home, Level 4 Extended Care Units	Extended Care Units Private Hospitals	Chronic Hospital	SNF Chronic Hospitals

[a] All 4 levels are part of Personal Care Home program of the Manitoba Health Services Commission.

[b] Access to all 5 levels is controlled by the Long-Term Care Program, which monitors care in the lower 4 levels. Extended Care standards are still part of Hospital Program.

[c] The Homes for the Aged Program is administered by the Ontario Department of Community and Social Services; the Nursing Home and Chronic Hospital Programs are administered by the Institutional Services Program in the Ontario Department of Health.

REFERENCES

Canadian Governmental Report on Aging, Minister of Supply and Services, Ottawa, 1982.

Gibson, R. M. and D. R. Waldo 1982. "National Health Expenditures, 1981." Health Care Financing Review, 4(1):19–20.

Hatcher, G. H. 1981. Universal Free Health Care in Canada, 1947–1977. Washington, D.C.: GPO.

Maxwell, R. J. 1981. Health and Wealth: An International Study of Health-Care Spending. Lexington, Mass.: Lexington Books.

Mennie, W. A. 1982. "Health Care Cost Containment Policies in Canada." Paper prepared for Expert Group Meeting on Economic Efficiency in Health Care Delivery, sponsored by International Social Security Association, Turku, Finland, September 30, 1982. Mimeo.

Mueller, M. and R. M. Gibson 1976. "National Health Expenditures, FY 1975," Social Security Bulletin, 39(2):3–20

PTF (Parliamentary Task Force on Federal-Provincial Fiscal Arrangements). 1981. Fiscal Federalism in Canada, Minister of Supply and Services, Catalog No. XC2–327/7–01E, 1981.

Preserving Universal Medicare: A Government of Canada Position Paper. 1983. Ministry of Supply and Services, Ottawa.

Schwenger, C. W. 1983. "National Context—Canada," a compilation of materials prepared for the Commonwealth Fund Forum, "Improving the Health of the Homebound Elderly: Best Prospects from Five English-Speaking Countries." London, England, May 23, 1983.

Soderstrom, L. 1978. The Canadian Health System. London: Croom Helm.

Taylor, M. G. 1978. Health Insurance and Canadian Public Policy: The Seven Decisions that Created the Canadian Health Insurance System. Montreal: McGill-Queen's University Press.

Van Loon, R. V. 1978. "From Shared Cost to Block Funding and Beyond: The Politics of Health Insurance in Canada," Journal of Health Politics, Policy, and Law, 2:454–478.

CHAPTER 3

Long-Term Care in Ontario

AMONG the three provinces, Ontario's delivery system most resembles that of the United States (with the large exception of universal benefits that minimize charges to users at the point that they receive services). Like the other provinces we studied, Ontario provides a universal entitlement for nursing home care to any citizen who requires it. Although the provincial policy differs dramatically from United States policy on this key point, Ontario has struggled and continues to struggle with issues that are familiar to Americans. These include striking the proper balance in the delivery system between health and social service authorities; correcting a bias toward institutional rather than community care; monitoring and assuring quality in a system with a mix of proprietary and nonprofit providers; and controlling costs while targeting services to those who most require them.

Long-term care services in Ontario are delivered and financed by two governmental entities: the Ministry of Health and the Ministry of Community and Social Services (ComSoc). Both these provincial ministries are organized into regional and local units for direct service. Both sponsor residential care and long-term care services in the community. ComSoc programs are targeted for the poor, whereas health programs tend to have no income-based eligibility restrictions. (The Ministry of Education participates with the other two ministries in a project for enhancing service delivery to mentally retarded clients in nursing homes.)

The health-sponsored services for long-term care are presumably focused on debilitated clients who are eligible by dint of medical need. ComSoc programs serve a wider range of needs, since they provide shelter and social support as well as medical care.

The historical evolution of the two ministries has yielded duplications as well as gaps. Currently, planners in the province are considering how to create a coherent, efficient, and desirable program from the various components already in existence. Many officials in the Ministries of Health and ComSoc concur that the dual system is less than ideal, but a merger or a realignment introduces a range of issues highly pertinent to the United States.

Nursing homes (usually privately owned and capitalized but financed by the government) and homes for the aged (usually owned by local municipalities or charitable organizations) are the major sites of long-term care services in the province. The two ministries are now committed to designing a home-based system that might serve as the first line of service. To that end, medically oriented entitlements to home care, which were initially designed as hospital substitutes and/or supplements, have gradually been expanded to serve those with chronic care needs. Ontario's experience with that process is a major theme in our study.

Ontario's long-term care programs are much less controlled than those of British Columbia and Manitoba. As in the other provinces, the major approach to limiting use of publicly financed institutional beds is to control the supply. But efforts to allocate that supply of services to those in greatest need are weak and imperfect. There is no consistent case management or other rationalizing force imposed between the consumer and the provider. In recent years, various mechanisms have been developed to help coordinate services and set priorities. These include the District Health Councils (which are local planning bodies); in some districts, Placement Coordination Services (which are programs to manage the waiting lists for all long-term care institutions in a region); and care coordinators from the chronic home care programs, whose role is to assess applicants and purchase community service on their behalf. Each of these mechanisms exerts a force toward coordination or case management, but all fall short of a comprehensive and authoritative control. After describing the current system, we will discuss each force toward coordination.

The Province

Ontario is a vast province with a population about equivalent to the Greater Los Angeles area (approximately 8.7 million). The four Great Lakes (Lake Michigan is entirely within the United States) form part of Ontario's border with the United States. Ocean liners are able to serve Ontario's industrial cities, thanks to the St. Lawrence Seaway linking Ontario to the Atlantic Ocean. The southeast portions of the province are heavily industrialized.

Population

More than a third of Canada's population lives in Ontario, most of it concentrated in the southern part near the American border (see figure 3.1).

The bulk of the population is urban. At the time of the 1976 census, only 3.4 percent lived on farms. Two-thirds lived in ten communities of 100,000 or more (see table 3.1). More than a third of the provincial population is further concentrated in Metropolitan Toronto, the provincial capital. Only two other cities exceed 500,000 in population: Ottawa, the federal capital, and Hamilton,

Table 3.1

Ontario Population in Metropolitan Areas over 100,000, 1976

Metropolitan Area	Population	Cumulative Percentage of Provincial Population
Toronto	2,803,101	34
Ottawa/Hull	632,597[a]	42
Hamilton	529,371	48
St. Catherines/Niagara	301,921	52
Kitchener	272,158	55
London	270,383	58
Windsor	247,582	61
Sudbury	157,030	63
Oshawa	135,196	65
Thunder Bay	119,250	66
Communities over 100,000	5,468,499	66
(Ontario)	8,264,500	100

SOURCE: Extrapolated from information in the *Canada Year Book, 1980-1981,* tables 4.8 and 4.9, pp. 132-133.
[a]The Ottawa Metropolitan figures may be somewhat inaccurate; they were derived by subtracting 60,691, the population of Hull in 1976, from the population of the Ottawa/Hull Metropolitan area. Hull is a French-speaking city across the Ottawa river in the Province of Quebec.

an industrial city less than an hour from Toronto. Almost half the provincial population is found in Toronto, Ottawa, and Hamilton combined. With the exception of Sudbury and Thunder Bay, all other metropolitan areas shown in table 3.1 are within an easy drive of Toronto. Only ten other cities fall in the population range of 50,000 to 100,000, with the remainder of the province made up of numerous small towns and villages.

Figure 3.1. Ontario cities with over 100,000 population.

In Ontario, 10.1 percent of the population is over 65, close to the 9.7 figure for the country as a whole. Table 3.2 provides a more refined age distribution for older men and women in 1976 and 1981. In 1981, almost 40 percent of the 65+ group were over 75. Under assumptions of low fertility and an annual external migration of 30,000 people, it is extrapolated that, by the year 2021, Ontario will reach almost 10.5 million people; almost 27 percent will be over 65 and more than a third of the 65+ group will be over age 75 (SSD 1981).

Using 1976 data, Gross and Schwenger (1981) analyzed the residential patterns of older people in Ontario. Although the province's small farm-dwelling population is disproportionately old, people over 65 are for the most part distributed like the rest of the population in the province (see table 3.3). Great variation was found from county to county, however, ranging from 4 percent aged 65+ in Peel County, a growing "bedroom" community near Toronto, to 15.6 percent in Haliburton County, a rural "cottage" area. Some small towns and villages in southern Ontario also have remarkably high percentages of elderly, reflecting the move of the younger people to employment in the cities. In the populous areas of Metropolitan Toronto, according to Gross and Schwenger's documentation, the proportion of elderly in the inner city is decreasing relative to

Table 3.2

Population of Ontario Aged 65 and Over, by Sex, 1976 and 1981
(In thousands)

Age	1976			1981		
	Male	Female	Total	Male	Female	Total
65-74	207.0	251.2	458.2	241.8	294.6	536.4
75-84	84.0	136.0	220.0	98.8	160.2	259.0
85+	19.4	41.4	60.8	21.2	51.5	72.7
Total	310.4	428.6	739.0	361.8	506.3	868.1
All ages	4,096.9	4,167.6	8,264.5	4,246.8	4,378.3	8,625.1

SOURCE: 1976 figures from Secretariat for Social Development 1981:36; 1981 figures from *1981 Census Population*, Statistics Canada 1981.

Table 3.3

**Urban and Rural Concentrations of Elderly Persons in Ontario
at Various Ages, 1976**

	Aged 65–74		Aged 75–84		Aged 85+		Total Ontario Population (Percent)
	Number	Percent	Number	Percent	Number	Percent	
Urban							
100,000+	260,860	56.9	125,430	57.0	34,120	56.1	59.8
1,000–99,000	110,200	24.1	57,490	26.2	17,045	28.1	21.4
Total, urban	371,060	81.0	182,920	83.2	51,165	84.2	81.2
Rural							
Nonfarm	75,200	16.4	32,775	14.9	8,575	14.1	15.5
Farm	11,940	2.6	4,280	1.9	1,005	1.7	3.4
Total, rural	87,140	19.0	37,055	16.8	9,580	15.8	18.8
Total, Ontario	458,200	100.0	219,975	100.0	60,745	100.0	100.0

SOURCE: Statistics Canada 1976 data compiled by Gross and Schwenger (1981).

the concentrations in the suburban boroughs. This changing pattern is a result of the "aging in place" of those who moved to the suburbs decades earlier.

Government Structures

Ontario has had a remarkably stable provincial government over the years that its health and long-term care programs were refined. As we began our study, the Progressive Conservative party had enjoyed decades of uninterrupted incumbency. At the provincial level, several ministries (the equivalent of departments of state government in the United States) have some responsibility for policies and programs related to the aged. In addition to the most centrally involved ministries—Health and ComSoc—other relevant ministries include Municipal Affairs and Housing, Northern Affairs, and Culture and Recreation. A superdepartmental structure headed by a Provincial Secretary for Social Development attempts to coordinate many of these domestic program efforts. Additionally, an Advisory Council for Senior Citizens, whose members are appointed by the premier, serves as an official advocacy and watchdog group.

Ten percent of Ontario's land mass houses 95 percent of its population. This populous part of the province is municipally organized; the remainder of the vast territory is under direct provincial administration. The settled part of Ontario is divided into the Municipality of Metropolitan Toronto, ten regional municipalities (each including one or more cities), one district municipality, and twenty-seven counties and regional districts. There are 45 cities (counting each of the five boroughs of Metropolitan Toronto separately), 144 towns, 120 villages, and 467 townships; the counties comprise the towns, villages, and townships found within them. The ten regional municipalities have replaced the county structure for those given geographic areas. The national capital, Ottawa (unlike Washington, D.C.), is contained within a province, forming part of the Ottawa-Carleton regional municipality in Ontario.

For health-planning purposes, Ontario is divided into thirty-three District Health Council areas. As of 1984, twenty-six District Health Councils were in operation. The boundaries of these districts roughly correspond to the regional municipality or county structure, but the match is imperfect; in some instances, several counties are grouped together into regional health districts.

Historical Development

Health Programming

Ontario was instrumental in the political negotiations that led to passage of the two national health insurance programs. The province began insuring nursing home care as early as 1972, although it has lagged somewhat behind other provinces in developing a home-based long-term care benefit.

Before 1959, residents of Ontario were responsible for paying their own hospital and doctor bills, and the responsibility for the indigent fell upon the municipalities. By the 1950s, much of the general public had turned to nonprofit or for-profit insurance plans to cushion them against these expenses. However, the provincial government played a financial role during this period in several ways. A hospital building program was launched, heavily supported by the National Health Grants program begun by the federal government in 1948. Although at first the provincial government did not subsidize hospitals for day-to-day operating costs, by the mid-1950s, as hospitals experienced the pressure of escalating costs, the provincial government began making substantial contributions. The strategy was to help hospitals contain their charges rather than increase the patient's ability to pay. The Ontario Hospital Services Commission, which later became the vehicle for administering universal hospital insurance, was established in 1956.

The provincial government also provided a grant to the Ontario Medical Association's Medical Welfare Board to defray charges for medical treatment of the elderly and indigent. In 1965, payments from that fund on behalf of pensioners amounted to more than $1 million. The Ontario Medical Services Insurance Plan (OMSIP) went into operation in April 1964 to provide free or subsidized medical coverage for low-income persons. OMSIP, which was then made available on a premium-paying basis to all citizens, provided its beneficiaries with 90 percent of the charges under the Ontario Medical Association's fee scale. Enrollment was voluntary and the program therefore coexisted with the private plans for medical insurance.

In 1959, Ontario introduced its Ontario Hospital Insurance Plan and, a decade later, its medical insurance coverage as part of the National Medicare Plan. In 1972, the medical and hospital insurance plans became jointly administered under the Ontario Health Insurance Plan (OHIP). In 1974, the province added a drug benefit program for the elderly and for social assistance recipients. Unlike most provincial plans, OHIP requires payment of a premium, which, in 1984, was $28.35 a month for a single person and $56.70 a month for families of two or more. Premiums are waived upon application for persons over 65 and those with limited incomes.

In 1966, nursing homes were brought under the control of the Ministry of Health, and standards were established for their operation. The Nursing Homes Act of 1972 elaborated those standards and introduced an extended care benefit that entitled anyone needing such nursing home care to be covered under OHIP. The Act was revised in 1980 and added to in December 1983.

During the same period that nursing home care was becoming organized under the Ministry of Health, home health programs were becoming established with operating funds from the province. In the mid-1960s, "acute home care" programs were developed to provide specific professional services for those needing them for a short period (often to replace hospital care or for post-hospital convalescence). By 1975, acute home care was available in every health district and several "chronic" home care programs were piloted. These later allowed for more homemaker services and were intended to help those who needed continuing care to remain at home. By 1983, the chronic home care benefit was in place in all communities except metropolitan Toronto, which was covered by early 1984.

Social Programming

Parallel developments in the social service field after the turn of the century resulted in substantial provincial programming for the frail elderly both in homes for the aged and in the community. However, ComSoc began underwriting residential care earlier than did the Ministry of Health.

The Homes for the Aged Act of 1947 (amended in 1949) allowed the Ontario government to make grants to local municipal authorities and fraternal, religious, or other charitable organizations to subsidize homes for the aged. The 1949 amendment then made it mandatory for each municipality to provide suitable homes for the aged, with the province paying half the capital cost and a proportion of the operating cost. In 1950, the earlier Charitable Institutions Act was amended to provide provincial subsidies of $1000 per bed to private charitable organizations for construction of homes for the aged. Throughout the 1950s, the provisions were altered to provide ever more generous incentives to the municipalities and charitable organizations to upgrade, construct, and operate such homes. The provincial subsidy was increased to 70 percent for municipal homes, and charitable organizations were given $2,500 per bed for construction and reimbursed up to 75 percent of operating costs.

The bed capacity of homes for the aged increased dramatically under this provincial stimulus. In 1949, municipal homes operated 3,732 beds; by 1969, the number was about 15,000. By 1980, 89 municipal and 92 charitable homes operated a combined total of almost 28,000 beds. Admission to Homes for the Aged was based on functional need, but those able to pay were charged for the services.

As early as 1955, the Special Home Care Program was introduced to allow persons to receive care in smaller, more homelike facilities with the understanding that the individual could enter a home for the aged if more care was needed. Facilities under this program are known now as "satellite" homes. This option has not been heavily utilized thus far.

The Homemakers and Nurses Service act of 1958 gave municipalities discretion to operate programs of homemaking and home nursing for the elderly, the handicapped, and others, and provided 50 percent cost-sharing from the provinces. In 1968, the act was amended to increase the provincial and federal cost-sharing to 80 percent. Municipalities were able to use their own nurses and/or homemakers or contract with agencies such as the Victorian Order of Nurses, the Canadian Red Cross Society, and the Visiting Homemaker's Association. Charges for those services were established according to ability to pay. Over half the provincial expenditure incurred for nursing and homemaking under this provision was made on behalf of the elderly.

ComSoc also developed home services through direct programmatic support to social agencies. The 1961 Elderly Persons Social and Recreational Centers Act assisted nonprofit organizations with the costs of developing social and recreational centers for the elderly. In 1966 this was amended to the Elderly Persons Centers Act, which allowed provincial funds to be used for home support services such as meals-on-wheels, congregate meals, and home handyman activities. (This activity is somewhat analogous to the granting power available to states and localities under the Older Americans Act in the United States.) In 1979 there were 115 Elderly Persons Centers (EPCs) in the province, and the special grant for home services operated by EPCs had been raised to $15,000. That year, 40 ECPs were offering such services. Starting in 1977, the province began funding demonstration projects to provide a range of home support services similar to those offered by the EPCs.

Home support services in many communities are attached to homes for the aged and comprised under those budgets. By 1980, for example, seventy homes for the aged provided vacation care, day care was offered to 600 people through homes for the aged, thirty-three homes ran drop-in centers for the elderly, and seventy-five homes ran meals-on-wheels and other meal programs (SSD 1981).

Housing and Income

Ontario's Elderly Persons Housing Aid Act of 1952 stimulated the construction of low-income housing for the elderly under Canada's National Housing Act, described in chapter 2. By 1966, more than 3,500 low-rental apartments for the elderly had been constructed. When the National Housing Act was amended in 1964 so that the federal government paid 90 percent of the capital costs and 50 percent of the operating costs for provincially or locally owned and operated public housing, the Ontario Housing Corporation was established to administer the program. The low-rental units under the Elderly Persons Housing Aid Act were transferred to the management of the Ontario Housing Corporation. Over the years, the proportion of public housing built shifted until, in the mid-1970s, it was almost entirely for the elderly. By 1980, Ontario managed about 62,000 housing units for seniors (defined as 60+); this represented almost a sixfold growth in a decade. Most were public housing operated by the Ontario Housing Corporation, but one-fifth were operated by a separate Metro Toronto Housing Corporation.

Ontario's income maintenance efforts for the elderly shifted as the federal presence became greater. The 1929 Ontario Old Age Pensions Act was superseded by the 1952 federal Old Age Security Program. Ontario then passed an Old Age Assistance Act to cover those between 65 and 69 initially excluded from the federal program. Expenditures under that program decreased as the federal coverage became more generous. In 1974, Ontario introduced its GAINS program (Guaranteed Annual Income Supplement) for low-income pensioners. In March 1983, approximately 189,000 pensioners received supplements. The annual 1982–83 cost to the province was $89 million.

Table 3.4 provides a timeline for the major milestones that have led to the current situation, in which both the Ministries of Health and ComSoc offer institutional and home-based services to the elderly.

Table 3.4
Chronology of Selected Programs for the Elderly in Ontario

Year	Health Programs	Social and Other Programs
1929		Old Age Pensions Act
1947		Homes for the Aged Act[a]
1948	Hospital construction under federal grants	
1950		Charitable Institutions Act amended
1952		Old Age Assistance Act
		Elderly Persons Housing Act
1955		Special Home Care Act
1958		Homemakers and Nurses Service Act
1959	Universal Hospital insurance begins	
1961		Elderly Persons Social and Recreational Centers Act
1964	Ontario Medical Services insurance	
1965	Acute Home Care Program begins	
1966		Elderly Persons Centers Act allows in-home support programs
1969	Universal medical insurance begins	
1972	OHIP created	
	Nursing Home Act introduces a universal extended care benefit	
1974	Drug benefit for seniors introduced	
1975	Chronic Home Care Program begins	
1977		GAINS Program
		Alternatives to Institution-alization Program

[a]The Homes for the Aged Act was amended in 1949 and again in 1956 and 1958 to add further incentives for municipalities and nonprofit associations to build and operate nursing homes by modifying the arrangements.

Long-Term Care Overview

From this historical account of health and welfare provisions in Ontario, we move to a cross-sectional examination of long-term care. The purposes of this section are to examine the supply and use of the components of Ontario's long-term care system, the characteristics of providers and of persons served, the costs of the programs, and who bears those costs at present. In chapter 6, we discuss longitudinal patterns of supply, use, and costs in all three provinces.

Recall that we have defined long-term care as service of sustained duration to compensate for functional impairment. In Ontario at present, the major public cost centers for these services are the extended care program (which finances nursing home care) and the chronic hospital program—both in the Ministry of Health—and the ComSoc-administered Homes for the Aged program, which includes both extended care and residential care. Other components are the Ministry of Health's home care and day health care programs, and the variety of community-based services, including homemaking, that are underwritten by ComSoc.

As in the United States, any long-term care services that are largely privately financed are hard to quantify, although it is clear that private means are used to support in-home services. A substantial private Rest Home industry has also evolved. The Rest Home Association of Ontario estimated in 1982 that there were 50,000 to 70,000 rest home beds in the province, but only a small fraction of the owners belong to the Association. Rest home charges range from about $16 a day to about $45 a day. Some municipalities will finance the care of the poor in selected rest homes, and each municipality negotiates its own rates. For the most part, however, residents of rest homes are self-financing.

Levels of Care

Following the format developed by the federal government, Ontario uses five levels to classify *all* patient care: 1. Residential; 2. Extended; 3. Chronic; 4. Special Rehabilitative; and 5. Acute. Table 3.5 describes each level according to the characteristics of the persons served, the program characteristics, and the typical sites for delivery of service.

Note that level 1 is regarded as a "health-related *social* program." As such, it is offered in Homes for the Aged supported by ComSoc. But, as table 3.5 shows, extended health care (level 2) is also provided in Homes for the Aged. Therefore, residents of such homes who, by dint of disability, become eligible for an extended care facility, need not relocate to exercise their benefit.

Table 3.5

Patient Classification Levels in Ontario

Level	Characteristics	Patient Program	Delivery Sites
1. Residential	Independently mobile, needs supervision, ADL assistance and/or social and recreational service because of physical or mental frailty, medically stable	Health-related social program of activation-oriented residential care	Homes for the aged; boarding homes; rest homes, lodges, manors, hostels, etc.; day-care centers; community social support programs
2. Extended Health	Stabilized physical or mental chronic disease or functional impairment, a limited need for diagnostic or therapeutic services, needs personal care availability on 24-hours basis (with nursing supervision), condition expected to be prolonged	Reactivation-oriented maintenance care program with continuing medical and professional nursing supervision	Nursing homes; homes for special care; homes for the aged; a private home with home-care services
3. Chronic	Acute phase of chronic illness is over; patient may or may not be stable; requires a range of therapeutic services, medical management, and/or skilled nursing care; deviation of need unpredictable but likely to be months or years	Coordinated multidisciplinary rehabilitation-oriented program according to individual plan	A hospital for the chronically ill; a special "chronic unit" in a general hospital; a nursing home approved for chronic care; a private home with appropriate services
4. Special rehabilitative	Diagnoses established, acute phase over, specialized assessment, treatment adaptation and training needed related to an identified problem	Comprehensive program provided by team of rehabilitation personnel under direction of rehabilitation specialist	Specialized rehabilitation centers on inpatient or (given suitable living accommodations) an outpatient basis
5. Acute	Needs diagnosis, is critically or seriously ill, is precariously unstable, and/or is convalescing from illness or injury and requires a short therapeutic or educational program	Full gamut of specialized skills and treatment	Hospitals; outpatient health care; acute home care

SOURCE: Adapted from Ontario Ministry of Health brochure, "Patient Care Classification," 1978.

Note also that Ontario has used only one level (called extended care) for virtually all nursing home beds. This is in contrast to Manitoba and British Columbia, which have created additional differentiated levels within level 2.

The policy recognizes that care at any level can be provided in the community, assuming appropriate room and board and community support. Those who need level 1 care, therefore, might well be accommodated in social support programs such as day centers and meal programs. Day care for mentally ill persons is one example. Those at level 2 may be assisted by the chronic home care program as well as by an array of community support services. Interestingly, even those needing the specialized and intensive services of level 3 (Chronic Care) can be treated at home under suitable circumstances. Substantial numbers of persons requiring level 3 are younger than 65 and are managed at home through the good offices of spouses and other relatives. Even persons who might otherwise be receiving acute hospital care are sometimes managed at home. The acute home care program is credited with bringing about earlier discharges from hospitals and, occasionally, substituting for hospitals.

Levels 1, 2, and 3 directly concern long-term care (although access to specialized rehabilitation and acute care as appropriate is crucial to any long-term care system). The boundaries between these levels are somewhat arbitrary. The working guideline is that a minimum of 1.5 hours of personal and nursing care per day should be needed before a person is eligible for extended health care. When daily care requirements reach three hours a day, chronic hospital care is considered.

Programs and Benefits—Institutional Sector

First, we shall consider the institutional programs, their service, and charges as they would appear to a user. In the next section, we will describe the overall financing for the services.

Homes for the Aged. A home for the aged now exists in most municipalities. In early 1982, there were 180 homes for the aged, about half owned by municipalities and half by charitable societies.

Almost 15,000 beds were available for level 1 residential care, as well as about the same number of level 2 extended care beds.

Space permitting, any individual seeking residential service, regardless of income, is eligible for Homes for the Aged. In practice, the fee policies present powerful deterrents to admission for all those of moderate or greater incomes. Fees are charged according to ability to pay, and the equity in a person's own home becomes part of the fund for paying the home for the aged. Homes for the Aged seem *de facto* targeted at the poor.

Nursing Homes (Extended Care). The universal benefit for extended care is triggered by a physician's assessment. The doctor uses a standardized form that is reviewed by the Ministry of Health with a five-day guaranteed turn-around time. The form contains a variety of functional items and yields a score that indicates whether the applicant's needs are sufficient for extended care. Physicians readily learn how to "beat the form." The review occurs on paper only, and therefore the physician's endorsement is the single hurdle to overcome before a prospective user has a "license to hunt" for a facility. Facilities have the right of refusal, so the search for a mutually agreeable location with available accommodation may be taxing. In some geographic areas, Placement Coordination Services have been developed to make the process easier and fairer for both the users and the providers. (These are discussed below.) A residency of twelve months in the province is required before the extended care benefit takes effect.

As of April 1984, there were 332 nursing homes and 29,219 beds for extended care; at least 95 percent of these were in proprietary facilities. The resident pays a per diem charge to defray the room and board costs. This amount is fixed so that even those whose income derives solely from the OAS/GIS (described in chapter 2) will have at least a specified sum remaining for discretionary expenses. For example, as of March 1984, the copayment rose to $15.86 per day, and the personal allowance was $96.00 per month, a sum that far exceeds the most generous allowance for nursing home residents under Medicaid. Each resident is entitled to "standard ward accommodation," which may not exceed four beds in a room. Residents pay additional specified charges for semiprivate and private rooms unless dictated by their condition. Homes are required to charge "standard ward rate" for at least 55 percent of their beds—therefore, some residents in double rooms may be billed at the "ward" rate, depending on the facility design. Certain other delineated services and comforts also require extra payment, but the extra billing of residents is subject to rather strict rules. The patient's own physician may continue care in the nursing home.

In addition to the nearly 29,000 extended care beds in nursing homes, there were almost 13,000 extended care beds in homes for the aged in 1982. When a resident of a home for the aged qualifies for extended care, he or she no longer is responsible for any payment beyond the per diem just described for residents of nursing homes. Therefore, a resident has an incentive to be designated for extended care. The extended care beds in homes for the aged were originally intended to be limited to persons already in the residence, but, with the overall pressure on beds, admissions often occur directly from the community. Homes for the Aged tend to have their own staff physician, who assumes primary care responsibility for all the residents.

If a resident of a nursing home goes to the hospital, he continues to pay the per diem and the Ministry of Health continues to pay its portion to hold the bed for up to 14 days. After that time, the patient or family would need to pay *both* portions of the bill to reserve the space.

Table 3.6 shows the distribution of Level 1 and 2 institutional beds by ownership in 1981.

Chronic Hospital. In March 1982, there were about 12,200 chronic hospital and general rehabilitation beds available in Ontario. The majority were in chronic units of acute hospitals, but about 20 freestanding chronic hospitals were also in the system. Chronic hospital care is an OHIP benefit (i.e., part of hospital insurance) that is free to the user. However, long-stay chronic care patients begin paying the extended care residential fee after the 60th day in the hospital, as do others needing chronic hospital or extended care who are in the acute hospital awaiting an alternative arrangement. This provision removes any monetary incentive to remain in the hospital. Special rehabilitation beds (level 4) are scarce; in 1981, there were only 637 beds with that designation.

Table 3.6

Long-Term Care Bed Supply in Ontario in 1981
(Levels 1 and 2)

Type	Number of Facilities	Beds by Level		Total Beds
		Residential	Extended	
Homes for aged				
Charitable	91	6,977	2,683	9,660
Municipal	89	7,821	10,245	18,066
Total	180	14,798	12,928	27,726
Nursing homes	349	(a)	28,627	28,627
Total	529	14,798	41,555	56,353

ªNursing homes have a small number of residential beds, which are not covered by the extended care benefit.

Programs and Benefits—Noninstitutional

Acute Home Care. Since 1968, Ontario has offered a medically oriented home care program to OHIP beneficiaries. The following criteria must be met to be eligible for the service: The patient must be under medical supervision; the patient must need at least one professional service (e.g., nursing, physiotherapy, occupational therapy, speech therapy) on a regular basis; the physician must judge that the patient could be treated satisfactorily at home and the home must be deemed suitable for the care; the patient's professional treatment must be "reasonably expected to result in patient progress toward established goals for rehabilitation." (As home care programs have expanded, the coordinator/case manager from the home care program in conjunction with the physician has been designated responsibility for judging the suitability of home care, so by 1983 the nominal authority of the physician was reduced.) As with home health in the United States under Medicare, homemaking does not qualify as a professional service to trigger home care. Home care also is not offered if the individual is deemed able to receive the necessary service on an outpatient basis in a physician's office or outpatient clinic. Acute home care services may be provided to residents of facilities if the facility lacks the specialized therapeutic staff.

The acute home care program is free to the users. Often it is viewed as a hospital replacement—either in lieu of hospital admission or to shorten hospital stays. It is also used for post-hospital recuperation periods. Most home care programs are delivered through local health departments. Approval of the Ministry of Health was needed to activate the programs, and the Ministry provides each with an annual budget. There are thirty-eight programs; thirty are in health departments, four in Visiting Nurse Associations, three in hospitals, and one (Metro Toronto) in a freestanding nonprofit agency with a separate board.

Professional services (e.g., nursing, physiotherapy, occupational therapy, speech therapy) must be needed on a regular basis before the patient is eligible for the program. (Regular means at least weekly and likely more often.) When the need for professional services is established, the patient is then eligible for related assistance, including sickroom supplies, dressing, drugs, transportation, laboratory services, and homemaking. Homemaking is permitted to a maximum of 80 hours per admission and is meant to assist relatives or the person living alone with household tasks, particularly meal preparation and laundry. The Home Care Program may provide other services as well, such as social work, nutrition counseling, respiratory therapy, and enterostomal therapy. Residents of nursing homes and homes for the aged also can receive physical, occupational, and speech therapy from the Acute Home Care Program.

The Home Care Program purchases nursing services from agencies (especially the Victorian Order of Nurses) or secures them from the Public Health Nursing Division of the Health Department. The homemaking services are also purchased either from voluntary or proprietary agencies. In urban areas, there are usually multiple vendors including the Visiting Homemakers Association (a nonprofit agency). Outside the cities, the Red Cross is the major provider of homemaking services, although proprietary firms are gaining a foothold. The various therapeutic services are usually provided directly by Home Care staff, but contractual arrangements are also possible, particularly in rural areas.

A coordinator employed by the Home Care Program is responsible for care planning and managing all the services and facilitating communication among the various providers. The coordinator may be involved in arranging for other community social services, such as meal programs, friendly visiting, special clubs, day care, and so on. The coordinator is also responsible for assessing program eligibility—that is, whether the home is suitable for care and whether patient progress is feasible. In general, the home care coordinator determines that referred patients meet Home Care eligibility criteria and that reassessments are carried out at regular intervals. In the fall of 1983, the coordinators were renamed case managers, a reflection of the continuous monitoring role envisaged for them.

Chronic Home Care The Chronic Home Care Program is an extension of the acute home care program just described. Whereas the Acute Home Care Program provides for relatively intensive home care services that are generally short-term, the chronic program is designed to provide care to more typical long-term care users. A medical referral is still needed, but the amount of professional service required to maintain eligibility for chronic home care is reduced to three visits per month by one of the four professionals (nurse, physiotherapist, occupational therapist, or speech therapist) whose presence justifies the continuance of a health benefit. The amount of homemaking allowed is 80 hours the first month and 40 hours per month thereafter. The same vendors are used for home nursing, homemaking, and other services as in the acute home care program. As with the Acute Home Care Program, the Chronic Home Care Program provides direct therapeutic services (physiotherapy, occupational therapy, and speech therapy) to residents of nursing homes and homes for the aged if the service is not available through internal staff.

Chronic home care programs began on a pilot basis in the mid-1970s and gradually have been implemented throughout the province. With the planned 1984 implementation in Metropolitan Toronto, all districts will have a Chronic Home Care Program in place. Separate statistics are still maintained for the Acute and the Chronic Programs, although the two programs are expected to merge within another year or so. In 1982–83, more than 90,100 admissions to the acute home care and 21,500 admissions to the chronic home care programs were recorded.

If an individual needs homemaking and other social services in the home without any requirement for a professional health service, he or she may be eligible for programs under the auspices of

ComSoc. However, ComSoc programs are needs-tested and designed for the poor.

ComSoc administers a Visiting Homemakers' and Nurses' Services Program, which provides homemaking, assistance with meals, cleaning, and provision of personal care services. Visiting nurses also provide in-home medical care. Clients are needs-tested for services and may be required to contribute to the costs. Services are available to handicapped, convalescent, chronically ill, elderly, or otherwise disabled persons. In 1982–83 approximately 89,000 nurses' visits were recorded.

At this writing, the Ministry of Health and ComSoc are planning to pilot a "homemaker only" benefit to be administered by the same home care programs that coordinate acute and chronic home care now. Some authorities favor this as a more efficient way of delivering home care when professional services are unnecessary. Others worry about the ability to monitor the quality of care adequately if homemakers were to be visiting the case without the ongoing supervision of a health professional. The pros and cons of developing a homemaking service that is universally available to the functionally impaired and free at the point of use are widely debated. At this writing, it is planned that the Home Care Case Manager will assess persons referred to the Homemaker Service Program and reassess them at intervals, consistent with the Case Manager's function in the general Home Care program.

Utilization and Cost

Institutional Sector

Table 3.7 shows the pattern of use of extended care beds in nursing homes between 1973 and 1982. Over that period, the proportion of users over 65 increased from about 82 percent to 87 percent, and the total number of residents increased 46 percent. Table 3.8 presents the same data for the extended care beds in Homes for the Aged. The increase in utilization for this segment of the program was only 8 percent over the ten years and 10 percent for residents over age 65. The extended care beds in homes for the aged are almost exclusively occupied by persons over 65.

Table 3.7

Ontario Extended Care Program in Nursing Homes, 1973-1982

Year	Number Licensed Beds	Number Extended Care Residents	Percent Extended Care Occupancy	Number Extended Care Aged 65+	Percent Extended Care 65+ Occupancy	65+ as Percent of Nursing Home Extended Care
1973	22,505	19,123	85.0	15,671	69.6	81.9
1974	23,479	20,874	88.9	17,154	73.1	82.2
1975	24,887	22,873	91.7	18,844	75.7	82.5
1976	25,993	24,488	94.2	20,357	78.3	83.1
1977	27,308	26,031	95.3	21,727	80.0	83.4
1978	27,847	27,007	97.0	22,686	81.5	84.0
1979	28,079	27,614	98.3	23,417	83.4	84.8
1980	28,208	27,829	98.7	23,830	84.5	85.6
1981	28,295	27,478	97.1	23,684	83.7	86.2
1982	28,686	27,939	97.4	24,291	84.7	86.9

Summary of trends, 1973-1982:
Licensed beds increased 27.5%
Residents increased 46.1%
Residents 65+ increased 55.0%

Occupancy increased from 85.0% in 1973 to 97.4% in 1982 or +12.4%
Occupancy for 65+ increased from 69.5% in 1973 to 84.7% in 1982 or +15.1%
Percentage of clientele aged 65+ increased from 81.9% in 1973 to 86.9% in 1982 or +5.0%

SOURCE: Information supplied by Ontario Ministry of Health.
NOTE: Data refer to March 31 of each year.

Table 3.8

Ontario Homes for Aged Extended Care (HFA/EC) Program, 1973-1982

Year	Number HFA/EC Beds	Number HFA/EC Residents	Percentage EC Unit Occupancy	Number HFA/EC Aged 65+	Percentage EC Unit 65+ Occupancy	65+ as Percentage of HFA/EC
1973	—	11,196	—	10,704	—	95.6
1974	12,290	10,841	88.2	10,714	87.2	98.8
1975	12,920	10,868	88.4	10,283	83.7	94.6
1976	12,518	11,349	90.7	10,651	85.1	93.8
1977	12,794	11,722	91.6	11,106	86.8	94.7
1978	13,026	11,888	91.3	11,472	88.1	96.5
1979	13,094	12,380	94.5	11,653	89.0	94.1
1980	13,088	12,263	93.7	11,885	90.8	96.9
1981	13,118	12,323	93.9	11,975	91.3	97.2
1982	12,911	12,111	93.8	11,790	91.3	97.3

Summary of trends for extended care in Homes for the Aged, 1973-1982:
  Beds increased 5.1%
  Residents increased 8.2%
  Residents 65+ increased 10.1%

  Occupancy increased from 88.2% in 1974 to 93.8% in 1982 or +5.6%
  Occupancy for 65+ increased from 87.2% in 1974 to 91.3% in 1982 or +4.1%
  Percentage of clientele aged 65+ increased from 85.6% in 1973 to 97.3%
    in 1982 or +1.7%

SOURCE: Information supplied by the Ontario Ministry of Health.
NOTE: Data refer to March 31 of each year.

As already indicated, there are currently close to 15,000 residential beds in Homes for the Aged. The major building of Homes for the Aged occurred in the 1950s and 1960s, and the overall stock has therefore not increased in recent years. However, the proportion of extended care beds has risen, and subjective accounts suggest that the overall population in Homes for the Aged has become more frail.

Proprietary nursing homes and Homes for the Aged are reimbursed differently. The nursing home is paid a per diem that is negotiated annually between the Ontario Nursing Home Association and the province. The user pays a copayment as already indicated, and the provincial proportion covers the remainder. The per diem rate for standard ward accommodation was $42.35 in February

1984, with $26.49 paid by the government and $15.86 by the resident.

In contrast, the cost of Homes for the Aged is subsidized almost completely. The formula differs somewhat, depending on whether the home is owned by the municipality or a charitable organization. For municipal homes, the province pays 70 percent of the operating deficit, and the municipality pays the rest. For charitable homes, ComSoc limits reimbursement to 80 percent of the deficit on operating costs. The extended care portion of the Home for the Aged is also reimbursed somewhat differently in the two types of home. In municipal homes, extended care was reimbursed at 100 percent of costs up to a fixed per diem of $37 in 1982; 70 percent of any excess over that amount is paid by the province, with the municipality picking up the remainder. In 1982, the province paid a flat $39 a day for extended care in charitable homes. It would seem, however, that the distinction between extended care financing and residential care financing must become somewhat blunted as costs are affixed to one program or the other. The client's share of costs for residential care in homes for the aged equals more than half the total costs in charitable homes and less than half the total costs in municipal homes.

Table 3.9 shows the increase in expenditures for Homes for the Aged and nursing homes between 1977 and 1983. The increase in actual dollars is about 80 percent, with the nursing home sector accounting for a somewhat greater increase. Allowing for inflation, the actual rate of increase is much less. The Ontario government has been concerned, however, about likely future increases as a consequence of demographic shifts. Ontario planners have established guidelines for resource supply, as indicated in table 3.10. Table 3.11 compares the existing stock of extended care beds, as of mid-1982, with the number needed by these guidelines. The result is an excess of more than 10,000 beds. This excess exists only if the current utilization pattern can be brought under better control by developing other modalities of long-term care.

The Ministry is also concerned that the extended care program in the Homes for the Aged may be more expensive than the program in nursing homes. At this writing, no definitive data were available on case mix in the two sectors. Anecdotally, however, we are told that the extended care population in Homes for the Aged is older

Table 3.9

**Increase in Expenditures of Homes for the Aged
and Nursing Homes, 1977-78 to 1982-83**

Item	1977-1978	1982-1983	Percent of Total Increase	Accounting for Inflation
Homes for the Aged				
Operating	$103,905,880	$174,664,000		
Capital	1,838,837	8,290,300		
Total	$105,744,717	$182,954,300	73	4.4
Nursing Homes	120,198,092	218,600,000	82	9.7
Grand Total	$225,942,809	$401,554,300	78	7.2

SOURCE: Data provided by Ministry of Community and Social Services.

Table 3.10

Ontario Ministry of Health Guidelines for Bed Supply

Type of Bed	Number per 1000 Population
Acute hospital (excluding psychiatric)	3.5–4.0
Acute psychiatric	0.4
Chronic hospital	11.9 (per 1000 aged 65+)
Extended Care	3.5

SOURCE: Ministry of Health, Institution Division, March 1982.

Table 3.11
Extended Care Beds Available and Needed in Ontario as of May 1982

Item	Number of Beds	Beds per 1000
Current nursing home beds	28,627	2.7
Extended care beds in		
Homes for the Aged	12,911	1.5
Approval for construction	548	0.1
Total	42,086	4.3
Estimated need from guidelines	30,876	3.5
Excess supply	11,210	

SOURCE: Data Development and Evaluation Branch, Ministry of Health, 1982.

and frailer than in nursing homes. This may be due to market skimming by the nursing home industry.

The Ontario government controls the cost of institutional long-term care by controlling the supply. No new Homes for the Aged beds have been authorized, and the supply of extended care beds in private nursing homes is tightly controlled. When new beds are desired in a particular geographic area, the government initiates a "Request for Proposals," a competitive process whereby prospective operators may submit proposals to supply the beds on the basis of their credentials and their construction and operating plans. Cost is not at issue, because the firms compete for the rights to use their *own* funds to build the home, with the allowable per diem rates remaining uniform throughout the program. Therefore, an interesting situation has developed wherein proprietary homes compete to build beds on the basis of the amenities they plan to provide. Although the nursing home industry complains that the reimbursement rate is unconscionably low, each Request for Proposals seems to prompt a flurry of competitive bids.

Community Care. The gradual way in which home care programs were implemented complicates examination of utilization trends. In 1981–82, when thirty-eight acute and twenty-one chronic programs were implemented, there were 102,684 home care cases, of which 85,937 were acute home care, and 16,747 were chronic. In 1982–83, when the number of chronic home care programs implemented had increased to 34, there were 90,100 admissions to acute home care and 21,500 to chronic care. With Metropolitan Toronto added to the Chronic Program, almost a third of the province's population has become eligible; 1984 should show a marked expansion of clientele.

Table 3.12 presents data for the two years in which most Chronic Home Care programs were mounted. The Chronic Program clearly served an older population than the acute program, though both home care programs served substantial numbers of people under age 65 and in the 65 to 74 age range. The Acute Home Care population was most likely to be referred from an acute hospital and be discharged to the community, whereas Chronic Home Care patients had a good chance of being referred from home and a better than 50 percent chance of being discharged to the acute hospital. The amount of homemaking service given was quite parsimonious even in the Chronic Home Care program, where the average length of stay was a little more than 100 days and the average number of homemaker hours per case was only about 14. All the averaged statistics in table 3.12 mask the high degree of variability in every parameter among the program units. The program characteristics remained quite stable over the two-year period.

The statistics are somewhat difficult to interpret because persons with intervening hospital admissions would show up as new cases (a problem plaguing long-term care statistics in the United States as well). Also, the discharge disposition to nursing homes, chronic hospitals, and Homes for the Aged is somewhat misleading because some of that number is accounted for by persons originally residing in those facilities who were admitted to home care for a course of physiotherapy, speech therapy, or some other specialized professional service.

Until recently, home care programs have been funded according to prospective line-by-line budgets submitted to the Ministry of Health. The programs submit an operating statement every two months; this permits the provincial monitors to keep closer track of potential overruns. An internal study was conducted in 1982 to explore a number of options for financing home care, including

Table 3.12
Characteristics of Ontario Home Care Program, 1981–82 and 1982–83

	Acute Program		Chronic Program	
Item	1981-82	1982-83	1981-82	1982-83
Percentage of cases 65+	56.8	61.1	78.4	78.2
Percentage of cases 75+	33.4	35.0	56.00	54.8
Average length of stay (days)	33	30	104	135
Admissions per 1000 population	10.7	10.2	5.0	2.4
Average visits per case				
Nursing	4.8	5.5	5.6	5.4
Physiotherapy	0.8	0.9	0.5	0.5
Homemaking hours per case	5.4	5.6	13.9	13.7
Referrals by prior site (%)[a]				
Acute hospital	64.2	64.9	34.0	36.4
Community	28.5	26.9	38.7	56.0
Chronic hospital	0.7	0.7	0.7	2.3
Other home care	0.8	0.2	0.8	3.1
Nursing home	2.1	1.9	2.1	0.7
Home for Aged	1.8	1.5	1.8	0.2
Discharge disposition (%)[a]				
Home	62.0	60.9	24.5	26.1
Acute hospital	16.2	16.0	55.2	52.1
Chronic hospital	0.1	0.2	1.1	0.8
Nursing home	2.3	2.9	3.0	3.4
Home for Aged	1.7	1.5	2.5	1.7
Public health nursing support	4.2	4.5	3.5	3.6
$ per discharged case	$486.45	$509.33	$1751.93	$1550.63
$ per diem	$15.48	$17.04	$14.02	$11.47

SOURCE: Ontario Home Care Program Annual Reports, 1981-82 and 1982-83.

[a]Does not add to 100 percent because some small categories are omitted.

replacing line-by-line budgeting with partial or complete global budgeting, capitation systems, or block grants with an insistence on core services being performed. Municipal and/or user cost-sharing was also considered. After looking theoretically at the incentives and disincentives for each method according to quality, administrative feasibility, efficiency, monitoring ease, and community acceptability, the provincial program officials have decided to introduce partial global budgeting, with the possibility of later doing full global budgeting on some case-mix basis. Municipal and user cost-sharing were rejected at that time.

The costs per case vary enormously from region to region; for example, Windsor has a relatively low cost of $1,067 per chronic case, whereas Ottawa-Carleton has an average of $2,411 (well above the provincial average of $1,751). Some authorities speculate that the cost differential is related to the case mix; this is hard to substantiate, however, because the only case mix data collected are based on diagnosis rather than functional status. The price of service will also influence cost. Price of homemaking is negotiated by ComSoc in each municipality and will therefore differ from county to county. In 1982, the provincial average rate for homemaking agencies was $6.50 an hour, and the homemakers themselves were paid the minimum wage, which in April 1984 was $3.85. As of 1983, nursing agency rates have been negotiated through the Ministry of Health. In 1983, there were thirty-three different rates established with the different Visiting Nurses Associations, and for fiscal year 1983–84 the average provincial payment for home nursing ranged from $14.80 to $24.34 a visit.

The "homemaking only" benefit has potential to be either costly (if new clientele are added) or to save money (if professional services are dropped); projections on likely cost implications have been difficult. One study of the Chronic Home Care clientele in a particular area showed that only about 10 percent simultaneously received maximum homemaking (40 hours a month) and the minimum professional service (three visits a month). This was viewed as an indication of the maximum number of professional services that could be reduced under a "homemaking only" program.

Quality Assurance

Institutional Sector

The Ontario government's quality assurance mechanisms are much less elaborate than those in the United States. Private nursing homes are inspected regularly in visits that are "unannounced but not unexpected," and structural criteria are monitored. The Nursing

Home Act contains specific standards for the physical plant, but only general criteria for care, so that the legal grounds for enforcing explicit standards are somewhat murky. Considerable concern has been expressed about the quality of care and life in the average private nursing home, and the industry counters with an argument that is familiar in the United States—that quality is a reflection of the reimbursement rate. Indeed, the flat reimbursement of $42.35 is low by United States standards, particularly because virtually no private market exists, and operators therefore cannot transfer costs to private-pay residents. The active response to Requests for Proposals for new nursing home beds has prompted the government to use the bidding process more deliberately to build in verifiable quality expectations.

The quality of Homes for the Aged, rightly or wrongly, is of less public concern because of their nonprofit status. The different reimbursement system permits the Homes for the Aged to develop much richer staffing ratios and employ more professional staff. On the other hand, Homes for the Aged are of older stock and many are designed in a way that impedes privacy and autonomy.

In the last several years, a new grass-roots consumer organization has arisen with a specific focus on the quality of institutional long-term care. The group, incorporated as Concerned Friends of Ontario Citizens in Care Facilities, Inc., was started in Toronto by relatives and friends of residents. Operating on a shoestring budget with no paid personnel, the group has nevertheless managed to prepare a detailed position paper (CFOC 1982), host conferences, and attract media attention. Concerned Friends also operates a confidential complaint service, and makes the information available to people to help selecting a facility. Most recently, Concerned Friends has sent a questionnaire to all provincial legislators, asking their views on matters such as whether they approve of proprietary facilities, whether they endorse small community-based programs rather than institutions, and whether they endorse an independent complaint commission.

Concerned Friends espouses specific positions: Nonprofit facilities are best; proprietary facilities should be forced into full financial disclosure of the use they make of public money; smaller facilities tend to have a superior quality of life. (The latter position is rebutted by the industry, which claims that facilities of 100 beds or more are needed for economies of scale.)

It is unlikely that Ontario could move in the direction of giving incentives to nonprofit nursing homes, even if the government so desired. The capital costs would be prohibitive, and cheap mortgage money is no longer easily available from the federal government to underwrite those costs. However, the presence of the organization serves a salutory purpose in continually dramatizing the plight of persons in nursing homes of lower quality. At this writing, additional chapters of Concerned Friends are being established outside the Toronto area.

Monitoring the quality of home care service has largely been the responsibility of the agencies paying for the care. The care coordinators in the Health Department encourage clients to contact them with any complaints as well. The impression thus far is that the volume of complaints received by the various home care programs and the provincial department is low. Care coordinators have relatively small caseloads (about 80) and potentially are available to follow up on problems.

As a prelude to implementing its Chronic Home Care Program, the Metro Toronto Home Care Agency undertook a competitive bidding process to establish a roster of home care vendors. Sixteen applications were received for 1984 and twelve received one-year contracts. This process permitted the program to establish quality criteria and exact compliance from bidders. The process is planned to repeat itself annually. This seems a promising avenue to quality control and seems particularly pertinent in metropolitan areas. (Chapter 5 describes a similar strategy in Vancouver, where competitive bidding was used not only to establish a list of approved vendors, but also to develop contracts for specified amounts of service for a given clientele at a given price.)

Coordinating Forces

The system just described exerts less authority over the user of benefits or the provider of services than do the long-term care programs that will be described in the next chapters. However, several mechanisms rationalize the system.

District Health Councils

Definition and Role. The District Health Council (DHC) is a mechanism for health planning and coordination at a regional level. The Ministry of Health began the program in 1974, creating health planning catchment areas and providing operating budgets for those communities that organized themselves and started a DHC. As of 1983, there were twenty-six DHCs, representing more than 90 percent of the province's residents.

A DHC's responsibility is advisory only. The Ontario government decided not to endorse regional control over funds. The DHC's role is to help government establish priorities and allocate resources equitably and efficiently. Quoting from terms of reference drawn up in 1983: "While a District Health Council does not have operational control over health services in its area, it does have responsibility for objectively assessing community needs, planning a coordinated health system to meet those needs, and advising the Minister of Health on the specific changes required in the community."

The DHCs represent a planned mixture of professionals (40 percent), lay persons (40 percent), and government officials (20 percent). Except in areas dominated by medical schools, the DHC leadership reflects the views of practicing rather than academic physicians. The influence of various groups of the Council varies considerably with three identifiable patterns: The physician viewpoint, the hospital viewpoint, or the consumer viewpoint may predominate. Each DHC negotiates its own operating budget from the government, which is supplemented by "special project grants." The entire DHC program cost about $3.8 million in 1980–81 and the typical DHC budget is about $100,000. This usually funds an executive director and one or more planners. Work is done, for the most part, by voluntary committees appointed by the board.

The DHCs vary in the vigor with which they approach their mission and their ability to exercise a key force in planning and social development in their communities. For the most part, the Ministry of Health will not fund any program unless it is recommended by the DHC, but a DHC recommendation is no guarantee of funding. Dixon's (1981) analysis of the DHC program points to particular difficulties in engaging social authorities in joint planning, a task that some DHCs have been able to approach better than have others.

Dixon also discusses a potential conflict between the goal of developing effective health plans and the goal of enhancing community involvement in health planning, both of which are part of the mandate.

Long-Term Care Activities. DHCs in many areas of Ontario have conducted extensive studies of the long-term care situations in their districts. (Long-term care was, in fact, the most frequently emphasized area for DHC study provincewide, with mental health and emergency care also generating studies.) The volume of the information produced is impressive. Several themes recur with noteworthy consistency, but there is some variation in the solutions proposed.

Almost twenty DHCs have completed detailed multivolume reports on long-term care,* the single topic most frequently studied by the DHCs. In general, virtually every report cites evidence of misplacement of long-term care clients. Information is usually derived from surveys of providers. In addition, the provincial Ministry of Health developed an optional reporting system to describe and assess the adequacy of resource use. The system, called the Placement and Support Services Information System (PASS), is used in half the DHC districts. Table 3.13 summarizes data taken from the PASS system for the last quarter of 1982. Of the 4,332 placements reported, 87 percent were to the type of care recommended, 3 percent to a higher level, and 10 percent to a lower level. The proportion of optimal placements was poorest for those judged suitable for independent living, suggesting a lack of community care services.

The other problems noted in DHC reports included inadequate linkages between hospital and community facilities, and the lack of community alternatives. Most reports paid special heed to the problems of heavy care patients in long-term care facilities—those who required assistance with multiple activities of daily living and who were frequently incontinent. Invariably, a need was cited for a special level of care, which provided additional funds to support such care. Several studies noted that these heavy care patients

---

*Our comments are largely based on our review of materials produced by the following District Health Councils: Waterloo; Ottawa-Carleton; Thames Valley; Lanark, Leeds, and Grenville; Durham; and Kenora-Rainy River.

Table 3.13

Extent of Optimum Long-Term Care Placements Made in Ontario in 1982

Item	Placement (based on 4,332 placements)					
	Super-vised[a]	Nursing Home	Chronic Hospital	Rehab. Hospital	Other	Indepen-dent[b]
A. No. of optimal placements needed	848	1389	991	972	34	98
B. Actual placements made	761	1144	956	928	100	445
C. No. of placements made at optimal level	682	1099	858	895	26	62
D. % of optimal place-ments actually made (C/A)	80	79	87	92	76	63
E. No. of placements made at other than optimal level (B−C)	79	45	98	33	74	383
F. % of placements made at non-optimal level (E/B)	10	4	10	4	74	86

SOURCE: Placement and Support Services Information System, October to December 1982. Optimum Placement is in the judgment of professionals.
[a]Includes: Residential, foster home, group home, half-way house, home for special care, and other.
[b]Includes: Own home, boarding home, senior citizen housing, subsidized housing, and other.

were found in chronic hospital beds, nursing homes, and extended care beds in Homes for the Aged in surprisingly similar proportions. Where chronic home care had been introduced, there was a perception that the proportion of institutional patients who represented heavy care had increased, but the waiting lists for institutional care had increased rather than shrunk.

All of the DHC reports reflected a high priority given to long-term care. Befitting the council's role in the health care system, all made a series of recommendations for more services and provincial funds to support these services. The pattern of recommended change, however, varied with the setting. Although all anticipated an immediate need for additional institutional care, some favored conversion of excess acute hospital bed stock. The replacement was generally not a simple conversion. Several reports noted the inappropriate physical design of acute hospital wards for long-term care patients. Some advocated more intensive assessment and coordination programs, others encountered strong resistance to any effort to impose a placement coordination system.

Placement Coordination Service

Beginning in 1971, the Ministry of Health established and provided a program of Placement Coordination Service (PCS) entities. The Ministry was willing to finance a PCS in a DHC region upon review of written expressions of cooperation from hospitals, nursing homes, and Homes for the Aged in the area. The PCS program was designed to address four problems: inappropriate placements; overuse of institutions; inequities in the ability of hospitals to place clientele in nursing homes; and the ability of facilities to generate referrals.

The official objectives of the PCS program as listed in 1978 were to:

- Provide a single channel through which all applicants for institutional care (whether in hospital or in the community) are placed into "suitable accommodation, programs or services" in a way that promotes suitable access of clients to placement situations and increases the number of clients placed in an optimum situation.
- Maintain a central registry of clients awaiting placement.
- Maintain a central registry of available accommodations, programs, and services.
- Arrange for assessment of community clients as necessary.
- Provide a mechanism to relieve administrators, physicians, and discharge planning services of the responsibility of finding placements.
- Make available to health planners the data accumulated from the operation of the PCS.
- Educate the community about appropriate placements.

The first PCS was established in Hamilton in 1971, followed by Thunder Bay in 1974 and Ottawa in 1976. By 1984, twelve PCS programs were in operation. Typically, each PCS has one or more staff coordinators and a small secretarial staff. The province funds the operation 100 percent according to an approved budget. Each PCS has a Board of Directors from the community. Agency auspices vary: Three are under the Victorian Order of Nurses, three under public health departments, one under a hospital board, one in a social service department, and two are separately incorporated bodies. The annual budgets are small, ranging from about $40,000 to about $180,000. Funding was based on a formula that assumed that 8 percent of persons over 65 in a region would require placement each year and that 1.5 hours of staff time is required per placement.

Essentially, the PCS functions despite its small staff and budget because of the advance agreement of the providers to channel all placements through the PCS. Therefore a single waiting list is developed. The PCS does not itself do the assessments of the need for care, but rather provides a consistent format for hospital discharge planners and community personnel to use in their own assessments. Each of the twelve PCS units developed its own assessment form to be completed by discharge planners and others making the referrals. Some collect detailed information about functional status.

By now all DHC regions with a PCS are required to subscribe to the PASS data system. PASS is designed to pinpoint accommodation deficits in communities, reveal inappropriate placements and delays in discharge from acute hospitals, and indicate the reason for both of these events. For the system to operate, a form must be completed for each instance when a referral to a hospital discharge planner or community agency results in discharge or transfer of a client to another accommodation. Monthly printouts and biannual aggregations are sent to all participating agencies. The PCS takes responsibility for giving feedback from PASS data and from its own data about placements to all interested planners and providers in the community. Typically, PCS monthly statistics will show how many people are awaiting placement for each category of care and the type of facility in which they are awaiting placement. Also, detailed data are available about bed use in each cooperating institution.

Evaluation. The provincial government and some individual programs have attempted to evaluate the effects of PCS. The province performed a three-part evaluation using 1980–81 information pertaining to six PCS programs. The first part of the evaluation was a comparison of matched communities—with and without PCS—on a set of community parameters. The results were somewhat inconclusive because no PCS community scored better than its matched partner on all the variables of interest. In four of six matched comparisons, the PCS counties had higher percentages of optimum placements for chronic care and for a total of all types of care. Overall, PCS counties also seemed to have slightly shorter delays for placement into extended care but slightly longer delays for placement into chronic care. One objective of PCS—to minimize the percentage of placements originating in hospitals—was clearly met. Achievement of this goal not only reduces the burden on hospitals—which was the original intention—but also removes the crisis atmosphere wherein individual consumer choice is least likely to occur. Another goal was to improve equity among the hospitals in their ability to effect placements; this was realized in only half the comparisons as measured by the amount of variability in placement rates among hospitals in the study communities.

The second part of the study inquired whether effectiveness differed according to the type of agency housing the PCS. This was essentially a case-study approach, with positive community feedback used as a criterion of management effectiveness. The study found no differences attributable to the auspice of the PCS. Instead, effectiveness was related to management features such as the involvement of persons in authority from user agencies on the PCS management committee, the clarity of communication channels, and the interpersonal skills of the PCS coordinator.

The third part of the study examined the extent to which four PCS programs achieved their objectives in the first year of operation. One major measure was the proportion of placements to each type of care setting that were actually coordinated by the PCS. As table 3.14 shows, the four PCS programs studied varied in their involvement in placement activities and that placement to chronic hospitals was largely out of PCS control. On the other hand, the placement to nursing homes was highly successful in the sense of PCS involvement, and the Home for the Aged area showed extreme

Table 3.14

**Extent to Which Four PCS Programs Were
Involved in Placements in 1980–81**

Placement Destination	Percentage of Total Placements Coordinated by PCS (range from lowest to highest)
To chronic care	4 to 36
To extended care	
Nursing homes	81 to 90
Homes for Aged	0 to 71
Residential	
Homes for Aged	19 to 63

SOURCE: Ministry of Health Summary
dated February 1982.

variability from high saturation to no involvement at all. The four
PCSs were also involved in making "other" placements, such as to
rest homes, but here the denominator of such placements was
impossible to calculate. Most of the placements made by the PCSs
were appropriate—only one of the four programs fell below the 90
percent optimum placements set as a criterion. The achievement of
equity of access to long-term care was examined by comparing the
average waiting times of persons waiting for particular types of care.
Because variability was high, the conclusion was that equitable
access remained largely unachieved, although there was evidence
that the situation improved somewhat in the second part of the
year.

These evaluative comments pinpoint the limitations of a voluntary
program. The lack of involvement in chronic hospital placement is
not surprising, because hospitals would have every incentive to
place their own acute care patients into their own chronic units
without referring to the PCS system. Some critics of the concept
fault the PCS on a more basic issue—i.e., the limitation of merely
organizing and rationalizing the flow to long-term care facilities
rather than directly monitoring the appropriateness of the placement
plan and suggesting home care or alternative community-based

plans. The Ottawa-Carleton PCS, in its periodic evaluation reports of its own program, points out that the provincial directives for the proper universe of a PCS are somewhat vague. For example, rest homes, boarding homes, and special services for the retarded or mentally ill may or may not be included. It seems that many PCS programs do coordinate with Home Care, but referrals to Home Care are not directed through the PCS.

In sum, the PCS seems to be a valuable but limited mechanism for bringing some sense of community order to a system wherein individuals become eligible for extended care on a physician's endorsement, after which they and their agents hunt for a placement. Under the aegis of PCS, hospitals, facilities, and other agencies meet and discuss common problems. A common language and a district-wide data set are made available in the service of planning. The system depends on the good will of all the participants and, when functioning optimally, makes the process more efficient and equitable. It does not, however, add a layer of case management to the individual care planning in any reliable way.

Home Care Coordination

A third force for potential coordination is found in the Chronic Home Care programs themselves. Care coordinators have caseloads of about 80 and a fairly clearly articulated mandate to arrange services on behalf of clientele, in addition to authorizing and purchasing services in the direct purview of the Home Care Program. Chapter 7, which compares case management in three provinces, goes into considerable detail about the evolving role of the Home Care Coordinator as a rationalizing force. Summarizing here, it would seem that the Home Care Coordinator could provide the focal point for case management. At this time, the scope is limited to the community care sector. The Home Care Coordinator has no clear role in assessing the need for institutional care and no authority to authorize or disallow such care. The Home Care Program will do assessments for the PCS, but there seems to be no formula for using that information to manage the waiting list. Even in the community care field itself, there seems to be considerable disagreement about whether home care coordinators are best situated to manage the entire system or whether that role would better be vested in social work authorities.

Concluding Comment

Ontario presents a model of insured long-term care benefits without a well-developed diversified structure of care. In fact, the care system in place contains redundancies. The insured health services are overlapped by a socially sponsored set of programs offered on a sliding fee scale.

Provincial planners are struggling to bring the system under control. They face an excess of extended care beds above the established norms. In the effort to bring down the costs of care, Ontario has begun to broaden the availability of community-based services and to take steps to establish a case management system.

Of the three provinces studied, only Ontario speaks of the growing numbers of elderly as specifically representing a fiscal crisis (SSD 1981). It is dangerous to draw rigid conclusions from a comparison of only three provinces, but it is provocative that the province expressing this perspective is the one with the long-term care system least under control. The next two chapters describe long-term care systems where use of resources by individuals is managed more centrally.

REFERENCES

CFOC (Concerned Friends of Ontario Citizens in Care Facilities) 1982. "Consumer Concerns and Recommendations Related to Nursing Home Care in Ontario," a brief to the Honorable Larry Grosman, Minister of Health, September 1982.

CYB (Canada Year Book, 1980–81) 1981. Statistics Canada, Minister of Supply and Services, Ottawa.

Dixon, M. 1981. *The Organization of District Health Councils in Ontario,* Report of a research project funded by the Ontario Ministry of Health Demonstration Model Grant 332, London, Ontario.

Gross, M. J. and C. W. Schwenger 1981. *Health Care Costs for the Elderly in Ontario: 1976–2026.* Toronto: Ontario Economic Council.

SSD (Secretariat for Social Development) 1981. *The Elderly in Ontario: An Agenda for the '80's.* Toronto, 1981.

Statistics Canada. *1976 Inter-decennial Census Publications.* Ottawa.

CHAPTER 4
Long-Term Care in Manitoba

MANITOBA is a large, sparsely settled province in the geographic heart of Canada. It extends from the border with North Dakota to Hudson Bay. The population is concentrated in a roughly eighty-mile strip along the border with the United States. Over half of the one million plus inhabitants live in the city of Winnipeg. The province is home to a diverse group of ethnic minorities, many of whom maintain close social ties within ethnic enclaves. The small population clustered in a few centers facilitates interaction among professionals. Government program officials seem to know virtually all the providers on a first-name basis. Such open, personal relationships make for informality, and foster accountability.

Manitoba's long-term care program has two major arms: (1) universal coverage for nursing homes (called personal care homes) under the aegis of the Health Services Commission; and (2) directly provided community care overseen by a separate Office of Continuing Care. The Continuing Care Program is at the hub of an assessment and care planning process that manages home-based services and mediates the use of the personal care home benefit. Unlike Ontario's system, the Manitoba system has a single visible point of entry to both community-based and institutionally based long-term care benefits. An assessment team examines functional need for care and, as an independent issue, whether that need coupled with the client's preferences, social situation, and availability of community service suggests home care or whether an application should be made for a personal care home. The Continuing Care Program is also in a position to weigh the competing needs of persons awaiting space in personal care homes in a particular community. A unique feature of the Manitoba program is a panel procedure whereby each application for personal care home admission is formally reviewed before being accepted and placed on the waiting list of any facility. This affords a safeguard against hasty processes and ill-advised judgments based on insufficient information.

Despite systematic requirements for medical information and review, Manitoba strikes us as having moved far from the much-maligned "medical model" of long-term care. No particular physical or mental diagnoses are used to determine eligibility for any level of institutional or home-based care, nor are physician referrals required. Client's preferences for facility care or home care are honored, as is choice of facility.

Hospitals and Physicians

A provincial system of hospital insurance was introduced in Manitoba in 1958. Medical insurance was added in 1969. The Manitoba Medical Services Insurance Corporation, appointed in 1967 to plan and administer the program under the Canadian Medical Care Act, became the Manitoba Health Services Insurance Corporation when the program was implemented in 1969. In 1970, the staff of the Manitoba Medical Service, a physician-sponsored medical insurance plan, became employees of the Corporation, and the Manitoba Health Services Commission was established to replace the Health Services Insurance Corporation and the Manitoba Hospital Commission.

The Manitoba Health Services Commission administers the provincial program of universal medical and hospital insurance. This commission is responsible to the Minister of Health of the provincial government. Care in personal care homes was legislated under the insured program in 1972 and became effective in July 1973.

In 1974, the Office of Continuing Care was created within the Department of Health to coordinate home-based care. That provincial office is separate from the Health Services Commission but works closely with it in establishing eligibility for personal care home admissions. Continuing Care services are delivered through eight departmental regional offices and their many local offices. The latter are housed in the umbrella health and community services (social services) offices. Other benefits are much the same as in other provinces.

Under Pharmacare, benefits to people aged 65 years and older are 80 percent of the cost of allowable prescription drugs in excess of $50 per year. A program to provide eyeglasses on a similar basis has been in effect since 1982.

In 1983, Manitoba had 5,256 funded, active treatment hospital beds in public general hospitals, or 4.8 beds per 1,000 population. In addition, there were 1,127 extended treatment beds (1.0 per 1,000 persons) and 8,128 beds in personal care homes (7.5 per 1,000). The distribution of hospital beds is shown in figure 4.1. Winnipeg, with 55 percent of the province's population, contains 58 percent of the acute beds, 73 percent of the extended care beds, and 54 percent of the personal care home beds. (The figure also shows the eight major service regions of the province, which are discussed later in the chapter.)

Five of the Winnipeg hospitals have developed geriatric services; these offer an array of programs, including both extended care and day hospital. The geriatric programs each provide physician staff to the panels that oversee placement into personal care homes. One facility, operated by the city, is devoted exclusively to geriatrics. A second is a former federal government Veterans' hospital, recently transferred to the provincial health program and now providing personal care and extended treatment programs. The other three are geriatric programs functioning within acute care hospitals.

In 1983, Manitoba had 1,300 actively practicing physicians (active practice being defined as billing $20,000 or more per year), for a ratio of one physician per 835 persons. The small cadre of geriatricians serve as directors and staff of the extended care units, usually located in the larger population centers. These units mostly provide only consultation and assessment services, but they maintain a few long-stay patients. The bulk of the care for geriatric patients is provided by primary care physicians. They, rather than the geriatricians, provide care to residents in personal care homes.

Personal Care Home Program

Eligibility for personal care homes requires consecutive residence in Manitoba for twenty-four months prior to admission, or previous residence for a total of thirty years. There is no age limit, and the program serves handicapped adults under 65 as well as the elderly. Anyone can apply on behalf of an individual, or prospective users

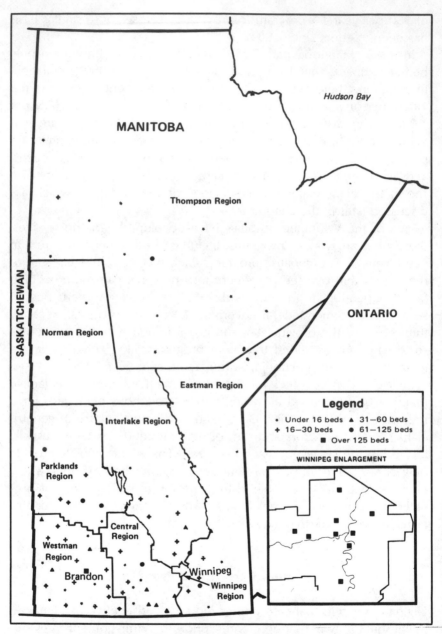

Figure 4.1. Distribution of hospitals in Manitoba according to size and health district.

can apply themselves. The Commission is responsible for developing assessment criteria. The Office of Continuing Care is responsible for the conduct of and quality of the assessment. Each application assessment includes a medical examination, a nursing assessment including a measure of dependency, and a social evaluation. One of the key features of the process is the review of assessment decisions by a multidisciplinary panel, which must approve any placement recommendation. However, the operation of the personal care home program rests with a unit of the Health Services Commission. Continuing Care responsibility ceases once the client is admitted to a facility.

Manitoba recognizes four levels of care, which are assigned by the assessor:

> Level 1. Indicates minimal dependence on nursing time. The individual requires weekly supervision and/or assistance with personal care and/or some encouragement or reminders to wash, dress, and attend meals and/or activities. He/she may need administration of medications on a regular basis and to use mechanical aids.

> Level 2. Indicates moderate dependence on nursing time for at least one of the following categories: bathing and dressing, feeding, treatments, ambulation, elimination, and/or support and/or supervision.

> Level 3. Indicates maximum dependence on nursing time for two or three of the following categories: bathing and dressing, feeding, treatments, ambulation, elimination, and/or support and/or supervision or maximum dependence for support and/or supervision and moderate dependence for at least two of the other categories.

> Level 4. Indicates maximum dependence on nursing time for four or more of the following categories: bathing and dressing, feeding, treatment, ambulation, elimination, and support and/or supervision.

The levels of care translate into staffing guidelines for personal care homes as follows:

Level 1—0.5 total paid hours of nursing care per resident day (10 percent RN and 90 percent nursing assistant).

Level 2—2.0 total paid hours of nursing care per resident day (10 percent, RN, 20 percent LPN, and 70 percent nursing assistant).

Levels 3 and 4—3.5 total paid hours of nursing care per resident day (20 percent RN, 15 percent LPN, and 65 percent nursing assistant).

Once a panel approves the application for placement in a personal care home, the individual goes on a waiting list. The prospective resident may choose any home that has beds at his or her level. Resident choice is honored, and persons can move to the facility of their choice once a vacancy arises. Because the staff person responsible for assessment and referral for placement is the same staff person who is responsible for assessment for home care, necessary services, supplies or equipment are often provided through the Home Care program during the waiting process, including homemaking as required. Priority for placement is given to people in hospitals and those with urgent need in the community. Authorities vary on whether the hospitalized or the community group should take precedence. As table 4.1 shows, personal care homes' waiting lists declined 40 percent overall between 1977 and 1982; the improvement was largely in the Winnipeg area, but the most recent data suggest a slight upturn.

Personal care home benefits to residents include nursing services, meals, drugs, physical and occupational therapy as approved, rou-

Table 4.1
Personal Care Waiting Lists

			Year			
Location	1977	1978	1979	1980	1981	1982
Rural	1179	946	1032	1079	893	717
Winnipeg	1238	988	892	711	519	727
Total	2417	1934	1924	1790	1412	1444

SOURCE: Office of Continuing Care, Annual Reports.

tine laundry and linen service, and any other services approved by the Commission. Residents pay a residential charge, which was $4.50 a day in 1973–74 and $13.00 in 1984. As in Ontario, the charge is set to be affordable to persons on government pensions and still permit an ample allowance for personal spending.

Personal Care Home Beds

Since the personal care home benefit was added in 1972 and became operational in 1973, the bed supply has followed the proportion of the population aged 70 and older (see table 4.2). The ratio has wavered between 94 and 101 beds per 1000 elderly. There has been some trend over time suggesting a decrease in the proportion of beds operated under proprietary auspices.

The personal care beds are further divided by the level of care they provide. Prior to 1972, a specific class of personal care home designed to serve ambulatory residents requiring a low level of care was developed. These units were referred to as hostels. They have been operated almost entirely as nonproprietary facilities. Because of their construction, they are usually unsuited for residents who

Table 4.2

Manitoba Personal Care Home Bed Summary, 1973–1983

Date	Total Rated Beds	Population Age 70+[a]	Beds per 1,000 Population Aged 70+[a]	Percentage Proprietary Rated Beds	Percentage Nonproprietary Rated Beds
July 1973	6,642	67,765	98.0	35	65
Dec. 1974	7,013	69,326	101.2	34	66
Dec. 1975	7,145	70,445	101.4	33	67
Dec. 1976	7,260	72,082	100.7	32	68
March 1978	7,393	74,449	99.3	29	71
March 1979	7,534	76,850	98.0	28	72
March 1980	7,480	79,250	94.4	28	72
March 1981	7,574	80,400	94.2	28	72
March 1982	8,038	81,550	98.6	29	71
March 1983	8,128	83,953	96.8	29	71

SOURCE: Personal Care Home Program, Manitoba Health Services Commission.

[a]All population figures are as of December each year except for program start as of June 1973; the 1981 figure is estimated.

require higher levels of care. The inclusion of these beds in the overall personal care home statistics tends to obscure more dramatic changes in ownership. For example, between 1972 and 1976, the personal care homes at levels 2 to 4 became more dramatically tilted toward nonprofit ownership.

Payment and Budget

Personal care homes in Manitoba are paid differently depending on their auspices. Nonproprietary homes are reimbursed on the basis of global budgets negotiated with the Health Services Commission. These budgets take into consideration the case mix and the various programs operated by the home. A sample 1981–82 budget for a 126-bed nonproprietary facility is shown in table 4.3. The average cost per resident per year in that home is just over $14,000, a rate comparable to the average costs of publicly reimbursed nursing home beds in the United States. The information provided indicates that salaries and benefits account for 75 percent of the costs. The wage rates for nurses ($23,000) are slightly above U.S. scale. Those for aides ($13,000) are well above. The food budget is about $2.25 per patient per day. Proprietary homes are paid on a fixed rate per patient-day, set at the average of the median rates for levels 2 and 3/4 among nonprofit homes. The staffing guidelines noted earlier constitute targets for the nonprofit homes, which may opt to exceed them; but they are the minimum standards for the proprietary homes, which are paid on a fixed rate basis based on a requirement to maintain staffing according to levels of care.

The costs of personal care homes have increased steadily. On a per capita basis, the costs have gone from $40 in 1975 to $58 in 1978–79, $74 in 1980–81, and $110 in 1982–83. This rate of increase is about the same as for health care overall. Table 4.4 indicates that, from 1976 to 1982, the proportion of the Commission's annual budget for personal care homes was relatively constant.

Provincial officials suggested that wages largely account for the increase in personal care home costs over time. For example, since the personal care home benefit was introduced, pension plans have been provided for the staff. Officials believed that there had been no increases in staff per level of care since the program's initiation. However, staff wages were very low at the beginning of the pro-

Table 4.3

Sample Annual Budget (1981–82) for 126-Bed Nonprofit Personal Care Home

Item	Full-Time Equivalents	Cost
Personnel		
Nursing		
Director of Nursing	1.0 ⎫	$162,088
Registered Nurses	5.7 ⎭	
Licensed Practical Nurses	9.2	159,257
Aides	31.9	407,573
Ward clerk	0.5	6,720
In-service	0.5	11,124
Total nursing	48.5	746,762
Activity	2.7	34,348
Transportation	4.2	7,252
Social service	1.0 ⎫	
General services and administration	31.2 ⎭	450,403
Employee Benefits		94,462
Subtotal	84.2	1,333,227
Other Expenses		
Food		103,500
Other		231,060
Debt structure		54,789
Other loans		51,120
Equipment depreciation		9,908
Reserve for major repairs		5,225
Subtotal		455,602
TOTAL		$1,788,829

gram, and have now been brought into parity with similar staff in hospitals. Currently, in fact, aides in nursing homes may be paid more than hospital aides. The pay rates for nurses are essentially the same in the two sectors. The other cause of the increase in the overall cost of the program has been the growth in the number of nursing home beds. These officials believe that the growth has probably reached a plateau. The average waiting time for a personal care home bed has decreased from about one year when the

Table 4.4

Health Services Commission Program Expenditures, 1972–1983
(In $ thousand)

Type	Year										
	1972	1973	1974	1975	1976	1977-78[a]	1978-79	1979-80	1980-81	1981-82	1982-83
Personal-care homes	106 (.06%)	11,435 (6%)	30,443 (12%)	42,548 (13%)	51,807 (14%)	73,877 (14%)	63,907 (14%)	70,559 (14%)	81,678 (14%)	99,958 (14%)	120,011 (15%)
Hospital services	121,448 (69%)	134,815 (66%)	159,390 (64%)	208,212 (56%)	236,850 (64%)	317,586 (60%)	262,536 (59%)	288,814 (59%)	342,492 (60%)	418,659 (60%)	487,985 (60%)
Medical services	51,541 (29%)	53,877 (27%)	58,496 (23%)	63,304 (20%)	72,971 (20%)	112,424 (21%)	94,616 (21%)	106,788 (22%)	117,220 (20%)	145,031 (21%)	166,650 (20%)
Pharmacare				4,000 (1%)	5,406 (1%)	7,732 (1%)	7,970 (2%)	8,742 (2%)	10,568 (2%)	13,611 (2%)	17,249 (2%)
Chiropodist, optometrist, prosthetic, and other services	2,576 (1%)	2,741 (1%)	2,659 (1%)	3,063 (1%)	3,520 (1%)	6,812 (1%)	6,023 (1%)	6,942 (1%)	8,512 (1%)	8,951 (1%)	11,743 (1%)
Other (including administration)						12,286 (2%)	10,170 (2%)	10,773 (2%)	11,842 (2%)	13,482 (2%)	15,947 (2%)
Total	175,565	202,869	250,998	321,126	370,553	530,717	445,222	492,618	572,319	699,692	819,585

SOURCE: HSC Annual Reports.
[a]Fifteen months.

program began, to about three to six months now. Part of this decrease is attributed to the tighter criteria applied to the assessment process.

Quality of Care

The Health Services Commission is responsible for assuring the quality of care in personal care homes. Inspectors from the Personal Care Homes Program visit the homes regularly. No formal system of quality assessment is used. The homes work with the government officials, sharing information about staffing, budgeting, and new programs. The Program has written guidelines for staffing, pharmacy, patients' rights, construction and physical plant, and other similar structural and programmatic features. Problems appear to be handled more by consultation than confrontation. The professional-to-professional contact is described as successful in maintaining standards.

Proprietary facilities are required to report monthly on hours of care and the professional/nonprofessional mix. In both proprietary and nonproprietary facilities, the same quality of care standards are applied. Nonetheless, the relationship with the nonprofit homes is different from that with the proprietaries because of the way the budgets are developed. With the former, the budgeting involves a commitment to achieve certain objectives. Increased scope of services is the basis for larger budgets.

Assessment and Paneling

Requests for admission to a personal care home are channeled through the Office of Continuing Care. Local continuing care operations (described more fully below) are housed in eight Department of Health regional offices throughout the province. Each region is further subdivided into districts.

The assessment for admission to a nursing home is multidisciplinary. In Winnipeg, teams of nurses and social workers employed directly by the Department of Health for the Continuing Care Program make home visits to do the core assessment, supplemented by medical reports and other evaluations that might be specifically required. Outside Winnipeg, the evaluation will be coordinated by the continuing care personnel (usually a nurse), and again, other input will be solicited. On the basis of the initial assessment, the applicant might be advised to consider an array of home services instead, but any citizen has the right to bring an application forward to an assessment panel.

The panel, therefore, is the necessary step for any placement in a nursing home. All patients, including hospital patients, awaiting placement are reassessed and brought back to panel to consider where care needs have changed.

Panels are organized by the Regional Coordinator of Continuing Care; the panel physician is usually the regional officer of health. In areas where geriatric medicine services are available (Winnipeg and Brandon), arrangements have been made for a geriatrician to provide the medical input for a panel. Four panels meet weekly in Winnipeg; in rural areas, the panels meet less often and are keyed to need (e.g., once a month with the possibility of special meetings).

Panels always include a physician, a nurse, a social worker, and the regional continuing care coordinator (or his or her representative). Persons with knowledge of the case, including the applicant's own physician, are encouraged to attend, as are applicants themselves and their families. The participation of the consultant is financed in two ways: Some are paid sessional fees; in other instances, the Continuing Care program contracts with the universities to provide service to the panel.

Each case is reviewed and discussed briefly. Considerable attention is given to the adequacy of the data base. Although some panel discussions will be a perfunctory acknowledgment of a self-evident decision, panels may also request a more complete evaluation of the patient's medical condition. This often involves a referral to one of the hospital-based geriatric assessment units. The costs of such evaluations are paid by the Health Services Commission. Panels may also request that the continuing care program explore the feasibility of some alternative arrangement before approving the application to the facility.

Most observers of the paneling process value it very highly. It is seen not so much as a mechanism for changing the decisions of the case managers as it is a means of integrating the case management process with the geriatric system. Informants state that the panels tend to approve the overall quality of the assessor's performance, but no study has formally reviewed the number of decisions changed as a result of paneling. Clients receiving home care who have not requested placement can also be reviewed by the panels at the request of the coordinator. In this case, the panel becomes a consultation resource. About one in four cases reviewed by urban panels is, in fact, a community care case. If placement is not at issue, the recommendations are advisory. This use emphasizes the value that the case coordinators place on these panels. The overall flow of the assessment process is shown in figure 4.2.

A person waiting for a personal care home bed may be in the hospital or at home. Once paneled and approved for placement in a nursing home, the hospital patient starts paying the approved daily charge for a personal care home to discourage waiting in hospital. If the person waiting at home for a personal care home bed requires home care services, such services are provided. These may exceed the cost limit otherwise observed; the other exceptions to this limit are for terminally ill persons, short-term episodes of care, or the provision of emergency family relief. People often prefer to wait for the personal care home of their choice. Manitoba, and Winnipeg especially, has many ethnic enclaves—e.g., Ukrainian, Icelandic, Jewish—and many homes have special characteristics corresponding to these ethnic interests. The availability of home care and the sense of a system in operation seem to prevent the panicky sense that the older person must accept any available bed.

The effort to provide personal care home residents with the opportunity to be housed in ethnically oriented institutions is at variance with United States policies. Here we encounter an interesting question about social equity. The Canadians choose to recognize the preferences of disabled elderly people even when those preferences may violate social norms for nonsegregation. In discussing this policy with Manitoba officials, we repeatedly heard the comment that the disabled elderly should not have to pay the price of social injustice, but should be permitted to spend their institutional days in a setting that was most conducive to their happiness and well-being. The importance of ethnic environments and cultural homogeneity was highly valued.

Waiting lists move in chronological order, with recognition that those in emergency situations in the community and those occupying hospital beds needed for acute care patients need some priority.

CONTINUING CARE PROGRAM

```
┌─────────────────────────────────────────────┐
│   Request/referral for home care/P.C.H. placement │
│     from person, family, physician, hospital  │
└─────────────────────────────────────────────┘
         │ In hospital          │ In community
         ▼                      ▼
┌──────────────────────┐  ┌──────────────────────┐
│ Hospital-based continuing care │  │ Community-based continuing care │
│    staff coordinator   │  │    staff coordinator   │
└──────────────────────┘  └──────────────────────┘
         │                      │
         └──────────┬───────────┘
                    ▼
┌─────────────────────────────────────────────┐
│              ASSESSMENT FOR CARE              │
│  Attending physician   Home care nurse   Home care social worker │
│  Clinical findings     Physical health   Social functioning │
│                                               │
│  Objective: to establish maximum potential for functioning in own home │
│       with available family and community resources. │
└─────────────────────────────────────────────┘
                    │
                    ▼
┌─────────────────────────────────────────────┐
│  Continuing care staff coordinator develops initial │
│     care plan with person/family/physician    │
└─────────────────────────────────────────────┘
         │ ─ ─ Consultation ─ ─ │
         ▼                      ▼
┌──────────────────┐  ┌──────────────────────┐
│   Home care      │  │   P.C.H. placement    │
│   required       │  │  requested or required │
└──────────────────┘  └──────────────────────┘
                              │
                              ▼
┌──────────────┬──────────────────────┬──────────────┐
│ May include  │  P.C.H. Assessment Panel │ May include │
│ referring physician, │      Physician      │ representative │
│ family, specialists │ Cont. care coordinator │ from P.C.H. │
│              │        +/or          │              │
│              │     senior nurse     │              │
│              │        +/or          │              │
│              │  senior social worker │              │
└──────────────┴──────────────────────┴──────────────┘
                    │
                    ▼
              ┌──────────────┐
              │   DECISION    │
              └──────────────┘
         ┌──────────┼──────────────────┐
         ▼          ▼                  ▼
┌──────────────┐ ┌──────────────┐ ┌──────────────┐
│ Not approved: │ │ Approved for  │ │  Defer for    │
│ continue on home care │ │ placement in │ │ further assessment │
│   or on own   │ │ home of choice │ │              │
└──────────────┘ └──────────────┘ └──────────────┘
                                         │
                                  ┌── Family or home
                                  │    assessment
                                  └── Consult attending
                                       physician
                                         │
                                         ▼
                                   May lead to
                              day hospital assessment or
                              geriatric unit assessment
```

Figure 4.2. Assessment and placement in Manitoba (personal care home and continuing care requests).

The decision about admitting a person not only recognizes the resident's preference but also must be accepted by the personal care home. We asked government officials what happens when a home is reluctant to take a particular person. The response suggested that negotiation is used rather than coercion. When a problem arises, the director of the Personal Care Home Program meets with the administrators of the home and tries to arrive at a meeting of the minds. She maintains that she has always received good cooperation and that few homes have ever consistently refused hard-to-place people.

For the purposes of our discussion, we separated the assessment process for personal care homes from the overall operation of the Continuing Care Program, discussed in the section below. It is important to note, however, that assessment and paneling rarely occur in a vacuum. In many instances, the applicant is known to the Continuing Care program and has been receiving services for some time. The application might be part of a planned process that has been worked out between applicant and case manager. If the need for an application arises in a previously unknown person, it is likely that the Continuing Care program will be providing home care during a transition period. If the application arises from an unknown person who is in the hospital, the usual assessment mechanisms for hospitalized patients needing long-term care come into effect. The main point is that the procedures for application for personal care homes are well integrated into a community-wide system of assessment and service allocation. No new cast of characters is introduced at a time of crisis.

Continuing Care

Organization

Policies for home care services are developed centrally by the Office of Continuing Care and implemented at the regional level by an operational arm of the Department of Health. This system requires a good deal of coordination and good will. The policy side of provincial government contains the following provincial programs: mental health, continuing care, public health, home economics, and dental health and health promotion. Each has a director who sets guidelines and reports to the Minister of Health. The home care program for Manitoba is the responsibility of the Director of Continuing Care.

Manitoba is divided into eight operational regions (see figure 4.1). Winnipeg, which constitutes the major population center, is considered a single region. The other regions are Eastman, extending to the Ontario border on the east and halfway up the province; Central to the west; Westman, extending west to the Saskatchewan border; Parkland; Interlake; Norman; and Thompson. The last four regions are sparsely populated, with Thompson representing a huge area that extends to Hudson Bay.

In rural areas, virtually all home care and home nursing services are provided under public auspices. Each rural region has some activity for each categorical program. They all operate out of regional offices and their district offices. The regional coordinator for each categorical program reports to the regional director for that region. In the seven rural regions, over half of the continuing care coordinators are public health nurses.

All regions are further divided into geographic districts, some of which are subdivided into local offices. In each district, there is a team manager and continuing care field staff. In Winnipeg, there is also a central regional office with a regional coordinator for each categorical function. The regional coordinator for Continuing Care for the Winnipeg region has a central staff of one social worker and one nurse, who monitor standards and provide multidisciplinary input to the field staff in district offices. She is parallel to coordinators of other functions and her staffing requests compete with theirs on the desk of the regional director of Health and Community Services. Her line of responsibility to the director of Continuing Care is dotted—that is, a program director accountability.

Roles and Functions

The Continuing Care field staff are responsible for assessing levels of care, arranging a coordinated array of community-based services, monitoring those services in a case-management mode, and authorizing specific components of care, especially homemaking, home nursing, and day care. Endeavors are made to incorporate existing community services (such as meal programs, transportation programs, and friendly visiting) into the care plan.

The Winnipeg program differs from those in outlying regions in two important ways: it is more resource-rich in both its team approach to assessment and the services it can draw upon; and a voluntary nonprofit organization, the Victorian Order of Nurses (VON), which does not exist in other areas of the province, has been allotted specific responsibilities in the Winnipeg system.

In Winnipeg, a team of nurse and social worker (the latter trained at or above the baccalaureate level) makes home visits to do the initial assessment. Other personnel are drawn into the assessment as needed, but one of the two assessors is assigned to serve as the case coordinator with primary responsibility for follow-up and coordination. Outside Winnipeg, a public health nurse is likely to serve as assessor and case coordinator, with some delegation as needed in rural areas. The case coordinator authorizes an amount and mix of in-home services as needed. Manitoba recognizes four levels of homemaking, ranging from light household maintenance to personal care, with slightly different pay scales for the four types of personnel. All homemakers work directly for the regional Continuing Care program, as do the LPNs. However, in Winnipeg, nearly all home nursing is purchased from the VON, whereas in the rest of the province the home nurses are also employees of the regional Continuing Care program.

Program organization in Winnipeg also differentiates between short-term and long-term home care needs. The coordination of assessment and services for those requiring care for more than 60 days is coordinated by the department's Winnipeg regional staff. For those whose need for care is not likely to extend beyond 60 days, coordination of assessment and care has been delegated to VON. In Winnipeg the Continuing Care program has staff located in the hospitals to facilitate the referral to home care at discharge. In most hospitals the Continuing Care staff are nurses contracted from VON. These hospital-based nurses coordinate assessment in the hospital for the initial care plan on discharge from hospital for those who may need either short-term or long-term home care. The discharged patient is referred to VON (short term) or the Winnipeg regional local office (long term), and community staff carry out a further community-based assessment for an on-going care plan within three weeks of discharge. This assures immediate service discharge and continuity from hospital care to community care.

The Continuing Care program in Winnipeg also has a placement coordinator who serves the eight hospital and hospital-based coordinators in assessment and paneling for those patients who require personal care home placement and who will remain in hospital pending placement.

The relationship between VON and the Continuing Care program appears complex to an outside observer, yet it seems to function smoothly. It emerged not as part of an ideal design but as a historical artifact. The VON, an agency analogous to the Visiting Nurses Association in the United States, was a well-established and respected provider of home care before the province-wide government home care program was implemented. It seemed rational and politic for the VON to be incorporated into the new system but be allowed to retain its identity. The role of case coordinator for short-term post-hospital cases recognizes that these cases usually have a pressing need for nursing and other therapeutic services. In contrast, as chapter 5 illustrates, the VON in Vancouver lost its special identity when British Columbia began its universal home care programs, and most of the employees began working directly for the provincial health units. The province of Manitoba is almost the sole purchaser of VON services, however, and the agency has therefore taken on a quasi-public function.

Therapeutic services such as physical, occupational, and speech therapy are purchased from a nonprofit agency. In Winnipeg a mixed system exists. Sometimes the therapeutic personnel work directly as salaried employees of the regional continuing care programs, and sometimes the services are purchased from private vendors. In isolated areas, improvisation is always the rule-of-thumb and therapeutic services are generally scarce.

Home Care

Authorized home care is free. There are no consumer charges. Unfortunately, the cost data for home care are rather scanty. The 1982–83 home care assistance budget for the cost of services provided in the home following assessment by care coordinators was $16.2 million for the whole province. The staff salary costs for the Central Office of Continuing Care represented about $190,000; the operational budget includes $94,000 for travel and supplies for these staff and for program supplies. The salaries of the coordinators in the various regions are combined into the overall regional budgets and cannot be directly ascertained. This will be improved as rural regions continue to separate Continuing Care staff from those of public health nursing.

The direct services money is allocated on a budget from the central office to each of the regional offices. Budgets are estimated on the basis of experience and forecasts, but the individual budgets are not rigidly enforced. The central office staff tend to monitor them on a month-to-month basis and generally have found that people are responsive and do not deliberately overspend their budgets to increase their portion. The central office maintains the clearing registry for all persons ever enrolled in the program. This provides data simply on those who are on home care and/or are being assessed for nursing home placement, with their names, addresses, some identification number, and the coordinating center. It is intended to prevent duplication of enrollment and facilitate continuity of care as clients cross regional boundaries for medical care or move their residences. It does not provide any real service data.

Although the cost data for home care are scarce, field personnel strongly believe that the case-management approach is valuable. They note that, when the case coordinators are overworked and unable to keep up with routine reassessments, they tend not to stop or reduce services; thus, an inadequate staffing for case management indirectly increases the overall operating costs. Moreover, when the case coordinators are pressed by heavy workloads, they tend to acquiesce to provider recommendations for expensive services with heavy professional components as opposed to less expensive nonprofessional services. Staff in the central office have observed that coordinators vary among themselves with regard to the length of the period for which they authorize services.

Some insights into the costs of continuing care at home are afforded by a study conducted by the Office of Continuing Care in January and February 1978. Records of all new admissions to the home care program were evaluated. Each client was rated as to the probable alternative level of placement to which he or she would most likely have been assigned if home care were not available. The staff designating the alternative level of placement were the same staff who would have been assessing for level of placement if nursing home placement were to have been considered for these clients. Average costs (including indirect costs and the costs of assessment) were calculated for each type of service.

As shown in table 4.5, of the 1,167 clients admitted during the month, 835 (72 percent) were elderly. On the basis of previous work on *expected* levels of need, these were divided into the young elderly (women aged 65 to 84 and men 65 to 79) and the old elderly (women 85 and over and men 80 and over). The younger clients were more likely to fall at one or the other end of the need spectrum; in the absence of home care, more of them would be expected to be at home without services or in the hospital.

Table 4.6 indicates the proportions of age groups that received nursing or homemaking services; clearly, some clients received both.

Table 4.5
Number and (Percentage) of Clients Admitted to Home Care by Designated Alternative Level of Placement and Age in 1978

Designated Alternative Level of Placement	Young	Middle-Aged	Young Elderly	Old Elderly	Total
Remain at home	33	81	181	50	345
	(28.9)	(37.2)	(29.5)	(22.5)	(29.6)
PCH Level 1	3	9	97	34	143
	(2.6)	(4.1)	(15.3)	(15.3)	(12.3)
PCH Level 2	4	19	112	76	211
	(3.5)	(8.7)	(18.3)	(34.2)	(18.1)
PCH Levels 3 and 4	3	4	35	15	57
	(2.6)	(1.8)	(5.7)	(6.8)	(4.9)
Non-acute hospital	38	38	97	39	212
	(33.3)	(17.4)	(15.8)	(17.6)	(18.2)
Acute hospital	33	67	91	8	199
	(28.9)	(30.7)	(14.8)	(3.6)	(17.1)
Total	114	218	613	222	1,167
	(100)	(100)	(100)	(100)	(100)

SOURCE: Adapted from Health and Welfare Canada, 1978.

When expressed as units of service in table 4.7, there is a clear pattern of increased care intensity through the various comparable personal care home levels. Hospital replacement care uses fewer units of service than do personal care home levels 2 through 4 but more expensive services, as reflected in table 4.8, which provides the average total cost per client in various designated alternative levels of placement categories according to the different packages of services. Table 4.9 summarizes the home care costs for the first month of care for each designated alternative level of placement category and compares them with the estimated costs for institutional care at that designated alternative level of placement. Even if one questions the designation of alternative levels as too theoretical, the average cost across all levels is less than the least expensive personal care home. The average home care client received only 22.1 units of service per month (including supplies). Those who received nursing services got an average of 7.3 units. Those using homemaking got 32.7 units per month. Overall, the intensity of home care was

Table 4.6

Number and Percentage of Clients Receiving Nursing and Homemaking Services by Age in 1978

Age	Nursing Services		Homemaking Services		
	Number	Percent	Number	Percent	(N)
Young (19–44)	89	78.1	36	31.6	114
Middle-aged (45–64)	185	84.9	52	23.9	218
Young elderly (Female: 65–84 Male: 65–79)	459	79.9	255	41.6	613
Old elderly (Female: 85+ Male: 80+)	167	75.2	96	43.2	222
Total	900	77.1	439	37.6	1,167

SOURCE: Adapted from Health and Welfare Canada, 1978.
NOTE: Percentages are percentages of people in each age group; those receiving both types of services are counted twice.

Table 4.7

Average Total Units of Home Care Received by Clients in the First Month After Admission, by Designated Alternative Level of Placement in 1978

Designated Alternative Level of Placement	Average Total Units Including Supplies		Average Total Units Excluding Supplies	
	Average	Standard deviation	Average	Standard deviation
Remain home without care	16.0	36.8	11.4	28.0
PCH Level 1	18.5	24.0	17.9	23.3
PCH Level 2	39.9	52.3	34.1	44.3
PCH Level 3/4[a]	82.5	115.9	56.5	104.6
Non-acute hospital	50.4	79.7	26.4	41.6
Acute hospital	72.2	81.5	16.3	9.9
All clients	39.7	66.3	22.1	40.5

SOURCE: Adapted from Health and Welfare Canada, 1978.
[a]The small total number of clients in this group (57) may distort the average, especially considering the large standard deviation.

Table 4.8

Average Total Cost of All Home Care Services in One Month, by Types of Services and by Designated Alternative Levels of Placement (Grouped)

Combinations of Types of Services	Remain at Home	PCH Levels 1, 2, 3/4	Hospital	All Designated Alternative Levels of Placement
Nursing, homemaking plus other types of services	$162	$260	$267	$252
Nursing and supplies	117	161	255	235
Homemaking plus other types of services (no nursing)	123	186	290[a]	198
Homemaking only	170	201	94[a]	174
Nursing plus other types of services (no homemaking)	66	101	164	120
Nursing only	73	65	163	103
Other types of services (no nursing or homemaking)	33	30	93	38

SOURCE: Health and Welfare Canada, 1978.
[a]In each of these cells, the total number is less than 15 and all have designated alternative levels of placement of non-acute hospital.

Table 4.9

Average Cost of One Month in Alternative Levels of Placement and of One Month of Home Care Services, by Designated Alternative Levels of Placement

Designated Alternative Level of Placement	Average Cost of Designated Alternative Level of Placement for One Month	Average Total Cost of Home Care for One Month	Difference in Average Costs
Remain at home without care	$ 0	$ 93	$ −93
PCH Level 1	399	98	300
PCH Level 2	524	186	338
PCH Level 3/4	805	249	556
Non-acute hospital	1,744	189	1,555
Acute hospital	4,012	244	3,768
All designated alternative levels of placement	$1,184	$161	$1,022

SOURCE: Health and Welfare Canada, 1978.

generally low, and thus the cost was modest. These costs are even more impressive when one recalls that the costs and services studied occurred in the first month after admission. Most clients enter the program with more intensive needs, which gradually lessen with time in the program.

Day Care

Day care is another major program administered by the Office of Continuing Care. One day care program is freestanding, but all others are housed and operated by personal care homes. Nonprofit personal care homes have been particularly encouraged to develop day care programs. Potential clients are assessed through the Office of Continuing Care. Day care is targeted at people with physical or mental dysfunction living in the community. It is primarily a social model, with supervised recreational and social activities for people whose care needs are being met at home. It also meets some of the need for relief of family members who are providing care. Criteria for admission include reasonable geographic proximity and assessed potential to benefit. Day care also allows older persons to experience the conditions of a facility before making long-term decisions for themselves, although this is not a primary objective of the program.

Day care users are expected to have virtually intact ability to perform activities of daily living and be able at least to ambulate with assistance, or in a wheelchair with ability to transfer. They should be able to follow simple instructions and either be continent or able to manage required devices on their own.

Day care programs are responsible for coordination or provision of safe, reliable transportation. They provide a noon meal and snacks. Other services that can be provided include counseling, pastoral services, nutrition, medication supervision, nursing supervision, and personal care. Programs operate a minimum of two days a week for six hours a day. An individual must attend at least one day a week and no more than three days a week (although exceptions are made).

A day care budget is added to the home's global budget to offset the marginal costs of the program. The home can also receive a transportation allowance to pay for those costs. Each client is expected to pay a set daily fee of $3.00, which in some programs equals about half the estimated cost of the program.

Housing

Housing is a component of long-term care. Some have argued that institutional care is often simply a poor substitute for sheltered housing. In Manitoba, housing assistance is available in several forms. Special public housing for the elderly provides low-rent accommodations. The need for such housing, at least in Winnipeg, appears to have been met at present. In 1978–79 Manitoba provided subsidized rent-to-income housing for persons 60 and over in 7,230 units (10 percent of the units are intended for couples) at a cost of $5 million. One complaint heard is related to the design of the public units: the vast majority were built as bachelor apartments that could not house couples. This inflexibility of design was cited as a deterrent to their use.

In a few pilot projects, the housing authority in Winnipeg has cooperated with the Office of Continuing Care to provide organized, on-site home care, but in general, persons receiving housing assistance apply for home care just like anyone else. Because admission to public housing is conditional on intact function, the general status of this group of elderly is probably somewhat better than the rest of the elderly population on admission, but deteriorates with time. As with other forms of admission policies in long-term care, the status on admission is not representative of the cross-sectional status. As these persons remain in public housing, their condition deteriorates, and many require assistance with daily activities.

Another form of housing assistance is available through the Shelter Allowance for Elderly Renters (SAFER) program. Modeled after a similar program in British Columbia, SAFER was introduced into Manitoba in 1978. It provides direct cash assistance to elderly persons to ensure that their rent does not exceed a fixed proportion of their total monthly income. (Limits on the maximum eligible rent are established. Persons paying higher rents may be eligible, but SAFER recognizes only rents up to the established limit.) In 1979–80, 3,000 units were eligible for rent subsidization within the provincial appropriation for the program. A 1981 study suggested that about a quarter of the estimated target population (defined by income, after excluding those in subsidized housing or personal care homes) were receiving SAFER benefits (Minuk and Davidson 1981).

As part of that study, a sample of SAFER clients were interviewed. Just over half reported no incapacity. A quarter had minor difficulty in getting about, communicating, or keeping house. About 15 percent had a noticeable handicap in one activity, requiring personal assistance, and about 4 percent were unable to accomplish daily tasks on their own. About a fourth of the SAFER clients received outside help (2 percent on a daily basis, 9 percent weekly, and 15 percent occasionally). Almost 10 percent of SAFER respondents received home care from the Office of Continuing Care, and another 5 percent paid someone directly for assistance. Only 2 percent were served by visiting nurses.

There is presently an excess of housing in Winnipeg; this is attributed in part to the economic recession. The availability of housing units has led to relatively low rents. Individuals in the housing authority noted that the availability of affordable rentals (especially with SAFER support), coupled with the limitations on unit size, has reduced the demand for public housing. New projects under consideration focus on the needs of specific groups by developing special facilities for independent living.

Concluding Comment

Manitoba has the most established long-term care program of the three provinces studied. Its benefit structure under the provincial universal health insurance program and the provincial universal Home Care program are generous. It now represents a steady-state condition. The use of services appears to have plateaued. The area where one might expect the highest degree of substitution of community services for institutional services is at level 1—those needing minimal care. This effect is detected in Winnipeg but not in rural areas. The lack of effect is directly related to the availability of institutional beds (in hostels), useful only for that level of care. The decision to preserve these beds has been periodically questioned. There is some belief that these beds meet an important social need, especially in rural areas.

The assessment process is in control of a nonmedical program, the Office of Continuing Care. Physicians have adjusted to their contributory role. The paneling procedures provide an opportunity for both a review of the case by a multidisciplinary team, including a geriatrician, and feedback to the assessors to maintain their skills. This approach is worth serious consideration by other groups looking into case management.

The Manitoba system deliberately separates the roles of the facility care program and the program responsible for community care. At one level, this separation seems to risk duplication and friction, but it appears to work smoothly. There seems to be close cooperation and a respect for jurisdictional boundaries. Responsibility for those in personal care homes is transferred on admission.

One cost of this separation between community care and institutional care is a gap in data available. The Health Services Commission provides a rich source of information about clients, which allows both detailed annual reports and longitudinal studies on utilization patterns of specific groups. Unfortunately, the recipients of community care are not specifically identified in this system, and thus the relationships between use of community services and traditional health services can be addressed only through special studies.

The separation of health and community long-term care has had no perceptible deleterious effect on the medical care received by recipients of both services. Hospital discharge planners work as part of the Continuing Care program to facilitate long-term care arrangements.

In population, Manitoba is a small province. Things get done on the basis of personal contact. The lesson should not escape those thinking about the structure of rearrangements for care in the United States. Decentralization into units of manageable size is critical to success. A population of a million persons can support a comprehensive system of care that is sensitive to the needs of the elderly and is also affordable.

REFERENCES

HWC (Health and Welfare Canada) 1978. Policy, Planning, and Information Branch. *The Manitoba/Canada Home Care Study: Comparing the Cost of Home Care with the Cost of Alternative Institutional Care*. Office of Continuing Care, Departments of Health and Community Services, Winnipeg.

Minuk, M. and K. Davidson 1981. *A Report on the Research Findings of the MHRC 1981 Shelter Allowance Programs Review*. Winnipeg: Manitoba Housing and Renewal Corporation.

CHAPTER 5
Long-Term Care in British Columbia

BRITISH Columbia's long-term care program was based in many ways on the Manitoba system. Building on the foundation of universal hospital and medical insurance that all provinces enjoy, British Columbia began insuring both nursing home care and community long-term care in 1978. The new program was heralded by widespread advertising to notify the general public of the new benefit. The British Columbia experience affords a chance for a case study of the simultaneous province-wide implementation of an immensely popular program of institutional and community-based long-term care benefit. The observations are reassuring. Despite the initial volume of referrals and applications, the programs were mounted relatively smoothly. Refinements in policy and procedure have been introduced continually over the first five years without altering the basic principle of the benefit.

The program is administered out of twenty-two regional health units. It has a case management system at its hub. Unlike their counterparts in Manitoba, the case managers in British Columbia are responsible for assessing and authorizing levels of ongoing care in facilities as well as at home. The competing requirements to implement this ambitious mandate and yet hold down the cost of case management creates an ever-present tension. The provincial government has invested substantially in a management information system that can be used to monitor providers and to help case managers track their performance with their clientele.

On the institutional side, British Columbia recognizes five levels of care. The institutional benefit is provided in both nonprofit and for-profit institutions. At the beginning of the long-term care program, the province instituted a deliberate policy to stimulate the growth of nonprofit beds. Currently, the wisdom of that direction is being questioned and the policy is shifting toward a more balanced approach between the two sectors. At this writing, a new reimbursement policy has been implemented to equalize the payment received by nonprofit and proprietary homes. How to deal equitably with the proprietary sector and yet keep profit within conscionable levels, while ensuring that residents receive adequate quality of care, is a critically important question with applicability to the United States. As long as the province or state is committed to the principle that private business has a legitimate role in long-term care, the nagging issue of how to keep profit in its place must be faced. In British Columbia the common view on this question shifts with the political winds, but the province has amassed experience suggesting that an unbridled nonprofit sector brings its own inefficiencies and problems.

In community long-term care, British Columbia took a somewhat different direction from Manitoba. Rather than hire homemakers directly as Manitoba's programs do, the long-term care programs in British Columbia purchase homemaking service from nonprofit and proprietary agencies. Over the last five years, considerable experience has been amassed about how such agencies respond to the purchasing power of government, and how government can become a prudent buyer of high-quality services. Our narrative gives considerable attention, for example, to recent efforts of the long-term care program in Vancouver to introduce a competitive system of contracting for homemaker service.

The Province

British Columbia is Canada's westernmost province. Stretching from the United States border to Alaska, it occupies about 9.5 percent of Canada's land mass. Numerous large islands are contained within the province, including Vancouver Island, where the capital city, Victoria, is located. The province is mountainous and rich in natural resources.

Although more than 2.5 times as populous as Manitoba, British Columbia is also sparsely settled. As of the 1981 census, the population stood at about 2.75 million. Almost 1.2 million people were located in metropolitan Vancouver and 250,000 in metropolitan Victoria. The approximately 1.3 million people remaining are scattered in small communities, some of which are quite inaccessible by land.

Using 1976 data, the 1980–81 *Canada Yearbook* reported that only three other cities in British Columbia exceeded 50,000 in population; these were Kamloops, Kelowna, and Prince George, each hovering around 60,000. Figure 5.1 shows the principal cities and the 22 long-term care regions. Seventeen of the LTC offices are located in provincial health department units and five are in municipal departments of health (four in the Metropolitan Vancouver area and one in Victoria).

British Columbia has experienced more rapid population growth since 1950 than any other province. Most of the surge was accounted for by in-migration instead of natural increase. The population grew 20 percent between 1951 and 1956, about 17 percent during each of the next three five-year intervals, and 13 percent between 1971 and 1976. Persons over 65 are part of this in-migration and also are mobile within the province. Table 5.1 compares the comparative mobility of elderly people in British Columbia, Manitoba, and Ontario by examining patterns of relocation between the 1976 and 1981 census periods. Fully a third of those 65 and over in British Columbia in 1981 had lived in a different home five years before, 10 percent had lived in a different municipality, and 7 percent came from outside the province.

Historical Development

Hospitals

British Columbia operates its hospital and medical insurance programs as two separate plans within the Ministry of Health. The hospital plan actually predates the advent of the national system of federally cost-shared hospital insurance programs. British Columbians had expressed a long-standing interest in universal hospital insurance, even endorsing the principle in a referendum held during the 1937 provincial election. In 1948, British Columbia passed a Hospital Insurance Act, and the following year universal coverage in acute hospitals began. The province paid 100 percent of the costs until, a decade later in 1958, the federal program for underwriting hospital insurance was enacted.

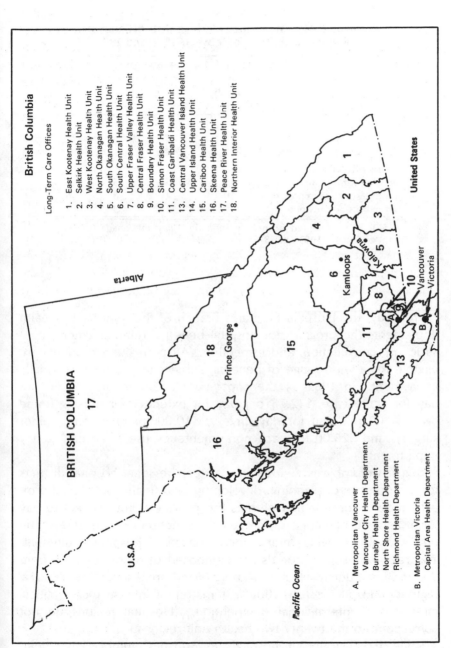

British Columbia

Long-Term Care Offices

1. East Kootenay Health Unit
2. Selkirk Health Unit
3. West Kootenay Health Unit
4. North Okanagan Health Unit
5. South Okanagan Health Unit
6. South Central Health Unit
7. Upper Fraser Valley Health Unit
8. Central Fraser Health Unit
9. Boundary Health Unit
10. Simon Fraser Health Unit
11. Coast Garibaldi Health Unit
12. Central Vancouver Island Health Unit
13. Upper Island Health Unit
14. Cariboo Health Unit
15. Skeena Health Unit
16. Skeena Health Unit
17. Peace River Health Unit
18. Northern Interior Health Unit

A. Metropolitan Vancouver
   Vancouver City Health Department
   Burnaby Health Department
   North Shore Health Department
   Richmond Health Department

B. Metropolitan Victoria
   Capital Area Health Department

Figure 5.1. Long-term care regions in British Columbia.

Table 5.1

Residential Mobility of the Elderly in British Columbia, Manitoba, and Ontario Between 1976 and 1981

	Province			
Moving Patterns	British Columbia	Manitoba	Ontario	Canada
Percentage of persons 65+ relocating	33	23	26	26
Percentage of movers 65+ by original location:				
Moving within municipality	15	16	15	15
From elsewhere in province	10	4	8	8
From outside province	7	3	3	3

SOURCE: Adapted from *Fact Book on Aging in Canada* (Government of Canada 1983), p. 23.

Presently, the Hospital Programs branch of the Ministry of Health implements the program for hospital benefits, reimbursement, construction, consultation, and inspection. All permanent residents are eligible for a wide range of benefits, subject to payment of a daily copayment. In 1983–84 the copayment amounts were $8.50 per day for acute care, $12.75 per day for extended or nursing home care, $8.00 per visit for day-surgery, $10.00 for emergency minor surgery, and $25.00 for each non-emergency use of an emergency department.

British Columbia is divided into sixteen regional hospital districts for the purpose of planning, developing, and financing hospital projects under a formula that permits the provincial government to pay for at least 60 percent of approved construction or renovation. The province also provides grants for purchase of hospital equipment. The regional hospital boards are composed of representatives from the various municipalities and unorganized areas located within the regions. Hospital construction is a matter of intense local political interest and interregional competition. (Hospital regions do *not* correspond to the twenty-two health unit regions.)

Since 1951, nonprofit hospitals in British Columbia have been reimbursed according to prospective global budgets adjusted for variable costs (e.g., supplies) that are related to the actual number of patient days. If hospitals have a lower or higher occupancy rate than anticipated, the budgets are adjusted accordingly at the end of the year, but the formula recognizes that most costs are fixed, whatever the occupancy rates.

As in all provinces, British Columbia's Hospital Act recognizes three categories of hospital: public hospital (i.e., nonprofit, primarily acute care hospitals; private hospitals (i.e., small privately owned hospitals in remote areas, usually operated by industrial concerns for their employees); and rehabilitation and extended care hospitals (which may be freestanding or may be part of an acute hospital). As of 1980, there were 96 approved public hospitals, six rehabilitation hospitals or units, thirteen extended care hospitals or units, and only two private hospitals in the province. The hospitals program also financed care in nine diagnostic and treatment centers and six outpost Red Cross hospitals. Administrative costs are modest. In Fiscal Year 1980–81, the provincial hospital program expenditures broke down as follows:

Payments for patient claims	$916,179,454
Capital and debt service	35,025,786
Grants in aid for equipment	8,754,673
Administration of program	5,317,086
Total	$965,276,999

Administration represented less than 1 percent of total costs.

Medical Services

Universally insured medical services in British Columbia were established in 1968 and are administered by the Medical Services Commission responsible to the Ministry. The plan provides insurance coverage for all medically required services rendered by physicians and osteopaths and for dental surgery done in hospital. Certain other services such as chiropractic, podiatry, optometry, and physiotherapy are covered with limitations and conditions. In January 1981, a Dental Care Plan of British Columbia was proposed, covering up to $700 a year for basic dental care and removable prostheses for specific groups: persons receiving premium assistance for their medical plan; all others over 65; others 14 and under; and some additional clients of the Ministry of Human Resources; however, it was canceled about a year after it commenced.

Premiums are charged for medical insurance; in 1984, a full premium was $16 per month for a single person, $30 a month for a family of two, and $34 for a family of three or more. All those whose taxable income falls below a specified amount are eligible for 90 percent assistance toward premium costs. More than one-quarter of the subscribers and about one-fifth of persons covered qualified for this 90 percent premium relief in 1979. In FY 1979–80, $214,765,821 was raised by premiums (with about $35 million accounted for by provincial premium assistance) and the remaining $323,110,941 came directly from provincial revenues.

As in the other provinces, the medical plan is run on a fee-for-service basis. Fees are established by the Commission in negotiation with the British Columbia Medical Association. British Columbian physicians have agreed *not* to opt out of the plan or to extra-bill. In 1980–81, $484.9 million was paid out to physicians for benefits, and another $28.5 million was paid to other professionals, including the new dental benefit. Administrative costs were held under $25 million. Expressed another way, the payments to physicians for fee-for-service care in FY 1979–80 amounted to $147 for each person insured, a rise from $130.50 the previous year.

Physicians receive a significant portion of the total health care dollar in British Columbia. Table 5.2 traces the increase in provincial health expenditures for various categories from 1974–75 to 1982–83. In 1974–75, medical services costs were 60 percent of hospital costs. By 1979–80, they rose to 64 percent, but fell to 56 percent the following year when the unions forced a major settlement in hospitals.

Pharmacare

British Columbia has a generous Pharmacare benefit. Oddly enough, Pharmacare is housed in the Ministry of Human Resources instead of the Ministry of Health. (Pharmacare was originally perceived as financial assistance and this may account for its place in the organizational structure.) Established in 1974, the program

Table 5.2
Health-Care Expenditures in British Columbia,
1974–75 to 1982–83
(In $ million)

Item	1974– 1975	1975– 1976	1976– 1977	1977– 1978	1978– 1979	1979– 1980	1980– 1981	1981– 1982	1982– 1983
					Year				
Hospitals[a]	373.4	486.7	542.5	577.8	631.4	700.6	965.3	1099.3	1211.6
Physicians	224.5	293.2	313.5	347.3	395.0	451.4	537.9	742.2	815.8
Long-term care	NA	NA	NA	18.3	97.0	143.0	168.2	220.7	258.3[b]
Total Health-Care Services	689.1	892.3	976.0	1094.4	1315.0	1490.6	1915.6	2328.0	2630.7

SOURCE: Annual Reports, British Columbia Ministry of Health.
NOTE: NA = not available.
[a]Includes administrative costs.
[b]Includes home care and homemaking.

covers the complete cost of prescription drugs and paramedical equipment (e.g., ostomy supplies, prosthetic appliances) for all persons over age 65, all residents of licensed long-term care facilities, and all persons deemed medically needy by the Ministry of Human Resources. The pharamacist is reimbursed directly for the drugs in the above cases. Other residents of British Columbia who do not fall into the listed categories are eligible to be reimbursed for 80 percent of their pharmaceutical and paramedical supplies subject to a $125 deductible in the calendar year. The Pharmacare program stands out as a model of a prudent buyer. The reimbursement to pharmacists is planned so that the pharmacist receives a professional dispensing fee over and above the cost of the drug but has no financial stake in the amount and price of drugs sold.

Beginning in 1976, the Pharmacare program altered its method of reimbursement for drugs provided to residents of long-term care facilities. Currently, a facility's drug service is restricted to a single pharmacy; the pharmacist uses a monitored dose system, makes regular visits to the facility to discuss drug safety and to establish procedures for storage and charting, collects unused drugs at the end of each month, consults with physicians, and monitors each patient's drug consumption. The pharmacist is paid on a capitated basis for this service. (In 1983, the rate was $21 per bed per month.) According to Tidball (1982) this system, featuring monitored doses from a single pharmacy and capitation payment, cost the province just over half the amount it projected for a system based on individual prescriptions provided by multiple pharmacies under the traditional fee-for-service pattern. The estimated saving was about $4.5 million. Equally important, drug use became much better controlled. From a baseline situation of an average of 72 prescriptions per resident per year, use fell to an average of 40 prescriptions per resident per year, and the actual amounts of drugs taken by the facility population were reduced by about a third.

Long-Term Care

Against this backdrop, we now turn specifically to long-term care programs. All adults, Canadian citizens, or landed immigrants who have been British Columbia residents for twelve months and who meet the physical or mental criteria established to define functional need are eligible for the nursing home and homemaking benefits bearing the name "long-term care." Any interested party or the person requesting the service may make the initial inquiry and activate an assessment process. The Long-Term Care (LTC) program consists of both institutional and home support benefits.

Organization

The LTC Program began in January 1978. The Ministry of Health has primary responsibility for the program but the Ministry of Human Resources has responsibility for ensuring that those in financial need receive funds for comfort allowances, user per diems, and any special services needed. The Ministry of Human Resources is also responsible for the program of special facilities for the mentally retarded, and it administers and monitors the Pharmacare program. The Department of Mental Health Services program within the Ministry of Health manages mental health boarding homes. The two ministries and various programs within them must therefore cooperate toward a smoothly functioning long-term care program.

The already existing Provincial Adult Care Facilities Licensing Board was legislatively mandated as the organization initially responsible to the Ministry of Health for the overall coordination of the new long-term care program. Its expanded responsibilities included: formulating policy and procedures; hearing appeals in connection with the program; recommending approval for construction of new long-term care facilities; licensing facilities that participate in the program; coordinating with the twenty-two health units responsible for administering the program and inspecting the local facilities; and liaison with other units within the Ministry. The Provincial Director of the LTC Program was also the executive for the Provincial Adult Care Facilities Licensing Board. By 1979, a single Executive Director was placed in charge of Long-Term Care and Home Care (the provincial home nursing program). In 1981 the Long-Term Care/Home Care Program was brought under the assistant deputy minister responsible for the hospital sector to facilitate consideration of trade-offs between these programs. In October 1983, the name of the provincial department was changed to the Continuing Care Division.*

Organizational units responsible for the LTC program at the community levels were created in the 22 regional public health departments. An LTC Administrator in each regional long-term care unit is the senior local program official. This individual is a member of the health department establishment and, as such, is responsible to the Medical Officer of Health. However, the LTC administrators are responsible also to the provincial program, from which they take overall policy direction and receive their administrative budgets. The province directly reimburses the providers of institutional care based on information received from local long-term care units. Homemaker agencies submit monthly statements to the long-term care units and these are audited and approved by the administrator before payment is made.

The provincial Ministry of Health undergoes perennial reorganization. Figure 5.2 shows how the various programs described interrelate administratively as of this writing. The Minister of Health is an elected member of the provincial legislature appointed by the premier (analogous to a state governor). The Deputy Ministers are the most senior civil servants within the government. Prior to the 1981 reorganization, Home Care/Long-Term Care was responsible to an Assistant Deputy Minister for Direct Care and Community Services, who also oversaw mental health services. After 1981 Long-Term Care/Home Care came under the Assistant Deputy Minister for Institutional Services, so that administrative trade-offs between hospital and long-term care programs could be better considered. Figure 5.2 illustrates the parallel positions of the LTC and Home Care components in each of the 22 regional units during the time we did our study. With the creation of the Continuing Care Division in 1983, a movement began to consolidate the LTC and Home Care

---

*The description below and the organizational chart in figure 5.2 reflect the pattern before the October 1983 change. Throughout this chapter, we use the term "LTC program" to refer to the homemaking and nursing home programs at the regional level and "LTC administrator" and "LTC case manager" to refer to regional program staff. However, as of 1984, a transition has been under way, and some regions are using the titles Continuing Care Administrator and Continuing Care Case Manager to connote the broader role implied by an administrative merger of LTC programs and Home Nursing programs at the regional levels.

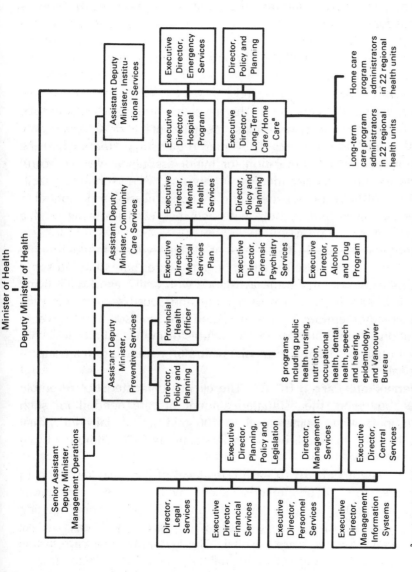

Minister of Health

Deputy Minister of Health

Senior Assistant Deputy Minister, Management Operations

Assistant Deputy Minister, Preventive Services

Assistant Deputy Minister, Community Care Services

Assistant Deputy Minister, Institutional Services

Director, Legal Services

Executive Director, Financial Services

Executive Director, Planning, Policy and Legislation

Executive Director, Personnel Services

Director, Management Services

Executive Director, Central Services

Executive Director, Management Information Systems

Director, Policy and Planning

Provincial Health Officer

8 programs including public health nursing, nutrition, occupational health, dental health, speech and hearing, epidemiology, and Vancouver Bureau

Executive Director, Medical Services Plan

Executive Director, Mental Health Services

Executive Director, Forensic Psychiatry Services

Director, Policy and Planning

Executive Director, Alcohol and Drug Program

Executive Director, Emergency Services

Executive Director, Hospital Program

Director, Policy and Planning

Executive Director, Long-Term Care/Home Care[a]

Long-term care program administrators in 22 regional health units

Home care program administrators in 22 regional health units

[a]As of October 1983, the Long-Term Care/Home Care Program became the Continuing Care Division

SOURCE: Adapted from the 1981 *Annual Report* of the British Columbia Ministry of Health.

Figure 5.2. Place of long-term care/home care program within the organization of the British Columbia Ministry of Health.

programs at the local level. As of July 1984, five health units, including Vancouver, had replaced the Long-Term Care Administrator and the Home Care Administrator with a single Continuing Care Administrator, and others are expected the make the transition as soon as feasible.

Institutional Care

Five levels of care are recognized:

Personal Care. Persons at this level are independently mobile with or without mechanical aids, mentally intact, or suffering only minor mental impairment. They may require a protected housing environment, social stimulation, or minor assistance with self-care, but do not need regular medical supervision. A personal care facility offers 24-hour-a-day supervision by nonprofessional personnel, a protective environment, help with activities of daily living, and a social/recreational program.

Intermediate Care I (IC-I). Persons at this level are independently mobile, similar to those requiring personal care, but will need some health supervision and some assistance with activities of daily living as well as the protected environment and social/recreational program already mentioned. It is estimated that a person at this level in institutional care would need 75 minutes of individual attention per day—15 minutes from a professional and 60 minutes from a nonprofessional.

Intermediate Care II (IC-II). The client's characteristics resemble those above, but the estimated amount of care needed for such clients in facilities is increased to 100 minutes of daily individual attention—30 minutes by a professional and 70 minutes by a nonprofessional.

Intermediate Care III (IC-III). This level of care was designed to recognize the psychogeriatric client with severe, continuous behavioral problems. The level is also used for persons needing more daily care than allowed under IC-II, especially those awaiting room in an Extended Care hospital. The assumption for care in this category is 120 minutes of individual care daily—30 minutes from a professional and 90 minutes from a nonprofessional.

Extended Care. An extended care hospital unit provides round-the-clock supervision of a registered nurse and the availability of regular medical supervision and a multidisciplinary therapeutic team. It is assumed the individual will need at least 150 minutes of care a day. The rule-of-thumb for eligibility is that this individual generally is unable to transfer independently.

The descriptions are taken from a more detailed discussion in the *Long-Term Care Program Administrative Manual* (an updatable compilation of policy directives). Despite the inclusion of examples, however, the distinctions among levels of care are not completely objective and clear, particularly between IC-I and IC-II levels.

The levels of care form the basis for accelerating daily reimbursement rates for proprietary facilities. As in other provinces, nonprofit facilities have been paid by a global budgeting procedure that reduces the significance of the level-of-care determinations somewhat, but the global budget is established partly on the basis of case mix by level of care. Some facilities at the Personal Care level resemble the hostels in Manitoba and cannot be readily adapted for higher levels of care. Typically, however, a facility can house multiple levels of care, especially those levels in the Intermediate Care range. Extended Care is provided in hospital units or freestanding extended care hospitals, subject to the management of the Hospital Program rather than the LTC Program. However, since 1978 the LTC program has done the assessments for eligibility to Extended Care and more recently has begun to control the waiting lists.

In 1984, the nursing home payment system was consolidated into a single system for both proprietary and nonprofit facilities. The new system sets recommended staffing guidelines for each level of care and pays up to 100 percent of these costs. For those with less than 90 percent of the recommended staffing, a lower rate is paid to encourage improvement. The staffing ratios, expressed as full-time equivalents per occupied bed, are:

Personal Care	.306
IC-I	.416
IC-II	.526
IC-III	.700
Extended Care	.700

Property costs are paid to proprietary facilities at a flat per diem rate and to nonprofit facilities as actual costs. Administrative supplies and other costs are paid to both as a flat per diem rate.

The individual user of an LTC facility pays a fixed per diem keyed to the amounts of the standard OAS/GIS benefits as in the other two provinces. (In 1983–84, the daily user charge was $12.75.) Clear guidelines are established for items that are to be included in the regular rate and the extra amounts that can be assessed for preferred accommodations (i.e., semiprivate or private rooms). Facilities are allowed to levy extra charges for specified items, such as personal telephone, cable television, personal drycleaning, hygiene and grooming supplies, newspapers and magazines, but they are prohibited from charging the resident more than cost for such extra amenities.

The LTC Program recognizes that the resident may be absent from the facility from time to time and has developed procedures to protect the resident, the facility, and the program in that regard. Two types of absences are recognized: paid temporary absences and unpaid temporary absences. In the former, the LTC Program pays the usual per diem and the resident is responsible for the user charges and any extra charges for preferred accommodations, whereas the resident is responsible for all charges in the latter situation.

Paid temporary absences of three days or less can be authorized by the administrator of the particular LTC facility where the client resides. Longer paid temporary absences may be approved at the discretion of the regional LTC administrator when the resident is in an acute hospital, when urgent personal reasons exist, or when "a reasonable period of absence is in the best interest of the client." A maximum of six weeks of paid absence is allowed if the resident is in a psychogeriatric assessment unit. The cumulative amount of absence for stays in acute hospitals or other illness reasons must be justified by the LTC administrator but has no arbitrary limit; the cumulative absence for non-illness reasons under the Paid Temporary Absence category is 30 days. In addition, the LTC administrator may approve Unpaid Temporary Absences of up to 30 days a calendar year if the client agrees to pay the full cost of the accommodation during the period. The combined force of these policies permits residents to take vacations or visit their families without losing their places in the facility. A standard form is completed by the residents with each absence to show that they understand the arrangements and their own financial liability.

In 1982 the LTC program spent about $1 million holding empty beds.

Home Support Service/Homemaking

The long-term care assessor may also authorize services that permit the individual to stay at home. Homemaker and handyman services are the primary benefits reimbursed directly by the LTC program, although some day care is also available. In addition, the LTC program attempts to coordinate home-delivered meals and other community services. The program assumes that most users would prefer home care and tries to arrange it whenever possible. The case managers also recognize the importance of informal help from family and friends and endeavor not to supplant it in authorizing public services.

Maximum hours of home care allowable under the program have been established according to the level-of-care assessment. Since 1979, the following maximum homemaker levels have been in place:

Personal Care . . .	up to 40 hours homemaking per month
IC-I	up to 46 hours homemaking per month
IC-II	up to 64 hours per month
IC-III	up to 98 hours per month
Extended Care . . .	up to 120 hours per month

Extensions to these limits are allowed under special circumstances, for example, to give respite to family caregivers, to provide for an emergency, or to provide service to someone waiting for an institutional bed.

Homemaking and handyman services are not free; those who can afford to do so pay for all or a part of the service. A rather elaborate calculation of income and expenditures is made to determine the amount an individual has available for his or her care. That sum is divided by 30 to derive a maximum daily rate that the person could be charged for homemaking. In theory, extremely well-to-do persons could end up with a daily homemaking charge more expensive than the costs of privately purchasing the help. Any such person would, of course, purchase homemaking privately. Perhaps the policy was meant to be a disincentive for high-income families to use the public homemaker benefit. In fact, despite widespread program utilization, the amounts of direct payments that the LTC program collects for homemaking and handyman services are negligible. In 1981, it was estimated that only about 3 percent of homemaking costs were recovered from fees. Most people receiving homemaking are well over 75, and their income tends to be well below the point at which fees are assessed. In 1981, a single person with a monthly income of $396 or a couple with $608 would have fallen into the noncharge category automatically.

Homemaker agencies are paid a daily rate negotiated with the regional LTC program. Standard budgetary forms are used for systematic description of expenses. The LTC administrator is responsible for working out these rates with the community providers. LTC administrators sometimes attempt to rationalize homemaking costs by instructing case managers to use specific agencies for clients in a certain geographic area or for specific types of clientele.

Home Care (Home Nursing)

The availability of home nursing service is an important aspect of any community-based long-term care provision. In British Columbia, home nursing is provided directly by public employees of the various regional health departments. As noted in figure 5.2, home nursing is at present administratively located in the Long-Term Care/Home Care Program, which in 1983 became Continuing Care Division. Each home care program has its own administrator in the twenty-two health units or municipal health departments. Patients may use home care without using long-term care and vice versa. The home care program serves many more people under age 65 than does its sister LTC program.

Home nursing was in existence before the advent of the long-term care benefits. Beginning in 1971, British Columbia developed a "hospital replacement" home care program that was free to the user because it served in lieu of hospital days coverable by hospital insurance. This program also made available homemaking and related services at no charge. Persons in a "nonhospital replacement" category (i.e., those needing care that would not otherwise require hospitalization) could also receive home nursing at no charge but needed to fund their own related ancillary services.

This already existing program of home nursing formed the nucleus of the nursing program for LTC clients. It continues to provide nursing and other therapy at home on both a hospital replacement and a hospital nonreplacement basis. The only difference in the hospital replacement program is that the home support is arranged for and purchased by home nursing programs, and no financial assessment is done because ancillary services are free regardless of income. The Home Care Program still keeps statistics that separate hospital replacement and nonhospital replacement categories, but financial differences to the user are blunted if functional impairments render them eligible for the LTC program as well. Very few LTC clients are charged fees for the homemaking services despite the financial reviews.

Home Care programs are located in the regional health departments alongside long-term care programs to comprise the continuing care division programs. Extensive mutual referral takes place; LTC receives many of its cases from home care and, in turn, requests home care for its clients from the local home care program. The extent of overlap in clienteles varies widely from health unit to health unit.

The Home Care program requires a physician's order for a nurse to continue giving care on the case. If a physician has not made the initial referral, the patient is asked to request it, or the nurse contacts a physician directly. Since 1963, a community physiotherapy program has been available as part of home care; the services are readily available in the municipal areas but limited by the supply of therapists in some provincial health units.

The potential for redundancy in care planning is present when both a Home Care nurse and an LTC case manager are involved with a client, but few problems in this regard have been reported at local levels. Combining the two programs—LTC and Home Care—into a single provincial department in 1979 clearly facilitated coordination. Note that the overall home support arrangements are under reversed auspices in British Columbia compared with Winnipeg: in the former, homemaking is purchased from multiple agencies, but home nursing is provided by public employees, whereas in Winnipeg, homemaking is provided directly and home nursing is purchased from a single agency—the Victorian Order of Nurses (VON).

In Fiscal Year 1982–83, the Home Care program saw 49,935 patients (31,489 on nonhospital replacement) and made 621,315 visits (466,548 on nonhospital replacement). Of these home nursing patients, 55.8 percent were over 65 and 33 percent were over 75. Statistics for FY 1982–83 show few discharges from home nursing to long-term care facilities (less than 3 percent). The largest category of discharge (52 percent) was "with no more care," followed by 20 percent who went to acute hospitals.

The Home Care program keeps statistics on the number of its clientele also on the LTC program. In FY 1982–83, 45 percent of home nursing visits were made to LTC program clients. That year the total expenditure for home nursing was a little over $17 million. At that time the community physiotherapy program made 17,443 visits to 1,802 patients at a cost of $580,000, and 42 percent of these patients were also on the LTC program. (Note that Community Physiotherapy Service data pertain only to the seventeen provincial health units and exclude the five municipal health departments in urban areas.)

The LTC program does not keep comparable statistics to show the proportion of its clientele that are also on home nursing. It is our impression, however, that a greater percentage of home nursing clients receive LTC services than vice versa. LTC serves many clients who do not require the sustained help of a nurse. Also, the home nursing program has a relatively short length of stay, and is likely to close and then reopen cases several times, whereas the LTC involvement is more sustained. This is in sharp contrast to United States policy, where a "skilled" nursing benefit triggers all home care under Medicare and usually under Medicaid as well.

The way home nursing is provided introduces some interesting issues. Clear advantages can be described for maintaining a cadre of public health nurses with general responsibility for home nursing procedures for people of all ages. The program personnel benefit by the good reputation and acceptability to clientele that public health nursing has historically enjoyed. As salaried government employees, they can be encouraged to use their time efficiently, making short visits when short visits will suffice, and doing training to help family and homemakers carry on with nursing procedures. However, because home nurses in British Columbia, like LTC case managers, are direct provincial employees, their positions are subject to cost-cutting measures and freezes on new hires. Direct personnel are much more vulnerable to such cuts than are purchased services, which in the British Columbia LTC/Home Care Program primarily means homemaking services. Ironically, measures for greater accountability in costs of public programs make the less visible purchased services seem attractive even if a shift to such vendors means less accountability for the program in the long run. British Columbia has thus far resisted the temptation to go to a vendor system for home nursing, but the economy of provincial (or state) government that deals in "positions" as much as "dollars" creates those pressures.

Then, too, when costs of community-based long-term care are considered in British Columbia (see chapter 6), the separately calculated costs of home nursing must be added to the homemaking and other costs that are kept by the LTC Program. Separate statistics make this accountability more difficult, particularly because the Home Care Program serves many who do *not* receive LTC.

Other Services

Nursing home care and homemaking services are the two major operations directly controlled by the LTC program, and home nursing from the Home Care Program is the major supplement to permit community care for the frail elderly. However, other services in the LTC program purview should be briefly mentioned. Adult day care programs are under steady development. At the end of 1980, twenty Adult Day Centers were in operation and thirteen more were in the planning stages. Family care homes are also available as an option. These are unlicensed homes that provide care to a maximum of two LTC clients in a home atmosphere. Family care homes are analogous to adult foster care in the United States; LTC programs have flexibility to develop and pay these resources as they see fit; as of July 1981, 175 family homes served 200 people. The LTC program also covers the cost of mental health boarding homes, although the supervision of those homes is under mental health auspices. (At this writing, plans are under way to remove mental health boarding homes entirely from the LTC program.) For skilled diagnostic work, the program can use three hospital-based geriatric assessment and treatment centers, two in Vancouver and one in Victoria. In 1981, these centers had a cumulative capacity of forty-five. LTC case managers also direct their clients toward other services not directly provided by the program; these include meals-on-wheels, "wheels-to-meals" (i.e., transportation to congregate meals), Red Cross Loan Service for medical equipment, friendly visiting services, special transportation programs, senior citizens counselors, stroke clubs, and a wide variety of professional and volunteer services in the local communities.

Case Management

Because chapter 7 describes case management in all three provinces, we only briefly outline it here. The centrality of case management is an important feature of long-term care in British Columbia. (In most jurisdictions, the term "assessor" is in more general use; we use the term "case manager" because the functions performed are analogous to those of long-term-care case managers in the United States.) The line personnel in each LTC program are called care coordinators, and they exercise a case management function. (The terms "care coordinator" and "case manager" are used interchangeably in this chapter.) After the initial assessment, the care coordinator is expected to do reassessments at regular intervals—at least annually for those in facilities, every six months for those in the community, after any hospitalization of any client, and as requested by the client or a provider.

Coordinators are predominately public health nurses, except in Vancouver, where social workers and physical therapists also serve in the role. The caseloads have tended to be large (most frequently falling into the 300 to 400 range), making routine reassessments difficult. However, the care coordinators are usually assigned to specific LTC facilities within their geographic area, making coverage of the residents in the caseload easier and ensuring that the care coordinator will become a familiar figure in the nursing home. The care coordinator is expected to raise or reduce both levels of care and allocated hours as needed. Given the large caseloads, the likelihood has been that reassessments, usually at the request of a provider, have led to increased rather than decreased service.

Decision rules for service allocations involve professional judgment. Coordinators attempt to be parsimonious purchasers in their exercise of this judgment. However, many have told us that they will authorize a minimum (perhaps four hours a month) for virtually any persons in their 80's who live alone, as an investment to keep those persons connected to the system. (Manitoba case managers made similar comments.) In the last few years, LTC programs have been given a specific budgetary ceiling for homemaking hours; any increase requires special provincial authorization. This step has also helped accountability in the program.

Management Information System

A uniform five-page assessment tool is used province-wide as the basis for the care coordinators' evaluations. (See the appendix to this chapter for the complete assessment form.) The first part of the first page, containing identifying information on the applicant and the level-of-care determination, is keypunched by the province and used in the computerized information system. The form is completed in quadruplicate: one copy to the provincial registry, one to the local registry, one to the care provider, and one for the assessor's own record. In the roughly 10 percent of assessments that require no service, a record is also kept and a routine reassessment is supposed to be done.

A second simple form, called a Care Advice Form (figure 5.3), is pivotal to the system. The case manager completes a Care Advice Form any time a service is started, stopped, or changed in intensity. The information is used to verify payment and also serves statistical reporting purposes. Therefore, a record exists of each transaction in or out of a facility, on or off homemaker or day care service, or any change in service. The date for beginning and ending a service is noted as are starts and stops of paid temporary absence from facilities. Level of care changes are also noted.

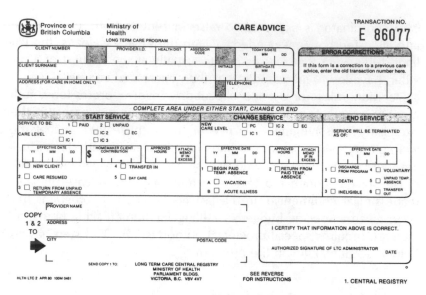

Figure 5.3. Care Advice form from British Columbia.

This information, combined with some basic descriptive information about each approved provider, permits quite detailed statistical analysis. Information is available by region on the work-flow of the case managers (number of new assessments, reassessments, reviews, appeals). Information is also available on specific clients (care currently and formerly received) and on specific providers (e.g., the distribution of their clients by level of care). The computerized system permits case managers at desk-top terminals to examine displays by client or by provider. Printouts are sent to each regional program quarterly, allowing them to compare their patterns with those in other regions.

Since 1982, homemaker utilization data have been sent to the regional programs in a highly readable form, permitting easy comparisons. One display ranks the LTC programs by numbers of homemaker clients in each level of care, and a second display rank-orders the programs by number of homemaker hours at each level of care. Table 5.3 illustrates an additional display that allows each program to compare its performance with others, adjusting for the population over age 65 in the region. As the table shows, 6.7 percent of those over 65 receive some homemaker service, but in June 1983 the range among the regions went from 4.9 percent to 12.8 percent, indicating a wide margin of local autonomy. Similarly, the average homemaker hours per client per month was 16.4 province-wide, but the range was 11.7 to 22.1. The next-to-last column shows a startling range in the percentage of persons over 65 using institutional long-term care: from 3.3 percent to 13 percent. There is no clear correlation between community care and institutional use. The final column shows that across the province about 16 percent of those over 65 used either the institutional or the community long-term care service, again with considerable range from region to region.

Experience With Supply and Demand

The LTC program became effective January 1, 1978. By October almost 42,000 applications had been processed and 39,880 applicants had been found eligible for care. These large numbers occurred partly because all those persons living in facilities when the program started needed to be assessed and most proved eligible for service. By October 1978, 17,618 persons were receiving the benefit in long-term care facilities and extended care hospitals, and 11,714 were receiving homemaker service.

Each nursing home had to choose whether to participate in the program or to remain outside it. Facilities were not permitted to accept a mix of private pay residents and provincial beneficiaries. Because all citizens regardless of income were eligible to receive care under the benefit, little private market for nursing home care remained. By the end of the first year, 95 percent of the homes, representing 86 percent of the beds, had joined the program—some 529 facilities with 15,082 beds; 7,531 beds were proprietary, 6,100 nonprofit, and 1,451 in mental health facilities. The program has grown since that time; by June 1983 the number of beds available in LTC facilities and extended care hospitals had risen to about 24,000.

The homemaking capacity in the local areas also expanded quickly. In 1978, 77 homemaker agencies were participating in the

Table 5.3

Homemaker Billing and Facility Client Analysis Report, June 1983

LTC Unit	Pop. Over 65	% of Total Pop. Over 65	Hmkr. Clients 19–64	Hmkr. Clients 65+	% of Pop. 65+ Receiving Hmkr. Service	Average Hmkr. Hrs./ Client	Fac. & E.C. Hosp. Res. 19–64	Fac. & E.C. Hosp. Res. 65+	% of 65+ Pop. in LTC Fac. & E.C. Hosp.	% of 65+ Pop. Receiving Hmkr. Serv. & in Fac. & E.C.
1	6329	8.7	153	814	12.8	18.8	31	398	6.2	19.19
2	3736	12.4	67	416	11.1	15.9	32	234	6.2	17.39
3	5856	12.6	81	506	8.6	16.0	26	322	5.4	14.13
4	10483	11.5	122	736	7.0	15.8	114	544	5.1	12.21
5	23251	15.9	261	1482	6.4	14.7	184	1166	5.0	11.38
6	7244	6.5	136	505	6.9	14.4	100	424	5.8	12.82
7	14099	12.1	120	804	5.7	16.1	122	1111	7.8	13.58
8	12047	9.9	143	733	6.1	14.8	188	1155	9.5	15.67
9	23638	9.7	225	1138	4.8	11.7	251	1713	7.2	12.06
10	13778	9.4	142	800	5.8	15.0	181	1016	7.3	13.18
11	4983	9.8	68	455	9.1	16.5	6	169	3.3	12.52
13	20079	12.0	317	1352	6.7	15.5	446	2615	13.0	19.75
14	6259	7.2	123	478	7.6	14.8	128	716	11.4	19.07
15	3264	5.0	76	300	9.1	20.5	34	144	4.4	13.60
16	3681	4.2	66	194	5.2	20.5	52	189	5.1	10.40
17	3094	5.2	70	273	8.8	18.5	32	187	6.0	14.86
18	4794	4.0	80	322	6.7	22.1	48	209	4.3	11.07
20	69993	16.6	1262	5048	7.2	19.1	1063	4879	6.9	14.18
30	17021	12.3	182	1307	7.6	15.5	116	1605	9.4	17.10
40	15829	11.2	82	851	5.3	15.0	82	1093	6.9	12.28
50	7280	7.3	108	410	5.6	13.5	14	395	5.4	11.05
60	44386	17.5	376	2199	4.9	14.7	295	3027	6.8	11.77
Province	321144	11.4	3709	21696	6.7	16.4	3106	31266	9.7	16.49

SOURCE: Example supplied by M. Halsall, Provincial Home Support Coordinator, Home Care/Long-Term Care Program, British Columbia.
NOTE: E.C. Hospital = Extended Care Hospital.

program, caring for 11,714 clients. In 1980 there were 102 nonprofit and 21 proprietary homemaking agencies serving about 24,000 homemaker clients. Three years later, the number of homemaker clients was much the same: it was 25,500 in July 1983. This suggests a stabilizing of the proportion of persons using the homemaking program which, in 1983, was about 6.7 percent of the population over 65 and less than 4,000 clients under 65.

Figure 5.4 provides an overview of the scope of the LTC program, according to the numbers and types of provider organizations in the program in July 1981, and the annual caseload associated with each category of provider. The bulk of long-term care costs is accounted for by facility care. For example, the estimated cost for care in nonprofit and for-profit facilities was almost $125 million. Another $13.5 million was expended in thirty-five private hospitals; this expenditure category refers to for-profit extended care hospitals where the LTC program occasionally purchases services. (These tend to be used when no bed can be found in a nonprofit extended care hospital unit.) The distribution of public dollars between home care and facility care is much more balanced than in the United States. The combined cost of payments to homemaker agencies, adult day care, and family care homes (i.e., adult foster care) was $63.4 million, whereas the combined costs of nursing homes and private hospitals was $137.3 million. Thus the facility costs were only about 2.2 times greater than the home care costs, and that ratio decreases further if home nursing is also added. (Group homes and mental health boarding homes are left out of this equation, as are assessment and treatment centers—the latter accounted for about $3 million, and the former about $9.3 million.) Above all, figure 5.4 shows the dramatic importance of homemaking, which served more than 60 percent of long-term care clients and received more than a quarter of the program expenditures.

In 1981, Penner (1981) performed detailed analyses of the utilization of facility care and homemaker care under the LTC program. Table 5.4 shows utilization rates as percentages of the population. The overall utilization of homemakers among persons over 65 was 7.8 percent but substantial differences occurred by age and region. The utilization rate was lowest in the greater Victoria area, where the population over 65 is about 17 percent, and highest in the non-metropolitan areas of the province. The low utilization for the

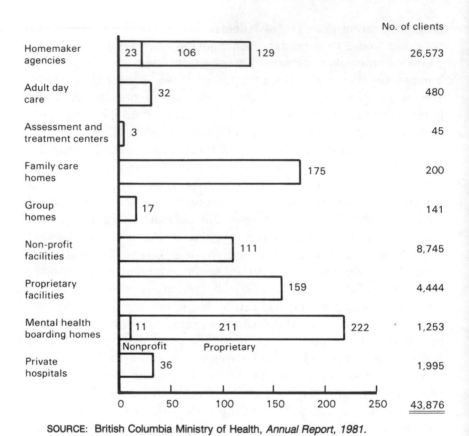

SOURCE: British Columbia Ministry of Health, *Annual Report, 1981.*

Figure 5.4. Number and type of organizations participating in long-term care program as of July 1981 by number of clients served.

Victoria region was accounted for by exceptionally low use among the youngest segments of the population over age 65 and may be related to greater wealth among retirees migrating to that area. The provincewide rate for facility use approached 6 percent and was quite similar across the regions. However, these rates rose sharply with age.

Table 5.4

**Utilization Rates of Long-Term Care Program by
Region and Age for Persons 65+
(In percent of the general population)**

Age	Vancouver Area	Victoria Area	Rest of British Columbia	All of British Columbia
Homemaker Utilization Rate				
65–69	2.88	1.62	3.23	2.86
70–74	5.63	3.27	6.44	5.63
75–79	9.44	6.34	12.14	9.96
80–84	14.45	11.24	18.29	15.16
85–90	16.59	17.76	21.52	18.30
90+	18.24	18.59	20.78	19.05
Total	7.66	6.14	8.48	7.75
Facility Utilization Rate				
65–69	1.36	0.83	0.93	1.12
70–74	2.50	1.82	1.94	2.18
75–79	5.30	4.08	4.86	4.96
80–84	11.63	8.98	12.21	11.37
85–90	20.66	18.42	23.72	21.20
90+	40.71	41.25	40.75	40.81
Total	6.34	5.76	5.16	5.81

SOURCE: Adapted from Penner 1981.

Table 5.5 shows the composition of homemaker and facility clientele by region and level of care. As expected, the homemaker clientele tended to be assessed as needing lesser levels of care. However, close to 10 percent of homemaker clients in all regions fell into either the IC-3 (i.e., psychogeriatric) or the extended care category. The facility clientele were assessed as much more impaired. The proportion of facility residents assessed as needing only personal care was particularly low in the Victoria area and the proportion assessed as needing extended care was particularly high.

Table 5.6 shows the composition of homemaker and facility clientele by age and level of care. Level of care rises with age, as one would expect, but it is noteworthy that the LTC program encounters persons at advanced age whose level of care is low. For example,

Table 5.5

**Composition of Homemaker and Facility Clientele
in British Columbia, by Region and Level of Care in 1981**

Level of Care	Vancouver Area	Victoria Area	Rest of British Columbia	All of British Columbia
Homemaker Clientele				
Personal Care	62.0	54.7	53.5	57.6
IC-1	18.9	24.7	23.6	21.5
IC-2	9.4	12.5	14.3	11.8
IC-3	5.5	1.8	4.3	4.6
Extended Care	4.2	6.3	4.3	4.5
Total	100.0	100.0	100.0	100.0
Facility Clientele				
Personal Care	28.6	16.4	21.5	24.5
IC-1	21.9	23.7	23.3	22.6
IC-2	14.6	20.0	18.7	16.8
IC-3	13.7	10.2	13.6	13.2
Extended Care	21.2	29.7	22.9	22.9
Total	100.0	100.0	100.0	100.0

SOURCE: Adapted from Penner 1981.

more than 50 percent of homemaking clients aged 85 to 89 fall into the personal care level, and more than 40 percent of homemaking clients *over age 90* also are assessed at the lightest level of care. Note that the assessed level of care reflects the actual functioning of the individual, not the amount of homemaker service ordered. The latter determination is a result of a further consideration of the need for help and the amount of informal help available.

Unit Costs and Cost Control

The average 1983 hourly charge of homemaker agencies was about $10. It is estimated that the homemakers themselves earn about $7 an hour in unionized agencies and $5 an hour in nonunionized agencies. Table 5.7 shows the average rates in the proprietary and nonprofit sectors and the range of those rates. The proprietary

Table 5.6

Composition of Long-Term Care Clientele in British Columbia, by Age and Level of Care in 1981

Age	Personal Care	IC-1	IC-2	IC-3	Extended Care
Homemaker (Rows = 100%)					
Under 65	48.1	22.0	14.7	6.0	9.2
65–69	61.2	20.9	10.8	3.4	3.7
70–74	62.1	20.7	10.3	3.7	3.2
75–79	62.9	20.9	10.1	3.4	2.7
80–84	60.9	21.5	11.0	4.1	2.5
85–89	55.1	22.0	13.5	5.5	3.9
90+	42.4	23.8	14.1	9.6	10.1
All clients	57.6	21.5	11.8	4.6	4.5
Facility (Rows = 100%)					
Under 65	30.0	25.0	17.1	14.5	13.4
65–69	26.2	23.9	17.6	14.5	17.8
70–74	25.1	24.0	16.7	14.0	20.2
75–79	25.7	25.5	17.0	13.9	20.9
80–84	25.2	21.0	16.9	11.6	25.3
85–89	25.2	21.0	16.9	11.6	25.3
90+	18.0	21.0	16.0	13.0	32.0
All clients	24.5	22.6	16.8	13.2	22.9

SOURCE: Adapted from Penner 1981.

Table 5.7

Charges of Homemaker Agencies Between 1979 and 1983

Year	Nonprofit Agencies		Proprietary Agencies	
	Average	Range	Average	Range
1979	$ 7.03	$5.83–8.89	Not available	
1980	$ 7.50	$6.16–11.73	Not available	
1981	$10.16	$7.10–13.06	$ 9.19	$8.35–10.00
1982	$11.18	$7.81–14.37	$ 9.64	$9.10–10.50
1983	Not available		$ 9.66	$9.45–10.80

SOURCE: British Columbia Long Term Care/Home Care Program.

average hourly rate is consistently under the nonprofit, but the range of the former rates is quite narrow. Although the charges for the nonprofit agencies were greater, the British Columbia government was able to evoke cost-sharing from the federal government on behalf of "persons in need" under the Canada Assistance Plan (see chapter 2). Depending on case mix of the homemaking agencies, this factor could make purchase from a nonprofit agency cheaper for the province.

Table 5.8 shows the per diem rates in the residential facility sector. The proprietary facilities were permitted to charge a fixed negotiated sum for each level of care, and this sum was held constant across the province. In contrast, the nonprofits were paid by a global budgeting process. As the table illustrates, the average per diem for nonprofit facilities exceeds the average per diem of the proprietary sector. The distribution of residents according to level of care is about equal across the five categories, so this comparison is best made by comparing the average per diem of the nonprofit facilities with the per diem paid the proprietary homes for the IC-2 level. The disparity between rates in the two sectors widens more markedly over time, especially because new nonprofit facilities were developed with higher operating costs. Interestingly, in view of the SNF/ICF distinction in the United States, the actual scheme equates

Table 5.8
Per Diems for Facilities Participating in the LTC Program, 1978-1983

Year	Proprietary per Diem					Nonprofit Average per Diem	User per Diem[a]
	PC	IC-1	IC-2	IC-3	EC		
1978–79	15.50	16.45	20.55	28.44	34.50	20.68	6.50
1979–80	14.20	18.20	21.75	35.00	35.00	27.51	6.50
1980–81	15.35	19.65	23.50	37.80	37.80	27.51	6.50
1981–82	17.20	22.00	26.32	42.34	42.34	36.31	8.50
1982–83	19.25	24.74	29.60	46.15	46.15	43.41	11.50
1983–84	20.20	26.00	31.10	48.45	48.45	43.91	12.75

[a]The user per diem is calculated into the daily rates for the proprietary facilities and the average daily costs for the nonprofit facilities.

IC-3 (largely psychogeriatric) behavioral problems and EC (largely heavy care, SNF-level residents). British Columbia recognizes a qualitative rather than a financial distinction between delivering IC-3 and Extended levels of care.

The stimulation of nonprofit societies to start long-term care facilities was a deliberate provincial policy in the early years of the LTC Program. The policy was particularly advantageous because low-interest federal loans were available through Canada Mortgage and Housing for nonprofit groups undertaking this activity (see chapter 2).

In the provincial government, a reaction has set in against an automatic assumption that nonprofit facilities are more desirable than proprietary ones. The reasons are twofold: (1) the higher costs paid to the nonprofits, and (2) some negative experiences with the performance of some nonprofit societies who were attracted into the nursing home business with no prior experience and sometimes with fixed ideas about the nature of the clientele.

The current plans of the government are to equalize the way the two sectors are paid so that the proprietary homes can receive individually calculated per diems keyed to their costs and patient mix, and the nonprofit homes can begin to assume some of the financial risks associated with inefficiency. The operating deficits of the nonprofit facilities will no longer be met by the LTC Program. The new reimbursement system is being phased in during 1984 along with studies to examine its effects.

Cost-control mechanisms for homemaker agencies must deal with the number of hours authorized as well as the charges. Many LTC Programs have been successful in getting agencies to temper four-hour minimum rules. Beyond that, the actual hours of service ordered by the case managers are the paramount factor in cost. In FY 1982, the provincial LTC Programs allocated a specific number of hours to each of the twenty-two regional programs. The majority of the districts (80 percent) were able to function within the allocation, and the rest were required to justify the need for more hours. Provincial officials were able to shave $8 million off the estimated program costs for that year had the rate of increase followed previous patterns.

The method of reducing services varied among the health units. Current analyses of homemaker utilization provincially show considerable variation in the age-specific utilization rates among the units in terms of numbers of clients served. This finding is consistent with a budgeting process based on hours, not clients.

Homemaker costs are also sensitive to the frequency and care of the case manager's reassessments. In 1980, the LTC Program commissioned a study of homemaker agencies in the province; one of the major recommendations received was to stop the practice of allowing provider agencies to reassess the client's need (Western Health Care Associates, 1981). Even if LTC Programs were not formally delegating the reassessments to the providers (who have the most to gain by increasing the levels of care and the least to gain by closing cases), this was happening *de facto* when caseloads became so large that routine reassessments were delayed and most reassessments were made at providers' requests.

Quality Assurance

In Facilities. Quality assurance responsibilities for facility care rest largely with the Community Care licensing officials within the Health Departments, but the LTC Programs and case managers play an intimate role in the process. The Adult Care Licensing Bureau in Victoria designates local units to do inspections or provides its own inspection team. In Vancouver, for example, the Community Facility Licensing Group is housed in the Health Department. The inspection teams include nurses, social workers, and public health inspectors. A complaint ombudsman also functions as part of the team, and the Assistant Director of the Vancouver LTC Program, who has responsibility for coordinating the institutional side of the LTC Program, works closely with the facility licensing group.

The licensure group operates with a minimum of regulation. The legislation enabling the inspections is brief and simply worded in contrast to the voluminous regulations spawned in the United States. The members of the Vancouver team expressed confidence, however, that the legislative mandate provided sufficient authority for full inspections related to the construction of a facility, licensure, and the quality of ongoing care. (Fire safety, plumbing, and electrical standards are the responsibility of the City of Vancouver.) Annual inspections are required, but the team visit a facility much more frequently if they have questions about the quality of care.

Enforcement by education is the preferred way of handling problems. Other options are to recommend that the licensing board in Victoria suspend or revoke the license or to go to court. Another possibility is to request that the LTC Program refrain from making placements in a particular facility until care improves. In seven years of licensing inspections, the head of the Vancouver unit estimated that four facilities had actually been closed.

The inspectors consciously emphasize quality-of-life issues. They try to eliminate terms like "Director of Nursing" in favor of "Director of Residential Care." They insist that sicker residents not be moved closer to nursing stations for the caregiver's convenience, but rather that patients retain their original rooms and have care brought to them. Rules for facility construction in effect since 1977 have required that new facilities be built primarily with single rooms!

Drug use, which accounts for so many quality-of-care problems in United States facilities, is monitored separately and vigorously through the Pharmacare program. Each pharmacist who successfully competes for a contract with a nursing home is expected to exercise a quality control function on drug use and that pharmacist, in turn, is monitored.

The ombudsman's function is to investigate complaints that involve infringements of the arrangements between clients and the LTC system. In Vancouver, where in 1982 there were about 6,000 LTC clients in facilities, the ombudsman works on four to six complaints at any given time and resolves most of them in a matter of days. About half the complaints are due to poor communication and misunderstandings, many involving the mechanisms for administering the resident's own comfort fund.

According to quality assurance personnel, the biggest lingering problems stem from poor selection of staff and administrators. Recently, the Vancouver LTC program established a rule requiring that newly hired administrators be approved by a committee from the program after review of credentials and an interview. (See table 5.9 for a list of the criteria used.) The community viewed this effort to ensure the quality of facility administrators through standardized procedures as controversial.

The licensing group and the LTC coordinators cooperate closely, at least in the Vancouver area. This works two ways: the case managers can call in the inspectors to investigate problems, and the

Table 5.9

**Criteria for Long-Term Care Facility Administrators
Established by Vancouver Health Department**

Academic	Experimental	Personal Suitability
(Incidence to be verified)	(Review and verify references)	(Consensus judgment of interview panel)
Recognized certificate or diploma in Administration or Personnel Management relevant to the health care field	Demonstrated ability and competence in administration and personnel management	Good physical and mental health
		Effective communication
Preferably a recognized degree or certification in a health related or social service profession	Demonstrated interest in knowledge and understanding of the frail, the handicapped, and the elderly	Response to supervision
		Ability to respect confidentiality
		Integrity, loyalty
	Demonstrated ability in establishing and maintaining effective communication and interpersonal relationships and working effectively with an inter-disciplinary team	Honesty
Eligible for registration in a recognized Canadian professional body or association		Initiative
Minimum of grade 12 or equivalent		Personal appearance (grooming, etc.)
		Outside interests
	Demonstrated ability to work effectively with community groups and agencies	
	Demonstrated leadership skills	

inspectors can ask the case managers to monitor the care of their clientele particularly carefully when the facility has seemed to be deficient in quality. Case managers who are liaisons to facilities are in those facilities often and have good capacity to observe. In Vancouver, the policy has been to switch the facility liaison every few years to avoid complacency and to provide a fresh look.

In Homemaking Agencies. The LTC Programs have approached quality of care in homemaking agencies by reviewing the care plans of homemaker agencies and requiring that the agencies present an accounting of actual services delivered. The accountability system is also geared to ensuring that the homemaking agency confines its activities to those authorized and approved by the program. For example, table 5.10 shows the rules established by the Vancouver LTC program for homemaker and handyman service.

In 1983, the Vancouver LTC Program instituted a competitive bidding process to award contracts with homemaker agencies for the following year. This procedure was designed to allow the LTC Program to introduce some quality standards as well as to encourage cost-effectiveness through competition. The Request for Proposals (RFP) required each competing agency to designate on a city map the geographic areas it was willing to serve and to indicate the maximum number of hours that the agency could supply. The scoring criteria for proposals awarded 25 percent for organizational capability and management expertise, 35 percent for technical aspects of staffing and service delivery, and 40 percent for cost considerations.

In advance, the LTC Program announced its intentions to award about ten contracts, evenly divided between proprietary and nonprofit concerns, and to purchase no more than 25 percent of the service from any one agency. The expectation was that the contracts would fall into a range of 25,000 to a maximum of 350,000 hours. The RFP explicitly suggested that some agencies might find it "advantageous to amalgamate into one larger agency" and this was encouraged as long as the proposal reflected the planned reorganization. In fact, part of the strategy was to use the award process to eliminate agencies that were marginal in efficiency or quality.

The RFP is of particular interest because it explicitly required the competing agencies to attach copies of their policies and procedures on a range of issues—e.g., checking references on those hired, establishing that homemakers are healthy, ensuring that client information be confidential, providing supervision, ensuring that homemakers do not get tasks beyond their competence, ensuring that homemakers facilitate client independence, and a host of others. Applicants were required to complete a detailed questionnaire on these items as well as to enclose copies of related material. Attachments to the RFP listed the range of personal assistance and

Table 5.10

Vancouver Long-Term Care Program Guidelines for Homemaking and Handyman Services Provided to Long-Term Care Clients

Cleaning services will be provided through long-term care only after it is assured that family, friends, neighbors and/or other community volunteer services are unable to carry out or arrange for the required service and only where not carrying out this function will result in a potential health hazard and/or damage to the client's residence.

1. Vacuuming and floor washing should be done a maximum of once every two weeks.
2. Dusting is to be done only when it is impossible for the client or family to do it.
3. Cleaning silverware, pet care and similar activities is the client's responsibility. It is not necessary for maintaining a safe environment.
4. Interior window washing to be done a maximum of once every six months.
5. Cleaning and defrosting fridge—a maximum of once a month.
6. Laundry for a person living alone (with no incontinence or odor problem), a maximum of once every two weeks.
7. Floor waxing or rug cleaning—only to be done in exceptional circumstances with prior approval by long-term care assessor.
8. No homemaker is to be placed exclusively for baking of cookies, cakes, pastries, etc.
9. Ceilings and wall washing a maximum of once a year and with prior approval.
10. Shopping—a maximum of once a week—and only for a person living alone with no family, friends, volunteers, or delivery service available.
11. Laundry being done in a laundromat by a homemaker is only a last resort when there is no family and no other resource available.
12. Delivery of milk, juice, eggs, cheese by dairy to be explored.
13. Banking or paying bills by homemaker only when approved by long-term care coordinator.

Handyman services will be provided only after it is assured that family, friends, neighbors, or community volunteer services are unable to carry out or arrange for the required services and only where not carrying out the function will result in a potential health or safety hazard and/or damage to the client's residence.

1. Grass cutting—a maximum of once every two weeks—two hours maximum.
2. Outside windows once a year.
3. Gutter cleanout once a year.
4. Hedge-trimming, pruning, refuse, and undergrowth clearing (only when it may represent a health hazard), maximum of twice a year.
5. Clearing of snow and ice from walks and stairs only as necessary to guarantee a safe and clear exit.
6. Minor repairs only when it is necessary to maintain a safe and healthful environment.
7. No fence work, garden digging, planting flower beds, major painting jobs, moving of client's belongings, major repair adaptations to a dwelling.

other purchased services included within the LTC Program (requiring that each agency clearly designate those services it chose *not* to provide); and a list of requirements of homemaker agencies regarding matters such as personnel practices, supervision, orientation, and so on. Because competing agencies needed to describe policy on matters of quality (e.g., policy to ensure that homemakers do not smoke on the job) and to describe their own agency on certain parameters (e.g., number of homemakers able to speak foreign languages), the agencies were forced to develop such policies and to consider their capabilities from the perspective of the LTC Program's external criteria. The hope was that successive years of competitive bidding would drive the quality of homemaking care upward.

In conjunction with its bidding process for homemaker contracts, the Vancouver LTC program instituted a formal quality assurance program for homemaking agencies. A community health nurse has come on staff to monitor the agencies for their adherence to the contracts and their quality of care. This official visits each agency and reviews its procedures; she also makes random visits to clients both to observe homemakers in action and to discuss satisfaction with the client. The type of sanctions to be imposed for quality breaches are not yet fully designed; however, the knowledge that the contract for the following year could be jeopardized is a strong inducement to cooperate.

Ensuring quality of homemaker care is a new area in the United States and one that is taking on increasing importance as state and local officials consider how to use the purchasing dollar wisely and guarantee quality despite multiple providers delivering care in the privacy of the client's own home. Because we consider the formulations embodied in the Vancouver RFP particularly useful, Appendix B reproduces the entire questionnaire for proposal submission and the attachments delineating standards.

Concluding Comment

British Columbia's program being a recently developed long-term care program, the province had the opportunity to build on the experience of others. Of the three provinces studied, it represents the highest level of coordination and formalization. We have therefore given more attention to some of its details. The LTC Program is housed in the the same ministerial unit with the hospital program. Within the LTC Home Care Program, virtually all aspects have been brought together. The same assessors determine client need and control facility placement and reassessment. The assessment process is relatively structured. An information system has been developed within the program, although it is not yet linked to acute care.

The consolidation of long-term care and home care at the local level promises to further rationalize the program. As of July 1984, only five units (three urban health departments and two provincial ones) have taken the step, and the changes are too recent to allow us to describe details. Under a unified Continuing Care program, however, there is the potential for a case manager to assess the need for *both* homemaking and home nursing. Unified record systems are feasible, and it may also be possible for regional Continuing Care Administrators to develop efficiencies and trade-offs in personnel between the two programs. Merging the LTC program, which relies on purchased service, and the Home Nursing Program, which is a direct service, calls for joining entities with different operational philosophies. The change should improve the information base and enhance overall monitoring of community services to the frail elderly.

The British Columbia program has used its control of the long-term care system to make changes. This philosophy can be seen in the recent changes in the reimbursement system for facilities and in the competitive bidding process implemented by the Vancouver region to secure homemaking contracts.

The program has not yet solved all its problems, however. The extended care units of hospitals are still administered separately, although there is a potential for coordination at the ministerial level. As with other case management programs that vest authority in the hands of assessors, the medical community may feel alienated. No system like the paneling approach of Manitoba has yet been proposed for the province but, at this writing, the Vancouver Health Department is considering a paneling system to screen facility admission requests.

APPENDIX

<table>
<tr><td colspan="2">Province of British Columbia
Ministry of Health
LONG TERM CARE PROGRAM</td><td>APPLICATION AND ASSESSMENT FORM
SECTION I
ADMINISTRATIVE AND SUMMARY</td><td>1 ☐ NEW ASSESSMENT
2 ☐ REVIEW
3 ☐ RE-ASSESSMENT
4 ☐ APPEAL
5 ☐ CORRECTION</td><td>HEALTH DIST.   ASSESSOR
CLIENT NUMBER</td><td>1</td></tr>
</table>

A   CLIENT'S PERSONAL DATA

1 CLIENT'S FAMILY NAME   FIRST NAME   INIT'S   PHONE (CURRENT)

2 LIST CLIENT'S ADDRESS FOR LAST 12 MONTHS. IF MORE THAN ONE, LIST ADDITIONAL ADDRESSES AND DATES IN PARA. F. SUMMARY. ENSURE PRESENT LOCATION OF CLIENT IS REPORTED IN SPACE PROVIDED.

CURRENT ADDRESS   FROM (DATE)

CITY   POSTAL CODE

CURRENT LOCATION OF CLIENT
☐ AS ABOVE
☐ OTHER

3   MARITAL STATUS
1 ☐ SINGLE
2 ☐ MARRIED
3 ☐ WIDOWED
4 ☐ DIVORCED
5 ☐ SEPARATED
6 ☐ OTHER

SEX ☐ M ☐ F   BIRTHDATE Y Y M M D D   MEDICAL PLAN NUMBER   DEP.   W/R   VETERAN ☐ YES ☐ NO   IF YES   SERVICE NUMBER

B A 'CONTACT PERSON' IS ONE WHO ASSISTS THE CLIENT WITH AN APPLICATION AND/OR A PERSON WHO IS WILLING TO MAINTAIN A CONTINUING INTEREST IN THE CLIENT'S WELFARE WITHOUT IMPLYING RESPONSIBILITY.

CONTACT PERSON'S FAMILY NAME   INIT'S   RELATIONSHIP

STREET ADDRESS

CITY   POSTAL CODE   HOME PHONE   BUSINESS PHONE

C GIVE DETAILS OF PERSON OR NEXT-OF-KIN WHO SHOULD BE CONTACTED IN AN EMERGENCY. ENTER 'CONTACT' IF PERSON IS NAMED IN PARA. B.

NAME   NEXT-OF-KIN: ☐ YES ☐ NO   RELATIONSHIP

ADDRESS   POSTAL CODE

D GIVE DETAILS OF PHYSICIAN RESPONSIBLE FOR CARE OF CLIENT. IF THERE IS SPECIALIST OR OTHER PHYSICIAN, ENTER IN PARA. F. SUMMARY.

PHYSICIAN'S NAME   OFFICE PHONE

OFFICE ADDRESS   POSTAL CODE

E   **APPLICATION**
I HEREBY APPLY FOR BENEFITS FOR WHICH I/CLIENT MAY BE ELIGIBLE UNDER THE LONG TERM CARE PROGRAM AND CERTIFY THAT THE INFORMATION THAT I HAVE PROVIDED IS CORRECT TO THE BEST OF MY KNOWLEDGE.

_____
CLIENT OR AUTHORIZED SIGNATURE

CLIENT'S PREFERENCE (SEE REVERSE)   PREFERRED FACILITIES
1 ☐ CARE AT HOME
2 ☐ FACILITY CARE   1 _____

21 ☐ STANDARD
22 ☐ SEMI-PRIVATE
23 ☐ PRIVATE   2 _____

F   **ASSESSMENT SUMMARY**   (TEAM REVIEW IF CARRIED OUT)

ASSESSMENT DATE   Y Y M M D D
REVIEW DATE
REASSESSMENT DATE

ASSESSMENT DONE:
1 ☐ CLIENT'S HOME
2 ☐ FACILITY
3 ☐ ACUTE HOSPITAL
4 ☐ OTHER

1 ☐ TEAM REVIEW
2 ☐ FOLLOW-UP

_____
ASSESSOR'S SIGNATURE

G   **APPROVAL OF CARE LEVEL AND SERVICES** (FOR ADMINISTRATOR'S USE ONLY) THE FOLLOWING SERVICES ARE APPROVED:

1 ☐ NOT ELIGIBLE
2 ☐ CARE DECLINED BY CLIENT
3 ☐ CARE AT HOME
4 ☐ CARE AT HOME;MENTAL HEALTH SUPPORT
5 ☐ FACILITY CARE
6 ☐ DAY CARE

1 ☐ PERSONAL CARE
2 ☐ INTERMEDIATE CARE 1
3 ☐ INTERMEDIATE CARE 2
4 ☐ INTERMEDIATE CARE 3
5 ☐ EXTENDED CARE

PREFERRED FACILITY   ALTERNATE FACILITY
FACILITY CODE   DATE ON LIST   Y Y M M D D   FACILITY CODE   DATE ON LIST   Y Y M M D D

LTC ADMINISTRATOR'S SIGNATURE   DATE SIGNED

LONG TERM CARE   SECTION II   HEALTH
ASSESSMENT   PROFILE

| CLIENT FAMILY NAME | CLIENT NUMBER |

A HOW LONG HAS CLIENT BEEN UNDER CARE IN A FACILITY? | HOW LONG HAS CLIENT RECEIVED HOME SUPPORT SERVICES? | IF NOT NEW CLIENT HOW LONG HAS CLIENT BEEN UNDER L.T.C. PROGRAM?

B   MEDICAL BACKGROUND   **1** MAJOR MEDICAL PROBLEMS   INFORMATION PROVIDED OR VERIFIED BY PHYSICIAN   1 ☐ YES   2 ☐ NO

2 MEDICATIONS	DOSAGE	FREQUENCY	ROUTE	PRESCRIBED BY

3 TREATMENTS	FREQUENCY	PRESCRIBED BY

4 SPECIAL PROCEDURES   2 ☐ BLADDER IRRIGATION   4 ☐ TRACHEOSTOMY   6 ☐ RENAL-DIALYSIS   7 ☐ OTHER; STATE:
1 ☐ CATHETER CARE   3 ☐ TUBE FEEDING   5 ☐ OXYGEN THERAPY

5 ALLERGIES

6 CURRENT DIET
1 ☐ REGULAR   3 ☐ CULTURAL   5 ☐ THERAPEUTIC BY PHYSICIAN
2 ☐ INSTITUTIONAL   4 ☐ SELF-DETERMINED
IS CURRENT DIET APPROPRIATE?   ☐ YES   ☐ NO   COMMENTS:

7 ADDITIONAL COMMENTS. IF CLIENT WILL BE ADMITTED TO PUBLIC EXTENDED CARE, IDENTIFY ADMITTING PHYSICIAN

C   MENTAL HEALTH   INDICATE THE APPLICABLE STATE, FROM INSTRUCTION PAGE, WHICH CORRESPONDS BEST WITH CLIENT'S BEHAVIOUR ON MOST DAYS, AND COMMENT BRIEFLY. | STATE

1 COMPREHENSION

2 MEMORY

3 SELF-DIRECTION

4 REALITY ORIENTATION

5 EMOTIONAL STABILITY

6 ADDITIONAL COMMENTS: DESCRIBE ANY BEHAVIOUR SIGNIFICANT TO CARE IN A FACILITY OR AT HOME; NOTE FREQUENCY AND DURATION OF EPISODES.

7 CLIENT SMOKES ☐ Y   ☐ N
DEGREE OF PROBLEM
☐ NONE   ☐ MODERATE   ☐ MAJOR

8 CLIENT DRINKS ☐ Y   ☐ N
DEGREE OF PROBLEM
☐ NONE   ☐ MODERATE   ☐ MAJOR

9 PSYCHIATRIC DIAGNOSIS (IF ANY)

LONG TERM CARE SECTION II	HEALTH PROFILE		CLIENT FAMILY NAME	CLIENT NUMBER	3
ASSESSMENT CONTINUED					

D DENTAL CARE

1 DOES CLIENT CURRENTLY HAVE DENTAL PROBLEMS?	☐ YES ☐ NO	3 DENTAL STATE	4 ☐ PARTIAL DENTURE	4 IS CLIENT ABLE TO CHEW FOOD EFFICIENTLY?	☐ YES ☐ NO
		1 ☐ NO DENTURES	5 ☐ DAMAGED DENTURE		
2 IS CLIENT UNDER CARE OF DENTIST?	☐ YES ☐ NO	2 ☐ FULL UPPER	6 ☐ NO DENTURES, NO TEETH	5 DENTIST'S NAME	
		3 ☐ FULL LOWER	7 ☐ DENTURES NOT WORN		

E COMMUNICATION

E COMMUNICATION	1 ☐ WEARS GLASSES	2 ☐ USES HEARING AID	LANGUAGES USED	1 ☐ ENGLISH 2 ☐ FRENCH	3 ☐ CHINESE 4 ☐ ITALIAN	5 ☐ RUSSIAN 6 ☐
1 VISION	2 ☐ ADEQUATE FOR PERSONAL SAFETY	3 ☐ DISTINGUISHES ONLY LIGHT OR DARK	4 ☐ BLIND-SAFE IN FAMILIAR LOCALE	5 ☐ BLIND REQUIRES ASSISTANCE		
1 ☐ UNIMPAIRED						
2 HEARING	2 ☐ MILD IMPAIRMENT	3 ☐ MODERATE IMPAIRMENT BUT ADEQUATE FOR SAFETY	4 ☐ IMPAIRED — INADEQUATE FOR SAFETY	5 ☐ TOTALLY DEAF		
1 ☐ UNIMPAIRED						
3 SPEECH	2 ☐ SIMPLE PHRASES INTELLIGIBLE ONLY	3 ☐ SIMPLE PHRASES PARTIALLY INTELLIGIBLE ONLY	4 ☐ ISOLATED WORDS INTELLIGIBLE ONLY	5 ☐ NO SPEECH OR SPEECH NOT UNDERSTANDABLE OR NO SENSE MADE		
1 ☐ UNIMPAIRED						
4 UNDERSTANDING	2 ☐ UNDERSTANDS SIMPLE PHRASES ONLY	3 ☐ UNDERSTANDS KEY WORDS ONLY	4 ☐ UNDERSTANDING UNKNOWN	5 ☐ NOT RESPONSIVE		
1 ☐ UNIMPAIRED						
5 IF CLIENT CANNOT SPEAK INDICATE MEANS AND DEGREE OR EFFECTIVENESS OF METHOD	1 ☐ EFFECTIVE	2 ☐ MODERATELY EFFECTIVE	3 ☐ PARTIALLY EFFECTIVE	4 ☐ NOT EFFECTIVE		
6 ADDITIONAL COMMENTS ON COMMUNICATION						

F ACTIVITIES OF DAILY LIVING

F ACTIVITIES OF DAILY LIVING	1 ☐ USES CANE	2 ☐ USES WALKER	3 ☐ USES CRUTCHES	4 ☐ USES WHEELCHAIR	5 ☐ OTHER PROSTHESIS OR AID
1 AMBULATION	2 ☐ INDEPENDENT ONLY IN ENVIRONMENT SPECIFIED BELOW	3 ☐ REQUIRES SUPERVISION	4 ☐ REQUIRES OCCASIONAL OR MINOR ASSISTANCE	5 ☐ REQUIRES SIGNIFICANT OR CONTINUED ASSISTANCE	
1 ☐ INDEPENDENT IN NORMAL ENVIRONMENTS LIMITATIONS:					
2 TRANSFER	2 ☐ SUPERVISION FOR: ☐ BED ☐ CHAIR ☐ TOILET	3 ☐ INTERMITTENT ASSIST. ☐ BED ☐ CHAIR ☐ TOILET	4 ☐ CONTINUED ASSIST. ☐ BED ☐ CHAIR ☐ TOILET	5 ☐ COMPLETELY DEPENDENT FOR ALL MOVEMENT	
1 ☐ INDEPENDENT					
3 BATHING	2 ☐ INDEPENDENT WITH MECHANICAL AIDS	3 ☐ REQUIRES MINOR ASSISTANCE OR SUPERVISION	4 ☐ REQUIRES CONTINUED ASSISTANCE	5 ☐ RESISTS	
1 ☐ INDEPENDENT IN BATH OR SHOWER					
4 DRESSING	2 ☐ SUPERVISION AND/OR CHOOSING OF CLOTHING	3 ☐ PERIODIC OR DAILY PARTIAL HELP	4 ☐ MUST BE DRESSED	5 ☐ RESISTS	
1 ☐ INDEPENDENT					
5 GROOMING/HYGIENE	2 ☐ REQUIRES REMINDER MOTIVATION AND/OR DIRECTION	3 ☐ REQUIRES ASSIST. WITH SOME ITEMS	4 ☐ REQUIRES TOTAL ASSISTANCE	5 ☐ RESISTS	
1 ☐ INDEPENDENT					
6 EATING	2 ☒ INDEPENDENT WITH SPECIAL PROVISION FOR DISABILITY	3 ☐ REQUIRES INTERMITTENT HELP	4 ☐ MUST BE FED	5 ☐ RESISTS	
1 ☐ INDEPENDENT					
7 BLADDER CONTROL	2 ☐ ROUTINE TOILETING OR REMINDER	3 ☐ INCONTINENCE DUE TO IDENTIFIABLE FACTORS	4 ☐ INCONTINENT— LESS THAN ONCE PER DAY	5 ☐ INCONTINENT— MORE THAN ONCE PER DAY	
1 ☐ TOTALLY CONTINENT					
8 BOWEL CONTROL	2 ☐ ROUTINE TOILETTING OR REMINDER	3 ☐ INCONTINENCE DUE TO IDENTIFIABLE FACTORS	4 ☐ INCONTINENT— LESS THAN ONCE PER DAY	5 ☐ INCONTINENT— MORE THAN ONCE PER DAY	
1 ☐ TOTALLY CONTINENT					

9 ADDITIONAL REMARKS ON A.D.L. NOTE FREQUENCY OF GROSS PROBLEMS. COMMENT ON SIGNIFICANT SLEEP PATTERNS.

LONG TERM CARE SECTION III SOCIAL ASSESSMENT　　　　　　　　PROFILE	CLIENT FAMILY NAME	CLIENT NUMBER	4

A　HOUSING AND SOCIAL CONTEXT

1　HOUSING

MODE　　　　　　　　　　　　**APPROPRIATENESS**

1 ☐ HOUSE
2 ☐ APARTMENT
3 ☐ ROOM
4 ☐ FACILITY
5 ☐ OTHER

1 ☐ RENTAL　2 ☐ SELF-OWNED　1 ☐ CURRENT　2 ☐ PROPOSED

2　HOUSEHOLD COMPOSITION

COMPANIONS　　　　　　　　**DESCRIBE RELATIONSHIPS**

1 ☐ LIVES ALONE
2 ☐ SPOUSE
3 ☐ OTHER ADULT MALE(S)
4 ☐ OTHER ADULT FEMALE(S)
5 ☐ CHILDREN
　　　GIVE AGES

PRINCIPAL HELPER:

3　SUPPORTIVE RELATIONSHIPS (SEE GUIDE ON REVERSE OF THIS PAGE)

4　RELEVANT CULTURAL AND RELIGIOUS FACTORS

B　SELF CARE INDICATE CLIENT'S CAPABILITY ON MOST DAYS

1　FOOD PREPARATION
1 ☐ INDEPENDENT
2 ☐ ADEQUATE IF INGREDIENTS SUPPLIED
3 ☐ CAN MAKE OR BUY MEALS BUT DIET INADEQUATE
4 ☐ PHYSICALLY OR MENTALLY UNABLE
5 ☐ NO OPPORTUNITY OR DOES NOT PARTICIPATE BY CHOICE

2　HOUSEKEEPING
1 ☐ INDEPENDENT WITH HELP FOR HEAVY TASKS
2 ☐ CAN PERFORM ONLY LIGHT TASKS ADEQUATELY
3 ☐ PERFORMS LIGHT TASKS BUT NOT ADEQUATELY
4 ☐ NEEDS REGULAR HELP AND SUPERVISION
5 ☐ NO OPPORTUNITY OR DOES NOT PARTICIPATE BY CHOICE

3　SHOPPING
1 ☐ INDEPENDENT
2 ☐ INDEPENDENT ONLY FOR SMALL ITEMS
3 ☐ MUST BE ACCOMPANIED
4 ☐ PHYSICALLY OR MENTALLY UNABLE
5 ☐ NO OPPORTUNITY OR DOES NOT PARTICIPATE BY CHOICE

4　TRAVELLING
1 ☐ INDEPENDENT
2 ☐ NO PUBLIC TRANSPORT USES PRIVATE VEHICLE OR TAXI
3 ☐ CAN TRAVEL ONLY IF ACCOMPANIED
4 ☐ PHYSICALLY OR MENTALLY UNABLE
5 ☐ REQUIRES AMBULANCE FACILITIES

5　TELEPHONE
1 ☐ INDEPENDENT
2 ☐ DIALS WELL KNOWN NUMBERS
3 ☐ ANSWERS TELEPHONE ONLY
4 ☐ PHYSICALLY OR MENTALLY UNABLE
5 ☐ NO OPPORTUNITY OR DOES NOT USE PHONE

6　MEDICATIONS AND TREATMENTS
1 ☐ COMPLETELY RESPONSIBLE FOR SELF
2 ☐ REQUIRES REMINDER OR ASSISTANCE
3 ☐ RESPONSIBLE IF MEDICATIONS PRE— PARED IN ADVANCE
4 ☐ PHYSICALLY OR MENTALLY UNABLE
5 ☐ RESISTS

7　COMMENTS ON SELF CARE

C　SERVICE INVENTORY · SEE GUIDE ON INSTRUCTION PAGE

CODE	HEALTH SERVICES	Y/N	CODE	HOME SUPPORT SERVICES	N/Y	CODE	COMMUNITY SERVICES	N/Y
☐			☐			☐		
☐			☐			☐		
☐			☐			☐		
☐			☐			☐		
☐			☐			☐		
☐			☐			☐		

LONG TERM CARE SECTION IV ASSESSMENT 5 ☐ CORRECTION	CONFIDENTIAL INFORMATION	CLIENT'S FAMILY NAME	CLIENT NUMBER	5

A FINANCIAL AFFAIRS

1 DOES CLIENT RECEIVE "GAIN FOR SENIORS" OR "GAIN FOR HANDI-CAPPED"? 1 ■ YES IF YES ▶ 2 ■ NO	IF CLIENT IS 65 YEARS OF AGE OR OLDER, RECORD THE 9 DIGIT NUMBER WHICH APPEARS TO THE RIGHT OF THE PAYEE'S NAME ON THE 'GAIN' CHEQUE.	IF THE CLIENT IS UNDER 65 YEARS OF AGE, RECORD ALSO ANY ALPHA-BETIC SUFFIX AFTER THE 9 DIGIT NUMBER.	◢ START 9 DIGIT NO. HERE PLACE ANY ALPHABETIC SUFFIX HERE

2 IS THE CLIENT IN RECEIPT OF THE GUARANTEED INCOME SUPPLEMENT? 1 ■ YES 2 ■ NO	3 IS THE CLIENT IN RECEIPT OF WAR VETERANS ALLOWANCE? 1 ■ YES 2 ■ NO	4 IF ANSWER TO 1, 2, 3 IS "NO", IS THERE AN INDICATION OF FINANCIAL NEED FOR FACILITY PER DIEM AND COMFORTS? 1 ■ YES 2 ■ NO

5 MANAGEMENT 1 ☐ INDEPENDENT IN ALL AFFAIRS	2 ☐ INDEPENDENT IF TRANSPORTED	3 ☐ NEEDS ADVICE WITH BANKING OR MAJOR PURCHASES	4 ☐ CAPABILITY OF COMPREHENSION DOUBTFUL	5 ☐ AFFAIRS MANAGED BY PUBLIC TRUSTEE, COMMITEE OR POWER OF ATTORNEY

6 WHO MANAGES AFFAIRS? 1 ☐ SELF 2 ☐ CONTACT 3 ☐ OTHER: (STATE)	7 IS ARRANGEMENT IN PARA. 6 APPROPRIATE? 1 ☐ YES 2 ☐ NO	8 RESPONSIBILITY FOR COMFORTS 1 ☐ SELF 2 ☐ CONTACT PERSON 3 ☐ OTHER: GIVE DETAILS BELOW

9 ADDITIONAL INFORMATION

B ASSESSOR'S COMMENTS AND RECOMMENDATIONS

1 ASSESSOR'S COMMENTS ON CLIENT'S CURRENT SITUATION.

2 ASSESSOR'S RECOMMENDATIONS FOR CARE OF CLIENT

IF THE RESPONSE IN PARA. 3 BELOW IS CODE 5, MENTAL HEALTH ORIENTATION OF PROVIDER, DESCRIBE NATURE OF SPECIFIC PROBLEM.

3 RECOMMENDED OUTCOME 1 ☐ NOT ELIGIBLE 2 ☐ HOME MAKER 3 ☐ CARE IN FACILITY 4 ☐ HOME CARE PROGRAM 5 ☐ MENTAL HEALTH ORIENTATION OF PROVIDER 6 ☐ DAY CARE	1 ☐ PERSONAL CARE 2 ☐ INTERMEDIATE CARE 1 3 ☐ INTERMEDIATE CARE 2 4 ☐ INTERMEDIATE CARE 3 5 ☐ EXTENDED CARE	RECOMMENDED PROVIDER RECOMMENDED HOURS OR SERVICES

REFERENCES

Fact Book on Aging in Canada, 1983. Prepared for the Second Canadian Conference on Aging, October 24–27, 1983. Ottawa: Minister of Supply and Services.

Penner, R. 1981. "Utilization of Long-Term-Care Services," July 14, 1981 (mimeo).

Tidball, P. 1982. "Capitation Payment for Pharmacy: A Head Start on Fair Return?" *Canadian Journal of Pharmacy,* July 1982, pp. 271–273.

WHCA (Western Health Care Associates Limited). 1981. *A Review of Homemaker Services in British Columbia.* Victoria.

CHAPTER 6
Patterns of Care Across the Provinces

ADVOCATES frequently suggest that developing community long-term care programs will yield dividends by stemming the demand for institutional care. Early data from demonstration projects in the United States fail to support these contentions (Greenberg, Doth, and Austin 1981). Findings from the current channeling demonstration, when available, will further elucidate the issue (Baxter et al. 1983). A recent review of the situation by the Government Accounting Office (U.S. GAO 1982) concludes that increased home care services would benefit the elderly but would *not* control costs for nursing home care. Community long-term care also has the potential to contain hospital costs, although the fragmentation between Medicare and Medicaid has kept American policymakers from focusing on the trade-off between publicly funded acute hospital costs and long-term care costs.

The Canadian operations provide an extended time frame of wide-scale experience. Because the community programs in each province were introduced in different years, we have "before" and "after" data with different time lines. This minimizes the effect of historical change and allows us to look for at least presumptive evidence of cause and effect. This chapter examines the trends in utilization and resource supply to look for general trends and to try to shed some light on the substitution issue.

Each of the three provinces we examined experienced substantial growth in the elderly portion of its population (aged 65 and over) during the 1970s. The growth figures were 35 percent for Ontario, 27 percent for Manitoba, and 45 percent for British Columbia (see figures 6.1–6.3). However, this growth was not evenly distributed among persons over 65. The Ontario pattern resembled that of the United States, with the oldest segments of the population showing the greatest relative gains. The British Columbia pattern was almost the opposite, and Manitoba's was in between.

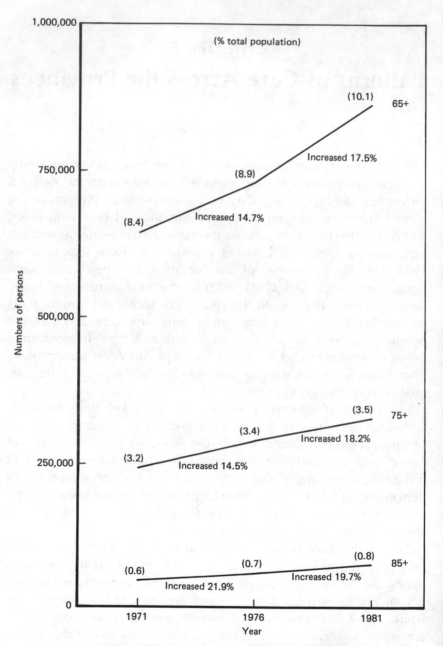

SOURCE: 1971 data from 1972 Census Catalog, Statistics Canada;
1976, 1981 data from 1981 Census Catalog, Statistics Canada.

Figure 6.1. Growth of elderly population in Ontario, 1971-1981.

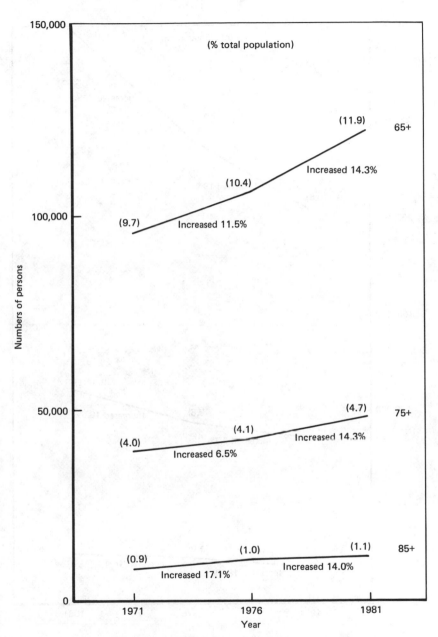

SOURCE: 1971 data from 1971 Census Catalog, Statistics Canada; 1976, 1981 data from 1981 Census Catalog, Statistics Canada.

Figure 6.2. Growth of elderly population in Manitoba, 1971-1981.

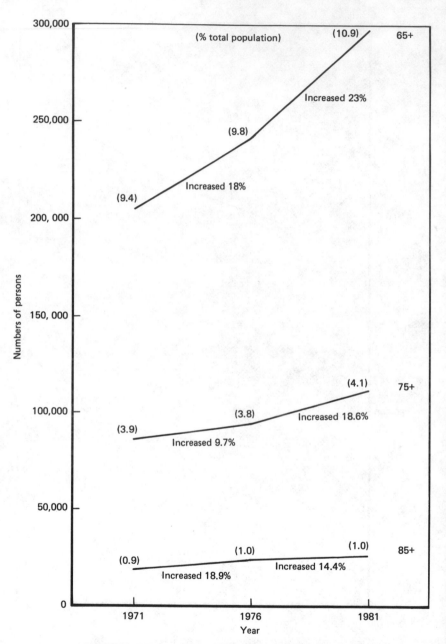

SOURCE: 1971 data from 1971 Census Catalog, Statistics Canada;
1976, 1981 data from 1981 Census Catalog, Statistics Canada.

Figure 6.3. Growth of elderly population in British Columbia, 1971-1981.

Because the older age groups use substantially more long-term care services, this uneven growth rate must be considered in interpreting the changes in patterns of long-term care use. To correct for the effects of population change, we developed an index of adjusted long-term care use based on age-specific 1978 rates of nursing home (including residential care) use in Canada (Wilkins and Adams 1983). National estimates from cross-sectional studies suggest that about 2.4 percent of those aged 65 to 74 are in residential facilities or nursing homes, compared with 10.6 percent of those aged 75 to 84 and 31 percent of those over age 85. (The corresponding United States rates were 1 percent, 7 percent, and 21 percent, respectively.)

The Canadian rates of nursing home use were applied to the populations in the three provinces to identify expected nursing home utilization rates, shown in table 6.1. The results from this approach closely approximate the simple growth of the elderly. The expected increase over the ten-year period, as a result of differential population changes alone, was 38 percent in Ontario, 26 percent in Manitoba, and 35 percent in British Columbia. Actual changes in utilization and supply of services should be viewed with these numbers in mind. An ability to hold utilization constant over the decade represents an impressive achievement in the face of increased demand.

Supply of Services

Utilization of services is directly related to their availability. We begin therefore by looking at the changes in supply. The numbers of places available is the result of policy decisions taken in light of expected demand. The relative index of expected long-term care use suggests substantial growth in demand for services. The changes in supply thus imply deliberate actions.

Table 6.2 summarizes information on bed supply in three types of hospital facilities, as reported to Statistics Canada. The changes over the decade from 1970 to 1980 are shown for three classes of beds: acute hospital beds, total long-term beds (rehabilitation, convalescent, and extended care), and extended care (or chronic hospital) beds. In some cases, these numbers disagree somewhat with other

Table 6.1

Expected Nursing Home Utilization Rates

Age	1971		1976		1981		Expected Increase in Utilization (%)	
	Pop.	No. in Nursing Homes	Pop.	No. in Nursing Homes	Pop.	No. in Nursing Homes	1971–76	1976–81
					Ontario			
65–74	399,235	6,388	458,200	7,331	536,485	8,584	16%	18%
75–84	195,335	20,705	219,970	23,317	258,995	27,453		
85+	49,845	15,452	60,745	18,831	72,710	22,540		
Total	644,415	42,545	738,915	49,479	868,190	58,577		
					Manitoba			
65–74	56,330	901	64,750	1,036	74,035	1,184	10%	14%
75–84	30,615	3,245	31,705	3,361	36,275	3,845		
85+	8,625	2,674	10,100	3,131	11,510	3,568		
Total	95,570	6,820	106,555	7,528	112,820	8,597		
					British Columbia			
65–74	119,160	1,906	147,880	2,366	186,500	2,984	14%	18%
75–84	65,955	6,991	70,505	7,473	84,600	8,968		
85+	19,895	6,167	23,665	7,336	27,075	8,393		
Total	205,010	15,064	223,355	17,175	298,175	20,345		

Table 6.2

Changes in Hospital Bed Supply for Acute and Chronic Care, 1970-1980

Year	Acute Hospital		Long-Term Care		Extended Care	
	Number of Beds	Percentage of 1970	Number of Beds	Percentage of 1970	Number of Beds	Percentage of 1970
	Ontario					
1970	39,040		10,302		8,708	
1980	34,395	88	12,441	121	10,182	117
	Manitoba					
1970	5,514		1,314		979	
1980	5,125	93	1,302	99	1,067	109
	British Columbia					
1970	11,098		2,605		1,982	
1980	10,983	99	6,491	249	5,358	270

SOURCE: Annual data from the Health Information Division; Department of National Health and Welfare.

data reported directly by the individual provinces, but they are adequate to illustrate a general point. In all three provinces, there was a decline in acute hospital bed supply and an increase in chronic hospital beds. Of the three provinces, Manitoba appears to have changed its supply the least overall. Ontario shows the greatest reduction in hospital beds, and British Columbia, a dramatic increase in overall long-term beds, especially Extended Care Unit (ECU) beds.

To estimate the extent to which these shifts may have resulted from differential population growth, we calculated a rate per 1000 persons aged 75 and over. This adjustment, shown in table 6.3, suggests reductions in the chronic bed supply in both Manitoba and Ontario, although the two provinces have pursued very different approaches to long-term care and began with different levels of beds per capita. British Columbia, which began with a bed/population ratio quite comparable to that of Manitoba, has moved in the opposite direction. It has virtually doubled its adjusted chronic bed complement over the same decade when the other provinces showed reductions. The pattern of this shift over

Table 6.3

**Changes in Supply of Long-Term and Extended Care Hospital Beds
per 1,000 Persons Aged 75 and Older**

	Long-Term Care		Extended Care Unit	
Year	Beds per 1,000 75+	Percentage of 1970	Beds per 1,000 75+	Percentage of 1970
		Ontario		
1970	42		35	
1980	37	88	31	88
		Manitoba		
1970	33		25	
1980	27	82	22	88
		British Columbia		
1970	30		23	
1980	58	193	48	209

time is portrayed in figure 6.4. It is noteworthy that the increase in British Columbia's ECU beds was accomplished by 1978, the year in which the community-based LTC began in that province. Thereafter, the supply of ECU beds in British Columbia remained relatively stable.

The long-term care data for Ontario show an interesting pattern. Although a major planning document suggests a more than sixfold increase in long-term care, institutional, constant-dollar expenditures between 1970 and 1980 (Ontario Secretariat for Social Development, 1981), the supply of beds did not change by anything approaching that amount. In 1970, about $70 million (in 1980 dollars) was spent on institutional long-term care. By 1980, that sum had increased to $455 million, of which $245 went to nursing homes, $185 to chronic hospital care, and $25 to residential care. The increase in health care expenditures on the elderly was almost as great: from $201 million in 1970 to $880 million in 1980, of which $650 million went to acute general hospitals and $230 million to physicians.

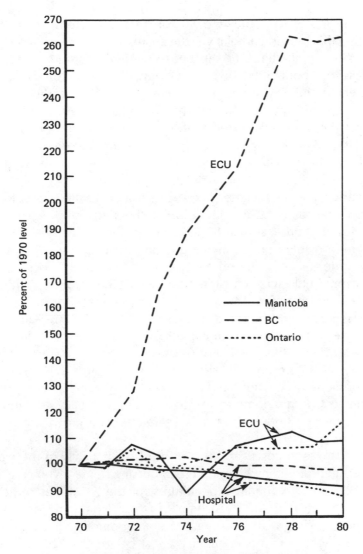

SOURCE: Data from various Statistics Canada reports, summarized by Health Information Division; Policy, Planning and Information Branch; Department of National Health and Welfare, August 1982.

Figure 6.4. Change in hospital bed supply in three provinces compared with 1970 level.

Figure 6.5 traces the growth of total long-term care beds. Because the plot is cumulative, the increase in nursing home beds gives the overall shape to the beds in Homes for the Aged. The increase of about 6000 beds, or about 27 percent of the original numbers of nursing home beds, occurred in the early and mid-1970s. Since 1977, the growth has essentially ceased. Moreover, most of the growth occurred in the nursing home (proprietary) sector, rather than in similar beds in Homes for the Aged, or in the residential beds in these latter nonprofit facilities. Beds in Homes for the Aged increased only 7 percent in this period.

Ontario's overall long-term care institutionalization rate for the elderly peaked in 1978 and declined thereafter as the supply of beds leveled off (see figure 6.6). Thus the growth in cost has resulted primarily from an increase in unit costs.

The other piece of the puzzle is shown in figure 6.7, which traces the hospital utilization rate for those aged 65 and over. While the general trend was for a continually decreasing rate for all ages, the rate for the elderly began to rise again after 1978, the same point when use of long-term institutional care declined. The coincidence suggests at least the possibility of offsetting effects. The pattern in Ontario is interesting because there was little corresponding development of community-based long-term care services during that time. Chronic home care programs did not really get launched in the province until at least five years after the growth in nursing home beds ceased.

The changes in costs can be seen most dramatically in the Homes for the Aged providing extended (i.e., nursing home level) care. Figure 6.8 traces the annual expenditures for the two types of homes, further subdivided by the types of care (i.e., residential vs. extended). The growth was greatest among municipally run homes, where provincial reimbursement is most generous. The difference in the rates of increase between extended care and residential care beds suggests the effects of unit-cost increases when no active price constraints are applied.

The Ontario experience is reinforced in Manitoba, the province with perhaps the earliest and best developed community care programs. Figure 6.9 charts the growth of Manitoba's personal care, or nursing home, beds from 1973 (the year prior to the community care program) to 1983. The number has increased steadily,

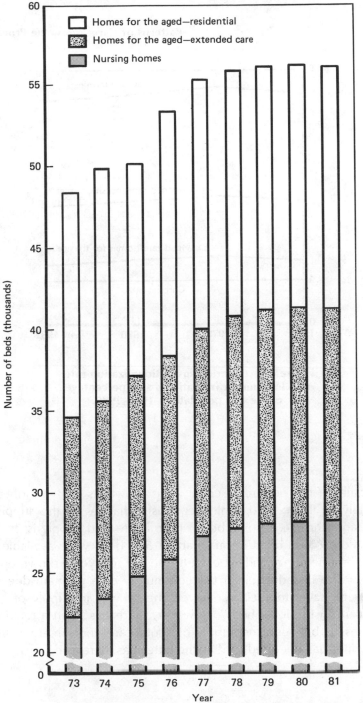

SOURCE: Data supplied by Policy and Program Development Division, Ministry of Community and Social Services, and by Ministry of Health.

Figure 6.5. Cumulative growth of long-term care beds in Ontario, 1973-1982.

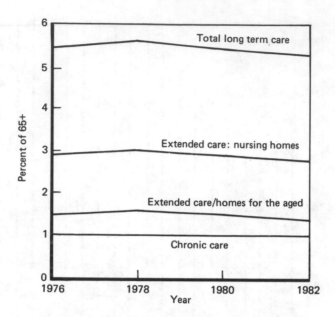

Figure 6.6. Ontario's institutionalization rate: 65+ long-term care patients as a percentage of the 65+ population, 1976-1980.

especially in the nonprofit sector. This growth is shown more dramatically in figure 6.10, which contrasts changes in the supply of acute and chronic hospital beds. (The acute bed supply is, in fact, even more constrained because about 500 beds were available but not given operating funds in each of the last five years shown on the graph.) The introduction of the community care program does not appear to have appreciably slowed the growth in supply of long-term care institutional beds. However, there has been a reciprocal relationship between the supply of acute care and long-term beds; the former has been reduced as the latter has increased.

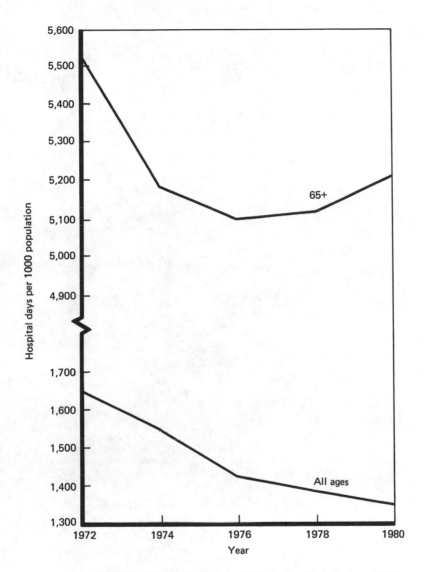

SOURCE: Data Development and Evaluation Branch, June 1982.
NOTE: Hospital service refers to combined acute and
rehabilitation hospital care.

Figure 6.7. Ontario hospital utilization rates for elderly and total
population, 1972-1980.

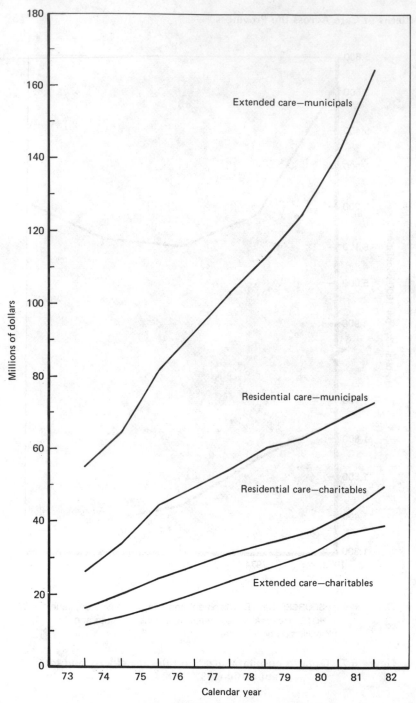

Figure 6.8. **Annual expenditures by Ontario Homes for the Aged, 1973-1983.**

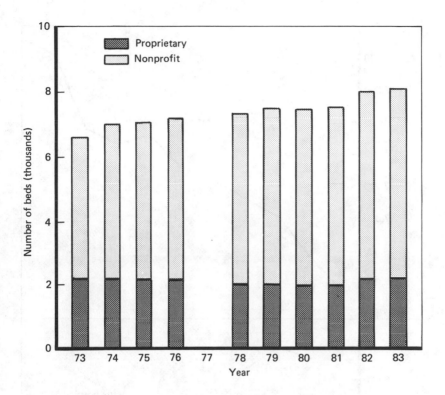

SOURCE: Management Information System of the Manitoba Health
Services Commission.

Figure 6.9. Growth in personal care home beds in Manitoba, 1973-1983.

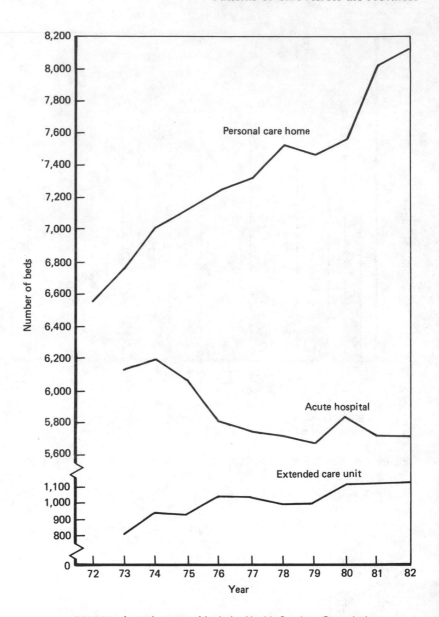

SOURCE: Annual reports, Manitoba Health Services Commission.

Figure 6.10. Changes in Manitoba's acute and long-term care bed supply, 1972-1982.

Potential Trade-Offs

The changes in numbers of beds reflects a shift from acute to long-term care in Manitoba. This pattern is also seen in the dollars spent. Because of the unit costs of hospital care, the hospital continues to receive the bulk of the health dollar, but its proportionate share has declined. From 1975 to 1982–83, hospital expenditures doubled, while personal care home expenditures quadrupled (see figure 6.11).

The lack of direct concordance between community-based long-term care services and institutional long-term care beds in Manitoba is further suggested by the data in figure 6.12. Here, data from Shapiro and Webster's analysis of the change in distribution of first admissions to Manitoba personal care homes are organized by level of care: the higher the level, the more nursing care required. Although it seems reasonable to assume that community care should achieve the greatest displacement of the lowest level of care (level 1), the pattern traced in figure 6.12 does not support this expectation. From 1974 to 1980, there is no clear change in the proportion of level 1 admissions. Rather, there is a shift from level 2 to levels 3 and 4. Part of this failure to observe a greater reduction in level 1 is attributable to the distribution of institutional beds in Manitoba. A number of facilities were specifically built to house only level 1 residents, who needed relatively little nursing care. These exclusively level 1 facilities, referred to as hostels, were poorly suited to accommodate residents at other levels of care. Thus a proportion of the nursing home bed stock was essentially nontransferable to other levels of care. In 1982, 1,690 (or 21 percent) of Manitoba's personal care beds were in such hostels.

The increase in personal care beds occurred despite an active program of community care in Manitoba. Figure 6.13 traces the growth of that program over the six years from 1975 to 1981. The number of clients served increased almost 25 percent. The growth has been primarily in homemaker services, as opposed to nursing services. By 1981, more than twice as many clients were served by homemakers as by nursing services.

The data from British Columbia suggest that home-based services there may have been somewhat more effective in displacing institutional care, but even here, the shifts are not dramatic. Because the community care program is more recent in British Columbia, the

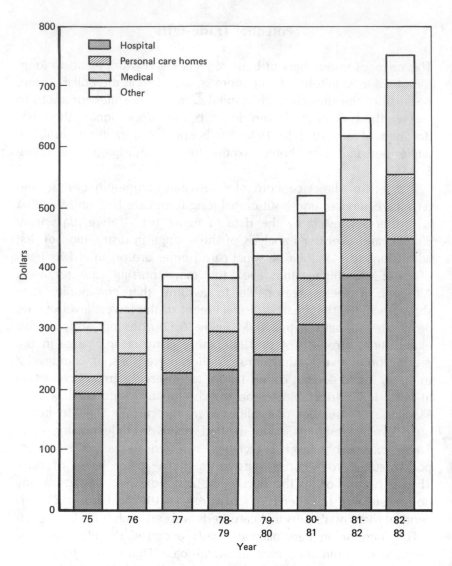

SOURCE: Annual reports, Manitoba Health Services Commission.

Figure 6.11. Per capita health care expenditures in Manitoba, 1975-1982/83

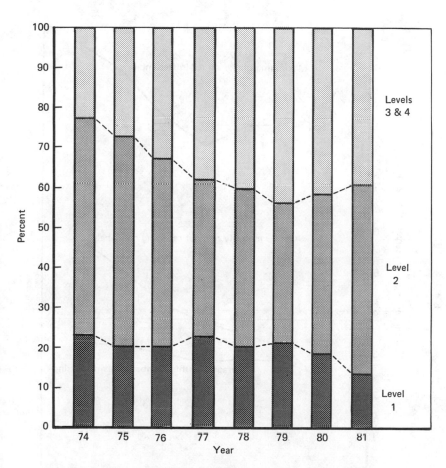

SOURCE: Data from Shapiro and Webster (1984).

Figure 6.12. Changes in the proportionate levels of care for first admissions to personal care homes in Manitoba, 1974-1981.

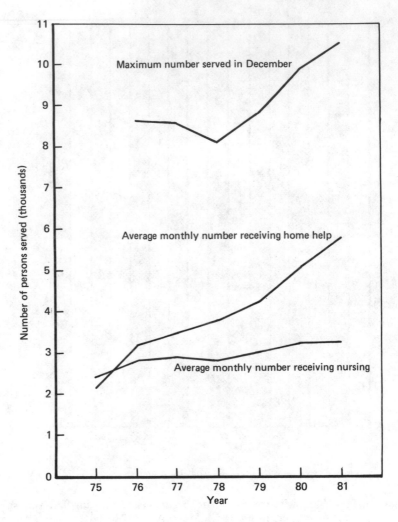

SOURCE: Statistical reports, Office of Continuing Care.

Figure 6.13. Volume of coordinated home care services in Manitoba,
1975-1981.

number of data points is smaller. Figure 6.14 traces the growth in numbers of clients served by nursing homes and community-based services since the latter began in 1978. For the most recent years, the data are available by level of care. The growth in the community-based program is apparent, while the numbers of nursing home beds have been held essentially constant. This issue of substitutability is still hard to resolve. Although the growth in homemaker services was largely in the personal care and IC-1 levels of care, the number at these levels in nursing homes remained virtually constant.

A difference in the clientele served can be seen in figure 6.15, which compares the age-specific utilization rate for clients using homemaker services with that of clients served by a variety of long-term care facilities. The curves are quite parallel until age 85, but then they diverge sharply, with facility use rising to almost 50 percent of the population aged 90 and over.

Because homemaker services do not require major capital costs, they can grow rapidly in the presence of financially supported demand. This response is shown in figure 6.16, which displays the change in amount of services expressed as total hours of homemaker care. Conversely, homemaker services can be more easily reduced in times of budgetary tightening. The figure also illustrates what happened when funds for community care were restricted in 1981. The numbers of clients continued to increase, but fewer hours of homemaker services could be afforded. The result, shown in figure 6.17, was a reduction in hours per client. This reduction was greatest among the heavier care clients, who were receiving more services. Not shown in the figures is the area of greatest reduction—efforts devoted toward reassessment of clients. Reassessments can change a client's designated level of care. As illustrated in figure 6.17, the intensity of service is related to level of care. Furthermore, reassessments can also lead to reductions of homemaker hours without reclassifying the patient to a lower level of care.

The addition of a community-based long-term care program had no perceptible effect on hospital expenditures, traced in figure 6.18. Long-term care expenditures dropped slightly in 1978–79, when the community-based program was introduced, but rose steadily in subsequent years. Hospital expenditure showed a steady increase,

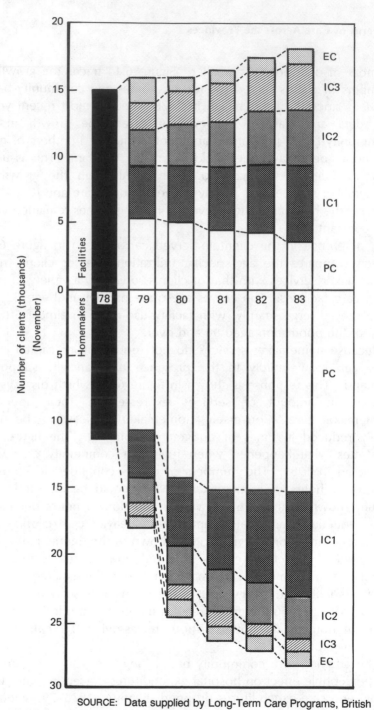

SOURCE: Data supplied by Long-Term Care Programs, British Columbia Ministry of Health.

Figure 6.14. Numbers of long-term care clients served by institutional and community programs in British Columbia, 1978-1983.

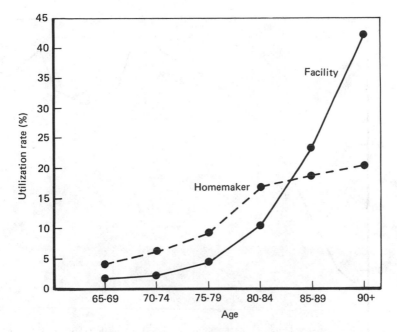

SOURCE: *Annual Report, 1981,* British Columbia Ministry of Health.

**Figure 6.15. Age-specific utilization rates by source of care,
March 31, 1981.**

with a dramatic jump in 1980–81 and 1981–82. This jump was not
associated with an increase in bed supply for either acute hospital
beds or extended care units in acute hospitals; instead, it was the
result of a massive union settlement that raised wages and reduced
daily hours worked per employee.

Concluding Comment

These data suggest that each of the three provinces made a substantial investment in long-term care at the same time that hospital sup
ply, but not hospital expenditure, was reduced. The case for a substitution of long-term beds for acute beds seems stronger than the
one arguing for a displacement of institutional long-term care by

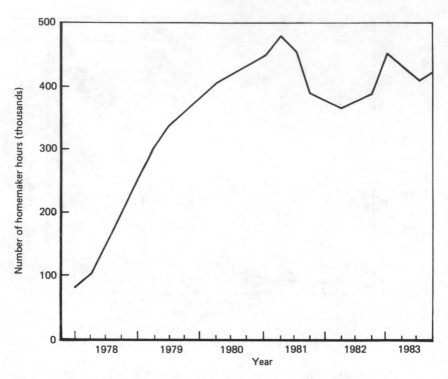

SOURCE: *Annual Reports,* British Columbia Ministry of Health.

Figure 6.16. Change in monthly volume of homemaker services, 1978-1983.

community services. Community care may itself contribute to reducing hospital care through shorter lengths of stay and elimination of some hospital stays.

The availability of community-based home care services was not invariably associated with a reduction in institutional long-term care. The growth in long-term care beds was no greater in Ontario, with a weakly coordinated community care system with minimal benefits, than in British Columbia, with a well-developed, more generous system. Moreover, the timing of changes in institutional utilization did not correspond to the expansion of community services. The case for substitution is no stronger when one looks at shifts in level of care within institutional care.

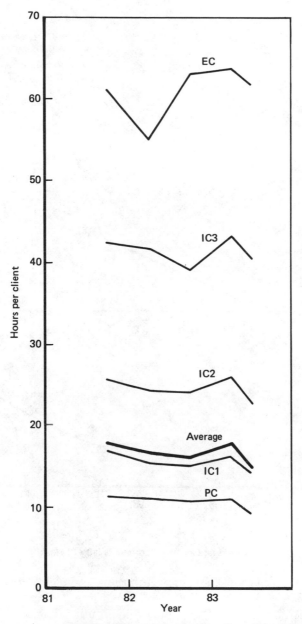

SOURCE: Data supplied by Long-Term Care Program, Ministry of Health.

Figure 6.17. Mean homemaker hours per client per month, British Columbia.

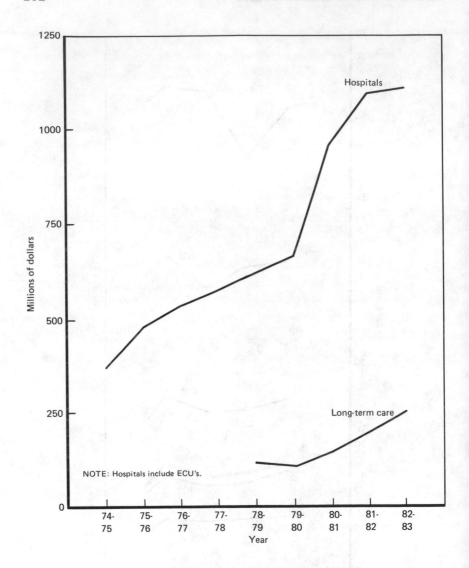

SOURCE: *Annual Reports*, British Columbia Ministry of Health.

Figure 6.18. Annual expenditures for hospitals and long-term care, British Columbia.

The increases in expenditures for both acute and long-term care are related largely to wages. In several of the provinces, union wage settlements resulted in shorter hours and higher pay. Work in long-term care facilities was brought into line with that in hospitals. In each province, there was some reduction in the extent of proprietary ownership of long-term care facilities, but each province retained a mixed market with both proprietary and not-for-profit. Part of this decision may have been based on a deliberate strategy of competition, but much of it was attributable to practical politics.

Nonetheless, in each province the growth in institutional long-term care beds was substantially less than that expected simply by the growth in the elderly population. Based on the estimates described at the beginning of this chapter, each province controlled its supply of nursing home beds. It appears that efforts to constrain supply must occur independently of developing new resources in the community. The presence of a community care system provides an enabling environment in which to take deliberate political action.

REFERENCES

Baxter, R. J., R. Applebaum, J. J. Callahan, Jr., J. B. Christianson, and S. L. Day 1983. *The Planning and Implementation of Channeling: Early Experiences of the National Long-Term-Care Demonstration.* Princeton, N.J.: Mathematica Policy Research.

Greenberg, J. J., D. Doth, and C. Austin 1981. *Comparative Study of Long-Term Care-Demonstration Projects: Lessons for Future Inquiry.* Minneapolis: University of Minnesota Center for Health Services Research.

SSD (Secretariat for Social Development) 1981. *The Elderly in Ontario: An Agenda for the '80s.* Toronto.

Shapiro, E. and L. Webster 1984. "Nursing Home Utilization Patterns for All Manitoba Admissions from 1974 to 1981." *Gerontologist* 24(6):610–615.

U.S. General Accounting Office 1982. *The Elderly Should Benefit from Expanded Home Health Care But Increasing These Services Will Not Assure Cost Reductions.* Washington, D.C.: GPO.

Wilkins, R. and O. Adams 1983. *Healthfulness for Life.* Montreal: Institute for Research on Public Policy.

CHAPTER 7

Case Management: Making Systems Work at the Local Level

A LONG-TERM care entitlement should be more than a license to hunt for scarce services. On the other hand, it should be less than a blank check for any practical assistance in one's own home or in a long-term care facility that many older people might find attractive. Case management is a mechanism to help strike the proper balance of service. In the United States, long-term care planners and policy-makers widely recommend the development of case management systems to allocate resources and plan and monitor long-term care.

British Columbia and Manitoba have predicated their long-term care systems upon a case management approach, and Ontario is considering the merits of a similar provision. This chapter reviews the experience of each province with case management, and draws inferences for policies in the United States.

What Is Case Management?

Let us anchor this discussion with a general statement about case management as it has been conceived in the United States. Case management refers to a system wherein a specified individual or group is responsible for locating, arranging, and monitoring a group of services. The purpose is twofold: For the individual, the case manager assesses functional need and arranges the necessary services to meet that need; and for the community, the case manager acts to promote efficient use of limited resources. A tension is inherent in the role: The case manager is simultaneously an advocate for the elderly and a gatekeeper for the community's resources. The functions of case management include case-finding, screening, comprehensive assessment, care planning, implementation of care plans, monitoring of service, and reassessment to repeat the cycle.

Over the past few decades in the United States, case management has been introduced in long-term care demonstration projects and to a limited extent in operational programs run by health departments, area agencies on aging, and welfare authorities. Little agreement has been reached about optimal characteristics of case management systems, and the scene is characterized by helter-skelter variation. Case management systems have varied in at least the following ways:

1. Their authority to confer or withdraw benefits.
2. The scope of their purview—e.g., health, social services, or both.
3. The target population—e.g., the elderly, the physically impaired, the developmentally disabled, the mentally ill—and the extent to which only the poor are targeted.
4. Their mandate to continue to manage clients in nursing homes.
5. Their separation from or integration with service delivery.
6. Their emphasis on client advocacy versus their emphasis on an efficient community system.
7. Their organization as a single-entry versus multiple-entry case management system.

Other variation occurs in the type of personnel who act as case managers, the size of the caseloads, and working policies.

Case Management in the Three Provinces

All three provinces have introduced some mechanism to coordinate and monitor community-based long-term care entitlements. The Manitoba and British Columbia systems go well beyond Ontario's preliminary efforts to develop a coordinated system, and their case managers enjoy more authority than their counterparts in the United States. Essentially, they control access to the universal nursing-home and home care benefits. In Ontario, the closest function to case management is the role of the home care coordinator, who authorizes home care purchases according to an assessment and a plan. As of March 1984, the *Ontario Home Care Program Policies* and *Procedures Manual* laid out expanded roles and responsibilities of "Home Care Case Managers," thus broadening the concept of the coordinator's function. In Ontario, placement coordination staff also exercise limited case management tasks. For the purposes of the chapter, we use the common term "case manager" to refer to the long-term care assessor in British Columbia, the continuing care case coordinator in Manitoba, and the home care coordinator/case manager in Ontario. The term "case manager" is actually used in Ontario and British Columbia, but rarely in Manitoba.

In all three provinces, the case management is provided by public entities located in the local health departments (or in Manitoba, in the departments of health and community services, combined at the field level) (see table 7.1). In each case, case management is a necessary step to gain entry into the long-term care system. Thus the programs have important responsibility and concomitant authority. The case manager authorizes the eligibility for care and determines the extent of care needed. Unlike the American system, the physician in Manitoba and British Columbia does not have authorizing responsibility but is expected to provide relevant information on the client's medical condition as part of the overall data on the client.

Case management is an administrative function; there is no charge to the user and the costs of case management are calculated separately from the costs of services provided. In contrast to the farming-out of case management sometimes suggested in the United States, the case management function is usually performed directly by the responsible agency. In the city of Winnipeg, however, the Victorian Order of Nurses (VON) is designated as case manager for short-term cases and serves as initial assessor for all cases originating in the hospital. The other exception occurs in rural areas of Manitoba and British Columbia, where it has sometimes been necessary for the case manager to delegate the initial assessments to a regular public health nurse or a hospital worker.

British Columbia and Manitoba have developed systems whereby the case manager can accept a referral from any interested party, including the applicant for care. A referral triggers an immediate standardized assessment, which leads to the assignment of a level of care. A second-level decision is then made about whether the home situation (i.e., the environment and the family support) will

Table 7.1

Characteristics of Case Management Systems in British Columbia, Manitoba, and Ontario

Item	British Columbia	Manitoba	Ontario
A. Access to system	Single-entry system through long-term care programs in each of 22 health districts	Single-entry system through continuing care programs in each of eight regions (except in Winnipeg, where short-term care is accessed by VON)	Home care services accessed through home care programs in each of 38 local Home Care Programs. Institutional benefit accessed by physician authorization approved by Ministry (Ministry approval function in turn is designated to the Home Care Programs)
B. Referral source	Self or any person or agency	Self or any person or agency	A physician's referral is required before services can begin
C. Services managed	Homemaking purchased from authorized agencies, a range of community long-term care services, and nursing home care; home nursing and therapies (PT, OT, etc.) are in a separate system; efforts made to arrange informal services before formal services are authorized	Homemaking provided directly by continuing care program, nursing provided directly (or in Winnipeg purchased from the VON), therapies (PT, OT, etc.), a range of long-term care services, and nursing home admission; efforts made to arrange informal services before formal services are authorized	Services managed include homemaking purchased from Red Cross and other vendors, nursing purchased from the VON and other vendors and therapies provided directly or purchased; the home care program even purchases PT, OT, etc. for persons living in long-term care facilities; efforts made to arrange informal services before formal services are authorized
D. Levels of care	Five levels assigned; decision about need for a care facility separate from level-of-care decision	Four levels assigned; decision about need for care separate from level-of-care decision	Two levels of care: acute and chronic home care; home care coordinator purchases nursing care according to assessment of need. Maximum homemaker hours established for both acute and chronic levels

Table 7.1 (continued)

	Item	British Columbia	Manitoba	Ontario
E.	Relationship to nursing home	Case managers assess level of care and authorize continuing service for those in facilities	Case managers cease activity once person enters a long-term care facility but are responsible for a panel procedure prior to authorizing an application and for management of waiting list	Home care coordinators have no responsibility for institutional access; in some areas, placement coordination services organize waiting lists for institutional admission
F.	Target population	All ages and income levels	All ages and income levels	All ages and income levels
G.	Background of case managers	Nurses, social workers, and physical therapists in Vancouver, and nurses and social workers in 3 other urban health departments; nurses elsewhere	Social workers or nurses—the latter predominate outside Winnipeg	Nurses historically, currently other personnel being considered, particularly therapists (PTs and OTs)
H.	Assessment form	Yes, province-wide	Yes, province-wide for continuing care program and for application to facility	No standard home care form for province, but some home care programs have developed their own forms; standard application for facility
I.	Timing of reassessments	After 90 days and then annually, after any hospitalization, and as requested by providers	Every three months or on request of provider in Winnipeg; outside Winnipeg, if home visit is impossible, telephone contact is made every three months	Varying, but reassessment occurs at least every six months and usually more often

permit the necessary level of care to be provided at home. (As a rule of thumb, home care is not authorized if it would be more expensive than institutional care over a sustained period.) The case managers are responsible, in conjunction with the providers of service, for monitoring the continued adequacy of the plan and the care provided under it, making reassessments as needed and also at routine intervals.

The main differences between the Manitoba system and the British Columbia system concern the boundaries of the case manager's authority. In Manitoba, case management ceases when a client enters a facility, but the case manager is responsible for the paneling procedure that precedes authorization of institutional care and for the management of facility waiting lists. The British Columbian case manager follows the client into the facility and conducts periodic reassessments to determine changing need, thereby having authority to authorize individual services both in the community and in the institution. However, in contrast to the Manitoba program, home nursing and other therapies (i.e., OT, PT, speech) are outside the scope of the long-term care case manager in British Columbia.

Compared with Manitoba and British Columbia, Ontario offers less in the way of case management. The closest analogue is the role of the home care coordinator (recently called "home care case manager") who assesses and authorizes services under both the acute and chronic home care programs. The authority of the case manager over resources is limited to authorizing purchases for home care and medical supplies and equipment under the rules of the home care program and monitoring the services provided. (Currently, in the chronic home care program, a physician referral and at least three professional visits from a nurse or therapist per month are required for program eligibility.) The case manager has no role in determining eligibility for institutional care and no official role in managing the waiting lists for such facilities. In some districts, a placement coordinator in the same health department manages the waiting list, and in those instances, the case managers cooperate with the placement coordination service. The March 1984 guidelines for case managers indicate that they should try to arrange and coordinate all resources on behalf of the patient, work with patient and family toward goals of maintaining independence, and help the patient plan toward discharge from the home care program with arrangement for necessary follow-up services. This emphasis on coordination and brokering without full authority is reminiscent of some case management approaches in the United States. Similarly, the new statement's emphasis on working toward planned discharge from home care shows a cost-consciousness that is also part of American case management programs.

As part of our study, we visited several case management programs in each province and conducted lengthy telephone interviews with all the remaining programs. The material in the rest of this chapter is based on these contacts with the administrators of the twenty-two long-term care programs in British Columbia, the eight continuing care regions in Manitoba, and all but one of the thirty-eight home care programs in Ontario, as well as comments from interested persons in the environment. The purpose of the inquiry was to explore how the case management systems worked in practice according to people actually involved with the tasks. We wanted to understand problems that arose and strategies used to address these problems.

Case Management Roles and Patterns

Who Does Case Management?

With few exceptions, case managers are nurses or social workers. In Ontario, the home care coordinators, whose roles are narrower than full-fledged case management, are all nurses; metropolitan Toronto is considering using public health nurses as coordinators once its chronic home care program begins (Metropolitan Toronto District Health Council 1984). We saw little evidence of multidisciplinary team case management as it is advocated in the United States, but multidisciplinary collaborative arrangements did occur in the four metropolitan Vancouver health departments and in Winnipeg. In British Columbia, the role differentiation of each profession seemed minimal, whereas in Winnipeg it was maintained as part of the assessment process and the procedures for reviewing nursing home applications.

Each of the seven regional units of the Vancouver Health Department had at least one long-term care team. A team included nurses, social workers, and physical therapists, each of whom interchangeably took intake, performed assessments, and maintained a case load. The multidisciplinary character of the staff presumably permitted mutual enrichment and crossover of skills, but team case management *per se* was regarded as inefficient. Most units agree with Vancouver that team management (whether interdisciplinary or intradisciplinary) is inefficient, but some rural units do use their assessment team to make all assessment decisions. Furthermore, many units have monthly team meetings to share information and discuss difficult cases.

Each long-term care team in Vancouver could also draw upon additional resource people who served more than one team—most notably, a nutritionist and a home support worker. The latter's role was to encourage the development of helping networks and other community long-term care provisions. Considerable discussion was taking place in Vancouver about whether this role was useful enough to justify continuance in lieu of reducing each case manager's large caseload. A team manager (either a nurse or a social worker) had overall responsibility for administrative matters and for coordination with the home nursing program and the preventive health care program in the health unit.

Winnipeg is divided into six districts, which represent fairly distinct communities; some large districts are further subdivided into local offices. There are eleven offices with continuing care teams in the city. A district manager is housed in one local office in each district and each local office also has one or more home care teams who are responsible to the district manager and programmatically to the regional care coordinator. Field staff is organized into nurse/social worker teams, with one to three teams located in each local office. The nurse and the social worker each make initial assessments on each case, but once the care plan is developed, one of them is assigned ongoing responsibility for case management and continuing reassessment. A homemaker coordinator at each office serves as a part of the care planning team, and most districts have a resource developer whose role is to facilitate community services.

Outside the major cities, the structure of case management becomes considerably less elaborate. Various patterns exist. In

Manitoba, some regions have already separated the long-term care program from the public health nursing program, and the rest are in the process of doing so. The case coordinator may be a nurse or a social worker. As needed, the case manager purchases evaluations from other professionals to round out the assessment process. Innovative forms of delegation seem to be used to ensure that assessment takes place for clients who live in isolated parts of the far-flung districts. Some districts also have resource developers who arrange for or make referrals to community voluntary programs or other services like meals-on-wheels or adult day care.

Outside Vancouver and Victoria, the British Columbian case management systems are located in long-term care programs, which are units in the local provincial health departments. Nurses do the case management, and their long-term care administrator is responsible for coordination with the home care program and preventive nursing program located in the same health department. Essentially, it seems that, outside the three principal cities, case management systems in British Columbia and Manitoba were successfully grafted onto already existing regional health care programs.

Recruitment of case managers seemed to pose few difficulties. Public health nurses and social workers were attracted to the position because it offered flexibility, autonomy, and interesting variety. Turnover was low. British Columbia has now amassed sufficient experience with long-term care programs to have observed some people moving through the ranks from case manager to administrator, and others developing a career pattern as administrator at successive posts.

Hospital-Based Referrals

About half the referrals for the LTC programs in British Columbia and Manitoba are made on behalf of hospital inpatients. A timely method of managing these referrals is a prerequisite of an effective system.

According to some of our informants, hospital social work directors perceived the advent of the LTC program in British Columbia as an invasion of territory. Perhaps because of the sensitivity of the issue, each LTC program was empowered to negotiate with hospitals in the region and establish its own working relationship. Consequently, the pattern developed for mutual coexistence varies considerably. Typically, in the rural areas, case managers come to the hospitals as needed to perform assessments, although hospital social workers and nurses may prepare preliminary materials. In larger referral centers, a liaison nurse from the health department is housed in each hospital to do both long-term care and home nursing assessments and complete paperwork. Then the regular case managers perform assessments soon after the patients are discharged to their homes or to facilities.

The Ontario health districts have developed various patterns for managing hospital referrals, but they fall into three general types: The case manager may be responsible for all the hospitals within her geographic district; each case manager may be assigned to a hospital (not necessarily in the catchment area) with the expectation that about 20 percent of her time will be devoted to in-hospital assessment; or one or more case managers may be assigned hospital work as their only function on either a permanent or a rotating basis.

Outside Winnipeg, Manitoba programs show similar flexibility in developing convenient patterns to handle hospital-based referrals. In Winnipeg itself, the hospital assessments are done by a representative of VON, contracted to work as part of the Continuing Care program. As chapter 4 indicated, the VON is responsible for case management for all short-term home care. On discharge from hospital, if the need has been assessed to be short-term (60 days or less), referral is to the VON. If the assessed need is for long-term services, referral is to the regional local office. In either case, the hospital-based coordinator establishes the initial care plan, which is reassessed and changed as necessary when the client is in the community.

Caseloads, Continuity, and Responsiveness

Each system has specified timelines for periodic reassessments to monitor change and adjust care plans and levels of care. The case manager is expected to perform regular reassessments, to reevaluate after any hospitalization, and to respond to requests by consumers and providers for reviews of the case. Our telephone interviews revealed that large caseloads, distance, and imperfect communication prohibited these ideals from being realized.

In British Columbia, the caseloads ranged from around 200 to more than 500. Realistically, this meant that compromises were made in the extent to which routine reassessments were done either for community-dwelling or institution-dwelling clients. Because reassessments were usually triggered by a request from a provider, the likelihood was that each reassessment would lead to an increase in service rather than a decrease. In some districts, clients with no evident deterioration were not seen for years. In contrast, when the Vancouver program declared a moratorium on new intake in July 1982 and instead asked case managers to reassess all existing community clientele, case managers recommended decreases as well as increases in service level. This exercise demonstrated the real need for periodic routine reassessments to make most appropriate use of the resources.

In British Columbia, the time from initial referral to assessment varied within districts, ranging from a matter of days to a matter of months. Six of the districts informed us that assessments were done within five working days of referral. Clients living in very rural areas might initially be assessed over the phone or by a regular public health nurse so that services could be ordered temporarily before the case manager could schedule a home visit. Seven of the districts told us that their assessments were done within two to four weeks, with a triaging function that permitted early attention to emergency needs. One agency falling into this category indicated a *preference* for doing assessments two to three weeks after the initial referral so that any crisis that precipitated the referral might be stabilized and the case manager would have a better idea of true functional capacity. Other districts had greater backlogs (even extending to six months) or had placed new referrals (except for emergencies) on temporary hold at the time we did our telephone interviews.

Caseloads in Manitoba and in Ontario have more manageable proportions. Precise figures were difficult to develop for Manitoba because the system outside Winnipeg was in transition. The earlier method used part-time nurses with other duties, and the change was toward a more consolidated and accountable method. The caseloads range from 80 to 140 with an average of about 100. Of course, the Manitoba caseloads are limited to community dwelling clients who generate higher activity per case than does the mixed caseload of facility residents and community residents held by case managers in British Columbia. Caseloads in Ontario ranged between 50 and 90, with the usual figure somewhere between 70 and 80.

Care Planning and Implementation

The British Columbia and Manitoba case managers base their initial determinations on a multidimensional assessment. The assessment considers functional abilities, cognitive abilities, and social circumstances as well as more traditional information about medical diagnosis and nursing needs. In Manitoba, multidisciplinary input is used for completion of the assessment material. Application for personal care home admission in Manitoba occasions a separate and extensive multidisciplinary assessment on standardized forms used for the paneling process. These assessment procedures in Manitoba and British Columbia can be contrasted to the practices presently used in Ontario's home care program. In Ontario, some programs rely entirely on clinical judgment, others use forms that deal almost exclusively with nursing needs, and only a few have attempted a multidimensional assessment based on functioning.

The mechanism for moving from assessment data to an actual plan is of particular interest. How reliably do case managers perform the assessments? Do they reach reliable conclusions about level of care and amount of service? Do case managers have flexibility to make innovative plans? What guidelines influence decision rules about how much service to offer and where? In the United States, the spectre has been raised of case management becoming an elaborate front-end assessment exercise leading to no significant choices for the older person. The thought of persons "all assessed with no place to go" is a realistic worry for program planners.

We should not idealize the science in the assessment process. Reliability is rarely tested, and it is uncertain that two assessors would reach identical conclusions. Stark, Gutman, and Brothers (1982) had occasion to computerize all four pages of the British Columbia assessment form and reported much missing and inconsistent information. Our informants from our telephone interviews believed that a high degree of reliability had been achieved within their own particular programs; many told us about strategies for orienting new personnel by having them observe experienced assessors. However, some expressed the opinion that the reliability across long-term care programs might differ.

The decision algorithm leading from assessment to service package is rather mysterious. Here, professional judgment is used to weigh the client's needs and resources and to determine how to fill the gaps. In Ontario especially, various administrators view themselves as more or less stringent than their peers about the allocation of services. In a society as litigiously inclined and as concerned about equity of benefits as the United States, the element of professional judgment might not find ready acceptance in the communities. Yet judgment must be exercised in accordance with the total need in the community and the amount of resources at the disposal of the long-term care program. Otherwise the important dual focus of the case manager—on the individual and the society—cannot be maintained. Some degree of trust in these individuals as agents of a benevolent social system seems essential.

Care planning in British Columbia and Manitoba, where the case management systems are refined, has common features. The plan is arrived at jointly with the client and the case manager, and the client's family is included when available and their participation is appropriate. The case managers reinforce statements about the purpose of the program that are also clearly expressed in the promotional literature. They emphasized that long-term care services at home are not designed to substitute for family care or to provide homemaking assistance in the luxury category. Case managers also attempt to arrange for existing community services before ordering services supplied or purchased by their own programs. For example, a homemaker will not be used to cook meals if a meal service is available. Similarly, a homemaker would not be used to transport the client if a community transportation system were available. In all three provinces, the care planners were especially clear that home nursing should not be used to substitute for ambulatory care that could readily be received in a physician's office.

The key service for allocation is homemaking. In British Columbia and Ontario, homemaking is typically purchased from agencies, whereas in Manitoba, homemakers are typically employed by the home care program. In either situation, the case manager attempts considerable specificity about the actual tasks needed.

In Manitoba, the tasks to be performed (dusting, sweeping, and so on) are listed. A translation from tasks to "hours" establishes the schedule for the homemaker. In Ontario and British Columbia, the agencies often have their own professional personnel who develop the actual plan, using the guidelines established by the provincial program.

The challenge for the programs that use vendors is to act as efficient purchasers while using the purchasing power of the program to stimulate a desirable balance of services in the community. Often agencies have minimum time rules (e.g., four hours), interfering with the home care program's ability to purchase small increments of service. One strategy is to use neighborhood approaches so that the homemaker can readily serve several people in the same apartment complex or city block within the minimum time allocation. In cities, the home care program may have an array of proprietary and nonprofit agencies competing for the business. Usually, the agencies differ in their charges and their particular competencies. The programs may develop rules to channel the purchasing strategy, which in turn removes from the individual case manager the decision about which agency to use.

Manitoba recognizes four levels of homemaking services, each requiring somewhat different skills and background. In ascending order of expertise and pay scale, these are (1) the sitter/attendant, with light housekeeping duties; (2) general maintenance and housekeeping; (3) assistance with personal care; (4) more skilled assistance with personal care under the supervision of a nurse.

Seemingly, both Manitoba and British Columbia allow the case managers considerable flexibility to arrange for and purchase necessary services. This flexibility is particularly welcome in rural areas, although some informants commented that the ability to innovate is limited by time considerations.

Clientele

All adults can receive the institutional long-term care benefit. Although even children can be served by the home care programs in all three provinces, nearly all the clients are over age 65, and their average age is often in the 80's.

When we asked the administrators to characterize their home care clientele, we received a considerable range of responses. The majority of the elderly clientele do not live with their families, but have family members in the vicinity who are prepared to be helpful. Manitoba administrators identified particular subgroups who tended to receive substantial family support—e.g., Mennonites and French Canadians (who rarely live with relatives) and Ukrainians (who often live with or very near their relatives). Particular subgroups *without* family support were identified in British Columbia, including elderly single men retired from the logging camps in the northern interior, a large native Indian population in the Cariboo area, and retirement communities in the central area and on Vancouver Island where many residents have migrated away from their families.

The Manitoba and British Columbia administrators described a frail elderly clientele of advanced age. Common diagnoses included arthritis, coronary heart disease, stroke, visual problems, and some terminal cancer. The Ontario informants most often mentioned circulatory and cardiovascular diseases, palliative care for cancer, diabetic and orthopedic patients, and post-surgical patients. Perhaps because most of the Ontario programs had recently phased into a chronic home care program, the prevalent thinking in Ontario was keyed to acute illness or convalescence from specific diseases rather than to functional conditions.

We were specifically interested in the ability of the home care programs to work with senile dementia. All agreed that those clients are the most difficult population to manage at home. Our Manitoba informants seem to do the most work in this area, maintaining senile clients at home if they are not violent or abusive, do not wander at night, and have family support available. Night attendants, respite care (i.e., care provided to give relatives time off for vacation trips and other personal needs) and adult day care were deemed particularly important to sustain a cognitively impaired person at home. One Manitoba regional administrator made the interesting observation that clients with senile dementia tend to be referred to home care programs only after the condition has deteriorated to the point where the family is drained. She speculated that earlier referrals to home care with earlier relief might delay institutional placement. Despite all efforts, most administrators observed that such a client usually ends up being admitted to a facility on an emergency basis. One informant summed it up for all by saying, "They represent only a small percentage of the caseload but the greatest problem in management."

British Columbia's experience was analogous. The administrators were dissatisfied with their ability to serve the confused and found that family support was the essential ingredient, combined with ability to purchase respite and attendant care.

In Ontario, administrators believed that they served few persons with dementia or incontinence and that, in general, the home care program was ill-equipped to serve such persons. However, several administrators commented that they see substantial "temporary" confusion among persons just returning from the hospital, and that a few weeks tend to bring about dramatic improvements. This observation provides another caution against the common practice in the United States of making nursing home placements directly from a hospital.

Socioeconomic status of the clientele varied widely in all provinces both between districts and within districts. Many people served had substantial assets in the form of property and some had the means to purchase additional services that were recommended. However, only a minority were believed to have sufficient income to purchase a full range of homemaking services on their own. In all three provinces, clients living in relatively affluent circumstances in self-contained, large homes tended to have the greatest needs for assistance. This underscores the relationship between environment and service requirements. Some administrators speculate that the senior citizen in a modern apartment or a seniors housing requires much less help, given the same level of impairment as a counterpart in a more complex setting.

Nursing Home Placement

One function of the case manager in both Manitoba and British Columbia is to organize the waiting list for nursing-home beds and certify the eligibility of applicants.

As chapter 4 indicated, a paneling process is used to determine eligibility in Manitoba. The client gives the case manager signed permission to bring the case to a panel. The case manager avoids bringing any cases forward unless he or she believes placement would provide the most appropriate mix of services. However, if a client is dissatisfied with community care and wishes to be considered for a personal care home, the case manager cannot deny that client the right to have a panel review the situation. A multidisciplinary review is performed as part of the panel process with input from the client's physician, a nurse, and a social worker. The panel includes geriatric physicians in Winnipeg and Brandon. In rural areas, the regular physician panel member is usually a district health officer. The patient's own physician is invited to attend the panel (but few do), and sometimes the administrator of the long-term care facility preferred by the client also attends.

The panel may recommend one of three courses: (1) approve facility placement and assign a level of care; (2) defer the decision, requesting more information or exploration of an alternative plan before reaching a decision; (3) deny the placement request. The deferral may include a request for a more complete medical evaluation by a geriatric assessment unit. If the panel approves the placement, the home chosen by the client is the one approved for placement unless it cannot meet the client's care needs. The client and family are given a list of facilities and encouraged to visit them before choosing one for placement. Case management and home care then continue until space in the desired facility becomes available. In Manitoba, each facility has its own admission committee to set admission priorities, and it is not immediately clear how the program ensures that certain kinds of applicants will not be dropped repeatedly to the bottom of the list. Because no program administrator identified this as a problem, however, the answer may be as simple as the following: The size of each facility's waiting list is restricted. If a facility puts off taking difficult cases, these cases stay on its waiting list and the facility will soon find that its list comprises only difficult cases.

In British Columbia, clients may request to be wait-listed for a facility placement at their level of care. Many administrators told us that clients are *not* placed on waiting lists unless they cannot be maintained at home, but in the absence of hard criteria, it seems unlikely that case managers could force that issue. The client considering a facility is encouraged to visit as many as possible before making a first and second choice. Once a vacancy occurs in either the first- or second-choice facility, some units require the client to accept it or be dropped from both waiting lists. If the second-choice facility is the one that first becomes available, the client must be admitted but is wait-listed for the first choice.

The waiting lists tend to move in chronological order. Several districts maintain emergency waiting lists for clients in "unsafe situations." Such clients must accept the first available bed in a suitable facility, but are wait-listed for facilities of choice with the option to transfer. One district administrator estimated that about 90 percent of placements in his district were from such an emergency list, a phenomenon that obviously compromises the ability to place people in facilities of their choice. In the Upper Island (i.e., Vancouver Island) district, three types of waiting lists are maintained—regular, emergency, and respite—and the lists move simultaneously with each taking every third vacancy.

Interestingly enough, *no preference* tends to be given to those in acute hospitals unless they were admitted to the hospital from a facility or they were admitted to the hospital because of a crisis that prevented them from being maintained at home (e.g., their primary caregiver died or became incapacitated). It is important to note that the long-term care programs were able to resist the slippery slope of prioritizing so-called "bed blockers" for immediate placement. In fact, on our visits to both Manitoba and British Columbia, we heard comments that giving priority to persons in the hospital creates a disincentive for persons to return home and try to manage with home care. Such persons need the security of knowing that their needs will not go to the back of the list should their home care not work out. The fact that hospitals are budgeted globally makes this policy feasible.

Demand for Service

Most informants from British Columbia and Manitoba reported that the demand for community care had reached a plateau. For most districts this steady state occurred within two to three years, though some indicated it took a little longer. Two of British Columbia's twenty-two districts reported that demand had not yet stabilized. One attributed this to lack of sufficient assessors to catch up with the backlog and the other to the development of a new market of young, terminally ill clients. Three of the Manitoba regions believed that the demand was not yet stabilized because of changes in the program, the demographics of the regions (more retired persons moving in), and the expectations of the users (more heavy care clientele wanting to stay at home).

The Ontario home care programs indicated that steady states were achieved in about two to five years for the initial acute home care program. The chronic home care program was too new to fully evaluate the start-up time. Almost all the informants told us that the advent of the chronic home care benefit had some effect on the use of the acute home care benefit, but the results were inconclusive. Some said that the use of acute home care *decreased* with the beginning of chronic home care (perhaps because chronic patients were formerly carried on the acute program), and others said the use of the acute home care program actually *increased* (perhaps because of the general publicity about home care). There is some indication that it took longer for demand to peak in rural areas. This was attributed to the paucity of community agencies and, therefore, the difficulty in generating referrals.

Referrals from clients and their families were common in both British Columbia and Manitoba. Rarely did more than half the referrals come from professionals (nurses, hospitals, physicians, social service agencies); often, about two-thirds of the referrals were from client or family. Seasonal variations occurred, with more referrals in the winter months. Some British Columbia informants also reported a greater demand for attractive new facilities.

Some informants had experienced what they considered unreasonable demands for services that were not justified by functional impairment. Many case managers were philosophical about that type of demand, viewing it useful for persons to be assessed and become known to the system. Approximately 10 percent of the applicants assessed in British Columbia were found to have no immediate need for service. However, in both British Columbia and Manitoba it seemed that case managers were willing to assign minimal homemaker hours to any very old person living alone. One case manager in British Columbia explained that any person over 80 living alone could probably profit by 4 hours of homemaking twice a month and that this service effectively links the individual to the system.

Supply of Service

All three provinces reported little difficulty in developing the necessary supply of homemaking agencies, although the two that used contracted services had more difficulty in developing plans with short increments of service. All had some problems supplying homemakers on weekends and in the evenings, partly because of availability and partly because of price. Some of the Ontario programs averred that care on weekends and evenings should be provided by families. Generally speaking, homemaking was viewed as a desirable occupation in British Columbia and Manitoba and turnover was reportedly low. In Winnipeg, in contrast, turnover was high. No sooner were they trained than the homemakers tended to take jobs in the hospital sector or in a personal care home.

Therapists of all kinds (PT, OT, speech) were in short supply in the rural areas. Ontario informants also would have liked access to personnel whose skills lie somewhere between those of a homemaker and a registered nurse to do simple nursing tasks. As one might anticipate, the rural areas had fewer organized meal services, day care, and other social services. Transportation was sometimes a problem, although many municipalities had developed low-cost ride programs. Several informants commented on housing shortages and remarked that apartment complexes that provide housekeeping and handymen would eliminate the need for some home care.

Quality of Service

In Manitoba, where the homemaker personnel are directly employed by the programs, all Continuing Care staff are trained, supervised, and monitored. A regular in-service education program is also offered by consultants, who travel from region to region. Additional mechanisms such as regular chart reviews and case conferencing were also introduced in several districts.

In Ontario and British Columbia, quality assurance is more difficult. Clients are encouraged to contact the case manager with any problems and, in addition, the caregiving agencies are expected to have their own quality assurance mechanisms in place. Some administrators expressed concern over the lack of a formal quality assurance program. The Vancouver Long-Term Care Program has demonstrated how a case management agency can demand quality of care from its contractors. In 1983, it developed the innovative bidding system for its contracts with home care providers and incorporated standards for quality assurance procedures into the requirements and the point scores for evaluating proposals (see chapter 5).

Although case managers in British Columbia continue assessing individual clients when they are in facilities, the formal responsibility for quality of institutional care rests with the provincial and municipal licensing authorities. However, the case manager comes to know the home well and is in a position to observe and report any lapses in quality that are noticed.

Consumer Choice

A deliberate effort is made to accommodate clients' preferences, both for the place of service and the choice of facility if an admission is planned. The administrators expressed respect for a client's decision to live at risk and a willingness to work to provide whatever services they could within the limits of the cost of a nursing home bed. One Manitoba district administrator indicated that the program sometimes contacts the police and the fire department to inform them of potential problems.

As already described, an honest effort is made to respect the client's choice of a particular facility.

Relationships with Physicians

The commonest difficulty experienced in the case management programs was winning the acceptance and cooperation of physicians. The physician is asked to play an unfamiliar role. He or she provides information, but the case manager makes the decisions.

Manitoba and British Columbia administrators indicated that physicians were slow to make referrals to the program, or that their referrals tended to be for placement rather than home care. In Manitoba, a physician working optimally with the program would be expected to refer appropriate clients, provide medical assessments, and work with the case manager in the ongoing determination of the client's medical and nursing needs. Physicians varied in how closely they conformed to that optimum. Generally speaking, problems were greater among rural physicians with a long history of solo practice, especially in those communities where they had long been virtually the only health care providers.

Administrators in British Columbia made much the same comments, but also deplored many physicians' lack of interest in the elderly. Some administrators pointed out difficulties that occurred when case managers needed to confront physicians with problems such as misuse or insufficient monitoring of medication, need for referral to a specialist, or additional medical problems identified by the project nurses. During a visit to Vancouver, we attended a meeting of physicians where the problems were discussed from the doctor's perspective. Physicians complained that case managers were preemptory, that they interfered in the doctor-patient relationship, and, most notably, that they required the physician to fill out health forms at no charge.

The underlying issue is the absolute necessity for physicians to be involved cooperatively in the case management process. Case managers are responsible for a functional assessment and for arranging services to compensate for observed functional deficits; but some functional problems may be remediable through medical interventions. Both physicians and case managers were concerned that remediable problems might be missed, but a smooth working relationship had not yet evolved. The panel method in Manitoba offered at least one built-in mechanism for communication with medical personnel. This feature was not part of the British

Columbia program, but is currently being considered by the Vancouver Health Department.

The Ontario home care programs required physician orders. Sometimes the home care program first identified the need and then requested the physician referral to start the service. Administrators commented that physician acceptance of the programs seemed to increase, the longer the program had been in the community. In the well-established Hamilton and Thunder Bay programs, for example, it was said that 95 percent of the physicians refer their patients. Younger physicians seemed more responsive than older ones. Reasons why some physicians fail to make referrals were suggested: too much paperwork; fear that they will lose control over their patients; fear that they too will be expected to make home visits. Many Ontario administrators also remarked that doctors were reluctant to make referrals to home care if hospital beds were empty, even if the patient could be cared for without admission or the hospital stay could be shortened.

Community Relationships

Cordial relationships are needed with other health providers besides physicians. Working out the relationship with the providers of home care and nursing care has sometimes been a problem. Agencies such as VON and the Red Cross maintained their own supervisors who arrived at their own plans of care. For the most part, the case manager would provide a general plan, which would then be reviewed and modified by the caregiving agency.

In a few areas, logistical problems arose because case managers were not informed when clients entered the hospital and therefore homemakers made unnecessary visits. Social service agencies sometimes indicated that because the case manager was a poor source of up-to-date information about a client, it was necessary to call the homemaking or nursing agency directly. This sentiment was most often expressed by hospital discharge planners. In turn, some administrators reported problems with "territoriality" among discharge planners.

Is Institutionalization Delayed or Prevented?

Most administrators believed that the case management along with the ability to purchase home services prevented or delayed admissions to nursing homes. Most of the evidence is impressionistic, however.

All the Manitoba administrators expressed that confidence. The consensus was that more clients were remaining home until death but that those entering facilities needed heavier care than ever before. The Parkland area had stopped making level 1 facility placements entirely at the time of our interviews, and the Eastman area claimed that 60 percent of levels 3 and 4 clients and 80 percent of level 2 clients were awaiting placement at home rather than in hospital. The frequent monitoring done in Manitoba was believed to have a preventive effect, in that problems were caught and treated early before they led to deterioration.

The comments from British Columbia similarly emphasized the impression that those entering facilities were frailer than previously. Some areas have been able to keep wait-listed persons at home for long periods until an emergency occurs. There was also consensus that the home care program prevented patients from being hospitalized as frequently for periodic flare-ups of chronic illnesses.

Some administrators believed that the long-term care program did not prevent institutionalization, but instead almost encouraged it by providing an orderly way for persons to enter facilities. This was true in areas where new facilities had been built. Many agreed that a better job in preventing institutionalization could be done if more respite services were developed and if there were planned short-term admissions to facilities for convalescence.

In Ontario there was widespread agreement that home care accounted for shortened lengths of stay in acute hospitals and for eliminating some "revolving door" hospitalizations for exacerbations of chronic illness. Some administrators also believed nursing home care was reduced, especially care that would be used for convalescence after a hospitalization. The clamor for more chronic hospital beds is anecdotally linked to the ability of the home care programs to keep people at home until they are too debilitated for extended care.

Conclusion

The Canadian experience suggests that case management is feasible. At the very least, it provides a means for improving decisionmaking at points of crisis in long-term care and encouraging clients to consider their options more carefully. The process formalizes the role of an individual outside the medical system in making the decisions about service needs. The cost of this separation is the potential lack of adequate physician involvement. The Manitoba paneling approach offers one useful mechanism to improve coordination, but it is most effective when geriatric resources are available for further evaluation as indicated.

All of the program personnel interviewed believe they are making an important contribution. Although they could not confirm their impressions about changes in facility case mix with any clear statistics, the presence of a program to coordinate and oversee the work of service providers makes good sense. In some areas, this oversight function led to more deliberate efforts to reshape the pattern of community care.

The costs of case management, as performed in these provinces, seem more than justified by its role in facilitating decisionmaking and monitoring services. Patients in long-term care do get better, and reassessments can reduce services and prevent dependency. Nonetheless, case management is vulnerable. In times of budget crunch, the case management programs often elected to reduce their efforts to divert money into direct services. Although it is always difficult to justify administrative expense when services themselves are threatened, the contraction of case management seemed to be associated with lost efficiency.

The collective experience of these programs is reassuring. Community care is not an inevitable giveaway program. Families do not abandon their elderly at the first sign of government assistance. Elderly clients do not make excessive demands. Reasonable decisions can be made about service needs and institutional placement without convening a national assembly. The demand for care does level off.

How does this experience translate to the United States? The danger is ever-present that we may overdo case management by making it an industry instead of a service. Simpler may indeed be better. The heart of the program seems to lie in concerned professionals making deliberate assessments but using common sense and professional judgment. Could such an approach work in the United States? The litigious instincts of Americans argue that the assessment process would have to be more formalized and hence probably more expensive, but the basic premises appear to hold. A program somewhere between the Canadian models and the more elaborate models mounted in United States demonstration programs seems most likely. The role of the case management agency as a source of standards for providers and a critical step in assuring quality seems a logical extension of the efforts demonstrated in the long-term care channeling projects.

REFERENCES

Metropolitan Toronto District Health Council 1984. *Co-ordination of Long Term Care Services in Metropolitan Toronto*. Toronto.

Stark, A. J., G. M. Gutman, and K. Brothers 1982. "Reliability of Level of Care Decisions in a Long-Term Care Program." *Journal of Community Health* 8(2):102–109.

CHAPTER 8
General Observations and Conclusions

THE common factor in the three Canadian provinces studied is universal health insurance for hospital and medical care, to which each province has added a nonmeans-tested, long-term care benefit. A basic message emanates from this work: Universal long-term care entitlements are feasible and affordable. Many observers have noted that health care expenditures have grown less rapidly in Canada than in the United States. The extension of coverage to include long-term care has left that striking finding unchanged. It is possible to deliver long-term care without bankrupting either the country or, equally important, without bankrupting families.

Although long-term care emerged in Canada as a health care program, it has a distinct status and identity. Its attachment to health grew from a yet unproven expectation that expanding long-term care would reduce acute medical care use, especially hospital use. But Canadian long-term care is not exclusively or fully a health care program; it is a hybrid. For example, in the recent Canada Health Act of 1984, long-term care is not exempt from user fees. Indeed, all three provinces charged for a residential component of nursing home care and, in turn, guaranteed all citizens enough income to afford it.

The Canadian experience with long-term care has demonstrated the feasibility of achieving several socially desirable goals. It shows that expanded services can be provided within a controllable budget. This observation should not be misinterpreted to say that new resources can be created from old at no cost. Money was infused into the Canadian long-term care programs, but the expansion has been reasonably well controlled. Each of our three provinces developed a distinctive program of long-term care upon the foundation of its universal health insurance program. Whatever the provincial policies, universal long-term care entitlements did not lead to runaway utilization. Each province developed mechanisms to control use. The more generous the benefits, the more necessary was effective case management to ensure accountable allocation of resources.

The Canadian long-term care system allows for considerable exercise of consumer choice. With available options for home or institutional care and even variations in the ethnic composition of institutions, consumers are encouraged to express a preference and, within the limits of available resources, that preference is honored. The centralization of payment for long-term care provides an important element of control and makes planning possible. Standards can be established and supply regulated by authorizing payment.

At the same time, the Canadian approach has several shortcomings: The place of long-term care vis-à-vis social and health care services is not clearly fixed. There is evidence of both redundancy and omission. In the health care areas, for example, hospitals continue to operate the extended or chronic care units directly. Although every nursing home resident must have an attending physician, physicians in practice are too often not actively involved in planning for or delivering long-term care.

Although government monopsony allows control of long-term care,* specific programs for quality assurance are poorly developed. In part, this lack of a highly developed, formal quality assessment structure may reflect Canada's low rate of litigation in disputes between citizens and governmental agencies.

Harkening back to themes raised in chapter 1, this chapter discusses our conclusions about the selected general issues that underpinned our study of long-term care in the three provinces.

Control of the System

The elimination of multiple payment sources permits a great deal of control. Government monopsony facilitates more deliberate planning for long-term care services. The system of global budgets, in

---

*"Monopsony" refers to the consolidation of payment authority in a single entity; it is the counterpart to consolidation of suppliers, or monopoly.

principle, allows general allocation decisions across sectors to be made by a higher level of government while leaving to smaller units the opportunity to set priorities for the use of the supposedly fixed resources thus made available. Because decisions can be made about the amount of resources to be allocated to a program, there is a greater opportunity to control the level of expenditure. In practice, however, the government's control is far from absolute. Providers continue to exert substantial influence both on an individual level regarding planning for specific services, and on a larger collective level through lobbying efforts.

One is struck by the relative lack of regulatory apparatus in Canada. Compared with the United States, decisions seem to be made more by collaboration than by adversarial confrontations, with concomitantly less use of the courts as means of resolving differences. Representatives of the government seem to take a more collegial attitude toward provider institutions. Inspectors are expected to know their territories and to work with the facilities they inspect to improve quality. Of course, critics of the system are quick to label such an approach as laxity or collusion. Moreover, when tangible evidence of quality is needed, as in the current Ontario debate, it is unavailable.

Among the three provinces studied, there is variety in the extent to which services are provided directly or purchased. In some cases, the pattern seems to have resulted from historical accident— the presence of a strong organization already delivering a certain service; in others, it evolved by choice. In British Columbia, we encountered some strong sentiment in favor of purchasing services rather than providing them directly. The arguments favoring this approach addressed matters of administrative simplicity and control. Administrators felt they had more control with fewer headaches when they could contract for services and hold a third party accountable.

The strategy for controlling costs seems to revolve on two principal axes—controlling supply and controlling entry. In British Columbia and Manitoba, and to a much more limited extent in Ontario, an area of major control in long-term care is placed at the point of entry. Case management is used as a mechanism for controlling use and hence for controlling cost. Once a client enters the system, his or her utilization hinges primarily on available resources. Supply is controlled by limiting beds within institutions (both the numbers of new beds and the numbers of existing ones authorized for payment), and limiting dollars available to support community services. The role of case management then is to make the most effective use of the resources available.

As the twig is bent, so grows the tree; similarly, the most effective point at which to shape the course of a client's long-term care is at the outset or at critical junctures when a change in status may be required. Such truths seem clear enough; however, if we judge by actual behavior, they are often ignored. For example, when community long-term care funds were restricted in British Columbia, reassessments were cut back or eliminated, being the most vulnerable part of the program, despite the likelihood that such reassessments could have produced savings through reduced authorizations for expenditures.

Ontario has little control over individual access, although overall use is firmly controlled by curbs on supply. What, then, is the benefit to the government of developing a case-managed, single-access system such as Manitoba and British Columbia have? The advantages to the consumer seem clear enough; the systematic approach allows greater fairness in allocation of resources. But from a government perspective, Ontario officials might well ask whether case management will make their system behave more efficiently.

Our findings show no more institutional long-term care use in Ontario than in the other two provinces. Ontario's present system lacks some elements that make case management most necessary. First, home care benefits are still firmly in the health sphere—a "homemaking only" benefit now being discussed would introduce a difficult assessment chore to determine functional needs. New coverage will mean increased demand and a need to control access and distribution of new services. Second, Ontario now has no variability in level of care; case management permits more nuances to be introduced.

It is ultimately almost an article of faith to state that better control through case management would benefit the Ontario government. Case management can help rationalize the pattern of utilization but is not likely to affect supply directly. In the absence of some type of case management, however, simply reducing supply may lead providers to serve some at the expense of others.

Currently, individuals may seek nursing home care on solely a physician's approval; they are limited only by supply constraints. As the queues for nursing home care grow, the clamor for additional beds will be inevitable. Arguably, case management and coordination at the *patient* level prevents some unnecessary institutional placements and creates conditions of confidence that allow supply constraints to continue.

Consumer Choice

Spokespersons in each province were concerned that broad coverage and generous benefits might encourage overuse of the system. Moreover, potential inducements to use institutional care were present in the two provinces where community care was better developed. Because the client copayments for nursing home care were set at a low rate—more than covered by the OAS/GIS—such care could be viewed as highly subsidized housing. (One informant dubbed nursing homes "the cheapest rent in town.") The decision about the level of care needed was made independently of the decision about institutionalization, but case managers could be pressured to recommend a nursing home rather than home care. However, despite the perverse incentives inherent in the system, we were repeatedly reassured that most clients had a strong desire to remain at home as long as possible. This desire served as a deterrent to the financial benefits attached to institutional care.

Properly executed, case management should facilitate consumer choice, except when consumer preferences substantially vary from assessed needs. To permit a choice, there must be alternative modes of services. The greater the range of services and flexibility permitted, the greater the opportunity for choice. The two provinces with well-developed community services and case management provided both the means and the opportunity for choice.

In all three provinces, clients entering nursing homes had at least some opportunity for choice of facility. They were permitted to indicate preferences based on location, ethnicity, ambiance, or other factors. They were automatically placed on the waiting lists of the homes of their choice. Their acceptance of a less desirable, but available, place did not alter their waiting list position for their preferred home.

Conversely, the homes also had freedom of choice. They could accept or reject potential clients. Generally, homes paid on a cost basis were more malleable than those paid on a fixed per diem rate, where the problems of market skimming were akin to those in the United States. The case managers, or coordinators, often played a brokering role, negotiating a placement for difficult clients in exchange for a promise of some easier clients in the future. Again, when the case management system controlled access to nursing homes, the greatest leverage was possible.

One prominent area of consumer preference with regard to nursing homes was the issue of ethnicity. Many persons held strong views about where they wanted to be and with whom. Sometimes these preferences were based on language; more often they were cultural or religious or some combination of these three factors. Cultural preferences raise a basic issue of equity in a publicly funded program. To what extent should such discrimination be permitted? The Canadians appeared to have little difficulty in acknowledging the importance of ethnic difference and the right of the disabled elderly to choose their environments. Although all such preferences could not be accommodated because of space constraints, the principle was clearly recognized.

The philosophy with respect to the separation of the disoriented and the physically frail was less clear. Although client preference was honored here as well, the opportunities for clear choices were not as great because the institutions tended not to separate their clientele. One of the inevitable problems in developing a policy of institutional emphasis and consumer choice is how much specialization is feasible. If there is a strong sense of ethnic identity, it may not be feasible in a circumscribed area to provide separate types of care for each ethnic group. Conversely, clients who are severely disoriented may have less intense, and certainly less perceptible, preferences about the cultural aspects of their surroundings. Thus there is a logic in emphasizing consumer preference for those most able to articulate their choices.

Another set of policies reflect directly on consumer choice and decisionmaking—i.e., policies about retaining a facility bed while a resident is in the hospital or on a short vacation. In all three provinces, the nursing home programs deliberately allowed for such flexibility. The program continued to reimburse facilities while the resident was in the hospital and, to the extent possible, that facility was regarded as the resident's home, to which he or she would return, rather than a bed the client was "occupying." Furthermore, the universal benefit meant that individuals could, for the most part, maintain their own homes while trying out facility care—again accentuating a sense of choice. (This would not ordinarily apply to renters whose own income was limited to GIS/OAS, most of which would be needed to defray the copayment. Even in such cases, however, welfare officials in British Columbia will continue to pay people's rent as long as there is a reasonable expectation that they will return to the community from the hospital or nursing home.) The Manitoba and British Columbia policy of locating day care programs in nursing homes afforded another way for persons to gain first-hand familiarity with a long-term care facility before deciding to move in. "Respite" stays while family caregivers were on vacation provided yet another possibility of getting information in a low-risk way. These policies combined seem to offer more opportunity for legitimate choice and less likelihood that persons will be "placed" as though they are commodities rather than human beings.

Although we must be cautious not to idealize consumer choice in the Canadian programs, they do present a sharp contrast to current United States policies under Medicare and Medicaid. Our Medicare policy provides an incentive to enter a nursing home from the hospital, the worst possible place from which to do shopping. The client has the worst of all worlds; the client is "placed" in an available bed from the hospital with almost no real choice of facility; the client has a disincentive to return home to choose a facility because of the Medicare three-day rule and the limited availability of home care; and if the client finds a facility he or she likes, there is no guarantee that the bed will be retained for the client if he or she is rehospitalized.

Relationship of Long-Term Care to Health and Social Services

As the Canadian long-term care systems are being developed, officials are wrestling with organizational issues. The problems they face offer useful lessons to those working in less developed systems. We do not suggest, however, that all problems should be resolved before implementation, or even that any single approach is clearly best. Indeed, the programs we studied speak to the desirability of taking a policy direction before every detail is worked out. Some of our Canadian informants spoke admiringly of planning techniques and demonstration models used in the United States, and freely acknowledged that health planning in Canada was in a more embryonic state. On the other hand, the Canadian government and the provincial governments, it was pointed out, are more willing than their United States counterparts to commit to a course of action that seems right. They are then prepared to make changes in the context of an operational program.

In all three provinces, there was some fragmentation between health and social service responsibility for long-term care; the fragmentation was less in British Columbia because the unification of these responsibilities into a single provincial ministry and the integrated delivery system for many community health and social services at the local level. In all three provinces, the health components of the long-term care programs were administered separately from acute health care. Such separation resulted in problems both in policy formulation and operation. If both acute and long-term care fall to a single administration at the higher levels of policy-making, planning can better incorporate shifts from one area to the other. However, unless it is possible to trace individual clients in both systems, it may be difficult to estimate the savings that would accrue from various shifts. In practice, none of the provinces had an information system that operationally linked acute and long-term care even within the health department, let alone across the departments of health and social services.

The pattern of fragmentation varied from province to province. In Manitoba, the acute care program and the nursing home program were operated by the provincial Health Services Commission, with good opportunity for exchange of information about those two components. In contrast, the Office of Community Care, which provided case management and authorized both home care and admission to nursing homes, was a separate entity administered in the provincial Department of Health. Both the Health Services Commission and Continuing Care reported to the same Minister.

Similarly, British Columbia has recently evolved a unified long-term care program, which reports to the same Assistant Deputy Minister of Health as does the hospital program.

In Ontario, duplication and lack of coordination were most severe. The acute hospital program, the extended care program, and portions of the home care program are operated by separate entities within the Ministry of Health, but other components of the system, including Homes for the Aged, some homemaking programs, and some community long-term care supportive programs, are operated by the Ministry of Community and Social Services.

Whatever the provincial government's organizational structure, planning was most commonly done for each segment separately until the point where needed extra resources might be appropriated from other ministerially controlled funds. In British Columbia, for example, positions formerly assigned to the acute care sector for nursing services were transferred to long-term care when the latter program got under way. In Ontario, at this writing, a process is being undertaken to move all home care for elderly and physically handicapped individuals to the Department of Health, even if homemaking is the only service needed.

However the relationship between health services and social services is forged, cooperation at the local level is essential to a coherent program. Furthermore, the usual solution of considering long-term care a health program with enriched social service add-ons creates an ironic situation at times. If long-term care is too far separated from acute care, persons receiving long-term care services may sometimes not receive the full benefits of their medical and hospital coverage.

Relationship Between Hospital and Long-Term Care

The hospital is the giant in the health care delivery system, with a commensurate gigantic appetite for resources. There is always a danger that the smaller long-term care program will be reshaped to serve the ends of the hospital rather than to follow the program's own internal priorities. Hospitals in the three provinces had their own discharge-planning apparatus. Sometimes the long-term care programs delegated to hospital personnel the initial assessment of the need for long-term care. Conversely, as in Manitoba, the long-term care programs also locate staff in the hospital to do assessments. But even without formal delegation to hospital personnel, the long-term care program is still heavily reliant on information provided by hospital staff. The incentives of such persons are, therefore, important.

Hospital staff sometimes viewed clients in need of long-term care placement as blocking beds needed for acute care. At the same time, hospital personnel had an incentive to ensure that their *own* chronic or extended hospital beds were full and contained the mix of residents that the hospital preferred. Decisions of hospital personnel about post-hospital placement could be influenced, on the one hand, by the desire to free hospital acute care beds and, on the other hand, to fully deploy hospital chronic care beds. In either case, the functional needs of the elderly person and the best overall placement might have been judged differently by community-based personnel.

In the three Canadian provinces, nonprofit hospitals were paid on a global budget and therefore the long-term patients in the acute hospital bed were in an anomalous role. Although the elderly were sometimes branded as "bed-blockers," hospital administrators recognized that having some such persons in acute beds reduced hospital costs by altering the case mix. Therefore, especially if the hospital's occupancy rate was less than capacity, long-stay patients were not invariably perceived as problems. Indeed, in some areas of the provinces, the long-term care staff complained that referrals were delayed until the patient had been in the hospital for the maximum time allowed for acute care without a status review. Once a patient was in the hospital 30 days, he or she was reviewed for a long-term care designation, after which the hospital would be reimbursed at the chronic care level and the patient would pay a residential copayment. (In Manitoba this step occurs only after the patient is paneled and approved for placement.) Sometimes it would have been in the interest of the patient, however, to have had an earlier review by the long-term care assessor. In short, the pressure to discharge these alleged bed-blockers was less intense than might have been expected.

In Manitoba, the rhetoric about elderly bed-blockers escalated during the 1970s, but researchers examining the bed-blocking situation more closely concluded that the young disabled were as likely to tie up acute care beds as were the elderly (Shapiro, Roos, and Kavanagh 1980). Younger disabled tended to account for the very long stays, and most of the older "bed-blockers" had relatively short waits for discharge. The number of persons awaiting placement in hospitals on any given day might be large, but most of the waits were short.

The failure to link acute and long-term care can have other deleterious consequences. Not only may patients be more aggressively moved from hospital to nursing home, but the reverse may also occur. In none of the provinces are there any incentives to encourage treatment of acute conditions in nursing homes. The general expectation is that, when the patient's care needs exceed the capacity (or the willingness) of the nursing home, the patient will be transferred to the hospital. By contrast, the extended care units operated as part of a hospital are more likely to treat patients for a variety of problems incidental to their chronic debilities. Because nursing home beds are usually held for long periods for patients who might potentially return, no exchange of patients occurs to release acute hospital patients awaiting nursing home admission.

Relationship of Physician Care and Long-Term Care

Perhaps the weakest interface between the acute and long-term care systems relates to the role of the physician. Dominant in acute care, the physician must play an important but not necessarily central role in long-term care. The challenge is how to assure that the client receives appropriate medical attention without medicalizing all the care offered. In the main, long-term care clients are treated like other elderly persons in the society. They receive primary and specialist medical care as their conditions warrant. Institutionalized clients may receive their primary care from their original physician, or a single physician may care for all residents as a matter of convenience. In Manitoba and British Columbia facilities and in Ontario private nursing homes, residents usually retained their own physicians. In Ontario Homes for the Aged, the physician usually was employed by the facility. Patterns seem to differ according to type of community. In rural areas, the physicians doing community practice are very likely to attend in the facilities.

In Manitoba and British Columbia, the central role of the physician in determining the need for long-term care has been reduced. Whereas in Ontario, admission to long-term care is contingent on a physician's indicating the need for it, the case managers in the other two provinces make the decision. Medical information is considered necessary to such decisions, but not sufficient. Even in Ontario, developments suggest a movement away from physician dominance in placement decisions. The relatively new Placement Coordination Services, while still relying heavily on physician-supplied information, are making more systematic determinations about appropriate levels and sources of care. In Ontario, however, a physician's signature is still the necessary and almost sufficient trigger for both the nursing home and home care benefits.

In British Columbia, physician groups expressed alienation at having been deposed from their central position. Part of their hostility was due to their being expected to provide case managers with information on their patients' condition although they were not paid for completing the forms. In our telephone conversations with case management officials in British Columbia, we also discovered that case managers often obtained medical information about such matters as diagnosis, symptoms, medication, and prognosis from the client or the family rather than directly from the physician. This strategem may have represented the "course of least resistance," given physician attitudes, but clearly any strategy that bypasses medical input also does a disservice to the client.

Manitoba has developed its paneling procedure as a mechanism to improve medical input while overseeing case managers' decisions. The panel, which reviews all cases proposed for nursing home care, includes a geriatrician, and cases can be screened to identify those needing more intensive medical evaluation. The long-term care programs can contract with geriatric assessment programs to conduct the more extensive evaluations when indicated. Community physicians are invited to participate in the paneling sessions when their patients are discussed, but few do so. They also receive feedback about panel recommendations when they alter the management plans. The very existence of a paneling system provides an inducement to careful initial evaluations. Of course, once the system is in place, one needs to guard against its becoming perfunctory.

As in the United States, education of general physicians is an important agenda item. In both countries, model geriatric programs have been developed in major university medical centers. We found that Vancouver and Victoria in British Columbia, Winnipeg in Manitoba, and Hamilton, London, Toronto, Ottawa, and Kingston in Ontario all had achieved or were developing some capacity in geriatric medicine, often with the leadership of British-trained geriatricians (although some Canadian physicians have prepared themselves further in geriatrics). During our study period, the city of Ottawa consulted with a Scottish geriatrician, who proposed a regionalization of long-term care delivery in the city emanating from each of the hospitals with a geriatric team at the helm of each unit.

The various geriatric units serve important functions in the system. They literally deliver the geriatric evaluation and treatment services in selected hospitals (already discussed); they train young physicians and medical students and nurses in geriatric medicine; they are a resource to the governments in planning; they give consultation and feedback to community physicians on a case-by-case basis; they offer some medical legitimacy to the field; and they provide a medical reference point for case managers and other nonmedical long-term care personnel. The latter is extremely important; we found that long-term care personnel valued highly the opportunity to interact with the geriatrician.

As in the United States, geriatric medical personnel are few. On the positive side, this means that they are no threat to mainstream medicine. Their roles are *not* in primary care. On the other hand, insufficient capacity for geriatric and psychogeriatric assessment is a problem in the systems. Meanwhile, the gap between geriatric physicians and other primary care providers is considerable, especially in their knowledge of community resources. Physicians did not automatically recommend the various home-based, long-term care programs. All three provinces invested resources to inform physicians about available services. For example, some health units developed attractive brochures informing doctors what home care could do for *them*. Manitoba provincial officials told us that, even in a province as unpopulated and therefore personally oriented as theirs, it took about two years for most doctors to know how to work with the Continuing Care Program. The three provinces combined publicity to physicians with extensive publicity to potential users.

Any similar efforts to launch statewide long-term care benefits in the United States would probably profit by the ingredients we have just discussed: widespread public publicity; widespread physician publicity; some geriatric expertise to provide a focal point for consultation; and some specific mechanisms that *require* long-term care program personnel to communicate with physicians. The fact that the benefits in the three Canadian systems were universal also probably helped hasten the admittedly imperfect physician involvement—the programs affected *all* their patients, not just the poor.

Individual Patterns of Care

One measure of how a community-based system affects the delivery of long-term and acute care is the change in utilization patterns of persons served by such a system. We had hoped that the information systems developed in the several provinces would allow us to link records for individuals and thereby trace changes in utilization patterns. That way we could have determined, for example, whether persons using home care use more or less hospital or nursing home care than the average. Unfortunately, this expectation was not met. The separation of responsibility and jurisdiction noted earlier placed a low priority on such record linkage.

We therefore relied on more limited information derived from several research projects and some special analyses performed on selected samples and covering only portions of the total care spectrum. A small study by Chappell and Blandford (n.d.) suggests that a sample of Manitoba home care clients had significantly more acute hospital stays and more hospital days than did matched community controls, but were less likely to be admitted to nursing homes.

In British Columbia, a pair of health regions has been studied longitudinally to follow persons initially enrolled in the long term care program. Of clients newly enrolled into the program for home care during the first year, 30 percent entered a long-term care facility within the year (Gutman et al. 1979). This figure likely represents an overestimate because some individuals were put on community care as an interim measure associated with enrollment on a long-term care facility waiting list. Subsequent analyses estimated the annual probability of entering a nursing home from community care at about 9 percent for those classified at the lowest level—personal care—and 25 percent for those at higher levels (Lane et al. 1983). The data from the first year's experience suggests that, overall, 46 percent of clients experienced an increase in level of care and 14 percent a decrease during that year. Accurate data on acute hospitalizations were available only for long-term care clients in facilities. During the program's first year, 26 percent of institutionalized long-term care clients were admitted to an acute hospital. Of these, about 60 percent were discharged back to the same level of care and 12 percent died (Stark et al. 1982).

A three-year follow-up of these cohorts reveals some interesting findings. Personal care level clients cared for at home had a higher mortality rate than those treated in a facility; the converse applied to extended care clients. Very few institutionalized personal care residents went home; about 20 percent of those originally treated at home were admitted to a facility by year 3. Overall, about a fourth of those admitted to home care and a fifth of those in facilities were under the same auspices (i.e., home or institution) at the same level of care three years after admission (Stark et al. 1984).

General program data from the British Columbia Long-Term Care Program permit analysis of transition within the LTC Program system to hospitals or hospital-based Extended Care Units. Figure 8.1 illustrates the transitions in status for one representative period. At that time, transitions to and from extended care units in hospitals were outside the long-term care data system so that the extended care figures reflect only extended care level, home care clients, or those in nursing homes and private hospitals funded by the program. The changes over this six-month period show a general trend of movement to more intense levels of care, but in each case there are transitions in the opposite direction as well. The total amount of activity can be approximated by noting that there were 2,528 transitions among about 25,000 persons in nursing homes and 25,000 on home care, or about 13 percent a year. When we recognize that those changes in status occurred at a time when reassessments were curtailed by funding, this level of activity underlines the importance of

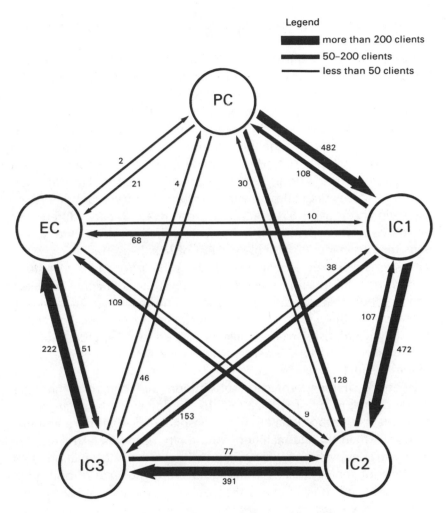

NOTE: This figure shows the number of long-term care clients who changed level of care in a six-month period; both homemaker and institutional clients are included. The levels of care are Personal Care (PC), Intermediate 1, 2, and 3 (IC1, IC2, and IC3), and Extended Care (EC).

Figure 8.1. Long-term care level changes in British Columbia, January 1, 1980 to June 30, 1980.

the reassessment in facilitating appropriate use of long-term care resources.

Researchers in Manitoba established a sample of elderly persons living in the community and in long-term care facilities in 1970. This sample has been used in a number of studies that trace longitudinal changes among the sample, and link such data to other records such as those of the Health Services Commission (Havens and Mossey 1979; Havens and Shapiro 1979; Mossey and Havens 1979; Mossey et al. 1981; Roos, Shapiro, and Roos 1984). Several findings confirm trends also seen in the United States. Hospital utilization increases dramatically with age; there is a threefold difference between those aged 65 to 69 and those 85+. But the differences are much less substantial with regard to physician use. Elderly persons tend to evidence a stable pattern of health-use behavior. Hospital use is clustered among a small group. Within a two-year study period, only 8.5 percent spent more than 30 days in acute hospitals and another 15.5 percent spent some time less than 30 days. In other words, three-fourths of the elderly did not use the hospital at all. Physician visits were similarly clustered; 23 percent of the elderly accounted for 57 percent of physician visits and 56 percent of the hospital days.

Evidence of long-term care substitution for acute care emerges from comparison of utilization by residence. Nursing home residents use proportionately fewer hospital days and more ambulatory visits than do age-matched community residents. This pattern, suggesting substitution, is reinforced by the observation that residents of senior citizens' housing have a higher rate of both physician visits and hospital days than do community or nursing home residents (Roos and Shapiro 1981).

Longitudinal data on nursing home residents suggests some improvement in client status despite the expected average deterioration. Although admission to a nursing home was generally a permanent placement with possible intervening acute hospitalizations, some residents moved to lower levels of care. Six-year survival data show a progression in mortality with initial level of care. Survival rates fall from 70 percent for level 1 to 30 percent for level 2 to less than 20 percent in levels 3 and 4. However, among the survivors, improved levels of care were noted in 8 percent of those admitted at level 2 and 19 percent of those at levels 3 and 4 (Shapiro and Webster 1984).

A possible indication of the impact of the community care program in Manitoba is suggested by data on the source of nursing home admissions. The proportion of residents admitted from home was 74 percent in 1974, the year the community care program began, and only 55 to 63 percent thereafter. This shift may reflect improved capacity to maintain persons at home.

Quality Assurance

Canada resembles Europe more than the United States in its approach to quality assurance. One encounters a much greater belief in the integrity of the system to perform properly. As already noted, there are fewer regulations and more collegial relationships between the regulated and the regulators than are found in the United States. Formal studies on quality of care are not as prevalent. Data on performance are not readily available to the public.

Because most provinces and districts are sparsely populated, most of the government staff feel a personal, direct knowledge about the providers and their strengths and weaknesses. They tend to talk like benevolent parents who use rewards, praise, and chastisement to improve behavior. Sometimes the situation deteriorates too far and stronger measures are needed, but harsh confrontation is rare.

The province in which we encountered the greatest dissatisfaction with quality was Ontario, and most of it was directed toward the proprietary nursing home industry. The system of nursing home inspections has been challenged as too weak. Prior notification allows the home to prepare for the inspection. The results of such inspections are not made public, thus preventing better consumer choice among homes. The voluntary system of accreditation operated by the Canadian Council on Hospital Accreditation is also challenged as self-serving and provider-dominated. Because accreditation is associated with less intense subsequent inspection, the overall effect may be to diminish quality assurance.

As a countermeasure to the provider-dominated lobbying efforts for long-term care, a consumer advocate group, the Concerned Friends of Ontario Citizens in Care Facilities, was formed. It has issued a number of position papers highly critical of nursing home care in Ontario. These reports include lists of deficiencies in all areas of care noted in the Ministry of Health's 1978 "Standards and Guidelines for Activation in Nursing Homes," including lack of a rehabilitative ethos, lack of privacy, lack of choice, unsanitary and unsafe conditions, and inadequate or demeaning social contacts.

Another group that serves an advocacy role for the elderly is the Ontario Advisory Council on Senior Citizens. Organized by the Secretariat of Social Development, it holds regular meetings around the province and publishes a series of reports on varied aspects of social gerontologic interest. It has not taken a strong reformist stance with regard to long-term care, but it has advocated on behalf of various community services for the elderly, including housing.

Auspices

The Canadian health care system reflects a general preference for nonprofit care, either public or private nonprofit. The proprietary institution has not gained as established a position in Canada as it has in the United States. But proprietary operations are not unknown in Canada, especially in long-term care. In both countries, data directly measuring the differences in care provided in institutions or programs operated under proprietary and nonprofit auspices are difficult to obtain. In at least two provinces studied, British Columbia and Ontario, policies about the desirable extent of proprietary long-term care were being reevaluated.

In British Columbia, the initiation of the long-term care program was associated with a deliberate policy to encourage the growth of nonprofit nursing homes. This decision was the product of belief in inherently better quality, but the implementation was catalyzed by financing opportunities for low-interest Canadian government loans to nonprofit organizations.

As in Manitoba, the institutional payment scheme in British Columbia addressed nonprofit and proprietary homes differently. The former were paid on a prospective global budget similar to that used for hospitals; levels of care were used as crude yardsticks but, in general, costs of care were met. There was thus no incentive to economize. By contrast, proprietary homes were paid a fixed rate by level of care. They were expected to provide necessary care within this negotiated rate. Pressures for efficient management, and dangers of skimping on care, were thus more intense. Anticipated complaints about underpricing and unfair competition were heard.

After four years of experience and several changes of government, British Columbia officials have begun to reevaluate the situation. They express open concern about the lack of strong administration, evidenced by many of the nonprofit organizations sponsoring nursing homes and a belief that these organizations have neither the motivation nor the technical ability to reduce expenditures. Although there remains an intrinsic belief that nonprofit groups provide a more attractive environment for long-term care, there are few hard measures of qualitative difference. More and more, we heard long-term care officials speak positively about the management skills of the proprietary firms and the desirability of linking them more effectively to nonprofit operations, perhaps by means of management contracts.

Less overt but still quite palpable was another factor: the nonprofit organizations were less easily influenced by the government. They seemed to exhibit an independent ethos, which contrasted sharply with the more market-oriented stance of the proprietaries, who were eager to find ways of meeting the government's needs.

In the area of community programs in British Columbia, the same distinction in style was evident. Proprietary firms priced their services consistently lower than nonprofit agencies and were usually willing to be more flexible. Despite occasional concern about the quality of some programs, many of the proprietary agencies were highly regarded. Up to the present, the British Columbia and Ontario governments have pursued a careful policy of protecting nonprofit agencies to assure that both types are represented in service delivery. The prevalent belief favors a mixed supplier market by which it is hoped the consumer will benefit in both price and quality.

As described in chapter 5, British Columbia has recently changed its payment system to consolidate the approach for proprietary and nonprofit nursing homes. Both are to be paid on a modified case-mix basis, with preset limits. Similarly, in community programs such as that run by the Vancouver long-term care program, proprietary and nonprofit agencies bid competitively for contracts.

The Ontario situation is quite different. Nursing home care is very heavily a proprietary industry, but that segment of it operated through Homes for the Aged belongs either to municipalities or nonprofit organizations. The latter are financed by the Ministry of Community and Social Services through a complex system that combines a per diem payment for nursing home care with global budgeting for residential care. At least it is more closely tied to costs rather than the fixed per diem rate approach used by the Ministry of Health to pay for nursing home care.

This discrepancy in payment methods and resultant per diem amounts has been the source of great controversy. As long-term care in general has come under closer scrutiny in Ontario, questions are raised about what is really purchased for the substantial difference in cost. The nursing-home industry is quick to argue that it is underpaid for the services provided, but when new franchises are opened, there is active competition for the business. Because the per diem rate is fixed, this competition takes the form of highlighting credentials and promising additional services over and above those mandated at the set price. Somehow the same industry that complains of underpayment is willing to promise to do even more for the same money.

As long-term care comes under closer scrutiny in Ontario, the dual nature of the institutional care has become more obvious. The discrepancy in costs has raised by now familiar questions about what is bought with the extra dollars paid to the nonprofit Homes for the Aged for their nursing home care. The nonprofits describe case-mix differences based on proprietary refusal to admit certain types of patients. They argue that the quality of care is palpably different in proprietary and nonprofit institutions, but the frustrations of similar discussions in other places and earlier times are reflected in the contemporary Ontario debate. Although there is active testimony from consumer groups about the inadequacies of proprietary facilities (and some nonprofit ones as well), systematic differences in services or measures of quality have not been demonstrated. A major study by the Ontario government purportedly comparing services and quality in nursing homes and homes for the aged has been undertaken but findings are yet unavailable.

The more anecdotal data of consumer groups on behalf of the elderly offer strident indictments of conditions in Ontario nursing homes. The Concerned Friends of Ontario Citizens in Care Facilities cite a long list of deficiencies. Their complaints go beyond the usual catalogue of concomitants of institutionalization to suggest a closed system that denies information to families, threatens retribution for complaints, and offers care to only the minimally impaired. They argue vehemently that compassionate chronic long-term care is inconsistent with profitmaking and urge community nonprofit sponsorship for nursing homes.

In the absence of hard data on differences in quality between proprietary and nonprofit institutions, the debate becomes primarily philosophic. The experience across the three provinces suggests that proprietary auspices are not *ipso facto* bad, but the potential for abuse is greatest where controls are weak or where the proprietary segment has a monopoly. The balanced-market approach of Manitoba and British Columbia (the former in the institutional sector and the latter in community care as well) represents a productive way of maintaining some of the potential advantages of proprietary management. This balance is achieved in Ontario by the use of Homes for the Aged as sources of extended care, but at the cost of confusion and inconsistency.

The most compelling argument for nonprofit sponsorship is the potential for public accountability. Board members of nonprofit organizations derive gratification from the esteem of their peers in the community. That respect is directly related to the reputation of the institution. Proprietary boards pursue different agendas related to profits and are accountable to a different constituency. However, the pride that motivates nonprofit agencies may also produce conflict with government agendas. The belief in what they are doing may render nonprofit organizations less malleable. By contrast, proprietary groups, viewing the government as the influential shaper of the marketplace, will make great efforts to accommodate to proposed changes as a means of increasing their market share. Governments may view the malleability of the proprietary sector as an unmitigated advantage, but checks and balances for an excessively parsimonious government may come best from nonprofit providers.

As pressures for funds grow, the tolerance for the more open-ended budgeting available to nonprofit organizations will diminish. We can already see this shift in Ontario and British Columbia. Nonprofits will thus be increasingly treated like proprietary groups and competition will be inevitable. It is not clear whether the nonprofit groups can survive such competition and retain their ethos without special protections. Their strength, their public accountability, becomes their liability in a price-cutting competitive environment where the quality of the service must be trimmed. Given the amorphous nature of long-term care but the fundamental belief that it must include items beyond those of basic technical quality, such a reduction becomes counterproductive. The best compromise from the perspective of both clients and government is a reorganized nonprofit sector that uses efficient management but preserves community accountability.

Pushing the Limits of Community Care

The experience with community care in Manitoba and British Columbia provides important lessons about the art of the possible. It is equally important, however, to appreciate what these observations have not shown. By a variety of case management strategies, they have controlled home care expenditures and utilization. Avid advocates of community care might ask about the effects of even more aggressive pursuit of this mode of long-term care. What might happen if more resources were deliberately shunted to community care?

In British Columbia, and to a lesser extent in Manitoba, case managers worked within budgetary constraints. The amounts spent on home care were considerably less, for individuals and in aggregate, than the sums spent for nursing home care. In exceptional cases, more generous community resources were expended for short periods, but the overriding goal was parsimony.

Rigorous experimental studies have established the feasibility of maintaining persons at home who would otherwise be admitted to nursing homes. At the broader programmatic level, the decision to increase the allowable allocations for home care seem destined to raise costs over the short run. Targeting services is always an issue.

The greater the resources available to expend, the greater the need for careful case management, with consequently smaller case loads.

The only foreseeable scenario by which substantially increased efforts directed toward community care would seem likely to reduce total long-term care costs is as part of a deliberate strategy to dramatically reduce the supply of institutional beds. This could be done most simply, but least easily, by removing a nursing home bed from the funded pool each time a well-supported community client is enrolled. Alternatively, one could pursue a longer-range investment strategy by committing the system to more community support and constraining any new growth in nursing home beds. Either approach must contend with the political and social realities, which currently push persons into institutions.

Even in the best-case scenario, a substantial number of people who require institutional care will remain. Extrapolations based on varied experience suggest that aggressive community care will not reduce the rate of institutional use by more than 50 percent, but halving the current rate would be no mean feat.

Concluding Comment

Our overall conclusions about the three Canadian provinces are positive. Collectively, they seem to show that persons and organizations of good will can grapple with long-term care and produce a program that both the country and the individual users can afford. A momentum can be developed for an ever-improving system in both qualitative and efficiency terms.

What of the translation to the United States? Clearly, we cannot adopt Canadian approaches bodily. We do not at present enjoy universal health insurance as an underpinning to any long-term care program that might be developed. The current atmosphere is one of intense cost-containment, and it is all too likely that any proposed additions in long-term care benefits—either universal or residual—will need to be sold on the basis that money will be saved in some other service sector. The concluding chapter takes us back to the world of Medicare and Medicaid and Diagnosis-Related Groups for hospital reimbursement and explores possible avenues for us in the United States to get from where we are now toward the sorts of long-term care programs that Canadians have today.

REFERENCES

Chappell, N. L. and A. Blandford, n.d. "Adult Day Care: Its Impact on the Utilization of Other Health Services and Quality of Life." Mimeo.

Gutman, G. M., A. J. Stark, and K. H. Sun 1979. "Transactions for Long-Term Care Clients in Two Study Areas, 1978: Analyses and Discussion." Mimeo.

Havens, B. and J. Mossey 1979. "Health Care Use Behaviors Among the Elderly." Paper presented at the Gerontological Society 32d Annual Meetings, Washington, D.C., November 26, 1979.

Havens, B. and E. Shapiro 1979. "Longitudinal Research of Health Care Utilization by Aging Manitobans." Paper presented at Canadian Association on Gerontology Meetings, Halifax, Nova Scotia, November 3, 1979.

Lane, D., D. Uyeno, A. Stark, E. Kliewer, and G. Gutman 1983. "Forecasting Requirements for Long-Term Care." Mimeo.

Mossey, J. M. and B. Havens 1979. "Health Care Use Among the Elderly: An 8 Year Longitudinal Study." Paper prepared for the Annual Meeting of the Gerontological Society, Washington, D.C., November 26, 1979.

Mossey, J. M., B. Havens, N. P. Roos, and E. Shapiro 1981. "The Manitoba Longitudinal Study on Aging: Description and Methods." Gerontologist, 21(5):551–558.

Mossey, J. M. and E. Shapiro 1982. "Self-Rated Health: A Predictor of Mortality Among the Elderly." American Journal of Public Health, 72(8):800–808.

Roos, N. P. and E. Shapiro 1981. "The Manitoba Longitudinal Study on Aging: Preliminary Findings on Health Care Utilization by the Elderly." Medical Care, 19(6):644–657.

Roos, N. P., E. Shapiro, and L. L. Roos 1984. "Aging and the Demand for Health Services: Which Aged and Whose Demand?" Gerontologist, 24(1):31–36.

Shapiro, E. and N. P. Roos 1981. "The Geriatric Long-Stay Hospital Patient: A Canadian Case Study." Journal of Health Politics, Policy and Law, 6(1):49–61.

Shapiro, E., N. P. Roos, and S. Kavanagh 1980. "Long Term Patients in Acute Care Beds: Is There a Cure?" Gerontologist, 20(3):342–349.

Shapiro, E. and L. Webster 1984. "Nursing Home Utilization Patterns for All Manitoba Admissions from 1974 to 1981." Gerontologist 24(6):610–615.

Stark, A. J., G. M. Gutman, and B. McCashin 1982. "Acute-Care Hospitalizations and Long-Term Care: An Examination of Transfers." Journal of the American Geriatric Society, 30(8):509–515.

Stark, A. J., E. Kliewer, G. M. Gutman, and B. McCashin 1984. "Placement Changes in Long-Term Care: Three Years' Experience." American Journal of Public Health, 74(5):459–463, 1984.

CHAPTER 9

Lessons for the United States

THIS chapter identifies lessons that might be exportable to the United States from the Canadian experience. A general note of caution is appropriate at the outset: importing anything from abroad, whether products or ideas, has its hazards. Both have to be modified to fit the peculiarities of the American situation.

America is a unique place. Its fundamental entrepreneurial ethos distinguishes it from other western countries. The comments of a British geriatrician returning from a visiting professorship in the United States reinforce this comment (Evans 1982). He remarked that despite humanitarian ideals, good research, and innovative programs, the United States is hindered in producing a system to deal with the needs of the elderly because of ideological barriers. Foremost among these barriers were two assumptions: (1) that people should provide during productive years for any disability, and thus using statutory social and health services represents a personal failure, and (2) that when services are to be provided, they should be contracted out to professionals or agencies rather than organized directly by governments.

Some extrapolations can follow directly from the observations made during our Canadian study. Other possibilities are suggested by what we saw in Canada, but the ideas require modifications before they can be translated into an American social climate.

The Art of the Possible

Even a cursory look at the Canadian experience provides much-needed reassurance. It is indeed feasible to expand long-term care without threatening national bankruptcy, and, given proper controls, this should be true in the United States context as well. Affordable long-term care can be offered as an entitlement rather than a welfare benefit based on personal insolvency. Although one may argue about the best way to organize such care, the Canadian experience suggests that we should move rapidly toward making it available in the United States, even if we have to refine the delivery system later on.

One key to the Canadian programs is the foundation of a universal health insurance scheme to which long-term care programs have been appended. Long-term care was viewed as another component of health care addressed to chronic illness. The strength of this approach lies in the centralization and unification of payment, which provides the government with a great deal of control in planning and promoting different types of care. It has also avoided the welfare stigma.

A corollary of establishing feasibility is examining how problems are defined. The difference between the Canadian and American responses to essentially the same demographic pressures is instructive. The aging of the United States population has been looked upon as a fiscal crisis. The effectiveness of programs is measured by their ability to control costs. In the determined effort to reduce expenditures, it is all too easy to forget that you cannot be efficient until you are effective. Less is not always better.

At risk of oversimplification, it appears that Canadians are more likely than we are to approach long-term care primarily as a question of how to meet the service needs of the functionally impaired. Some service is assumed to be needed for the elderly population; the issue is how to provide it decently and efficiently. Public and scientific statements in Canada are calmer than the crisis-oriented pronouncements in the United States. On both sides of the border, the projected growth of the "old-old" population is recognized; but Canadian analysts make frequent reference to offsetting reductions in the numbers of other dependent groups, especially children, when they write about the needs of the elderly over the next decades.

The way we shape questions about long-term care starts us on our search for answers. A favorite question in the United States concerns how to keep the Medicare trust fund solvent despite the approaching hordes of elders. But if we start from the question, "How can we save Medicare?"—and if we persist in the usual assumption that no general revenues should be used to save it—it is hard to generate a long-term care system. It is more meaningful to ask: What are the health needs and long-term care needs in the United States? How well does Medicare meet any or all of these needs?

Beyond the Demonstration Project

We looked at the Canadian experience as a means of complementing the results of circumscribed demonstration projects at home. It appears that the results are consistent, or at least compatible. Providing community-based long-term care does not inevitably reduce institutional care utilization. The use of nursing homes is essentially a product of their availability. Hence the most effective means of controlling nursing home use is by rationing supply.

Despite the centrality of supply in dictating nursing home use, community care can still affect institutional utilization in the long run. The additive vs. substitutive dichotomy is too simplistic a formulation. Indeed, social research results can easily be misinterpreted, given a failure to recognize the dynamic nature of the environment. In contrast to physical science, causal relationships are not fixed; rather, the major players adjust their behavior to adapt to changed circumstances. Although one cannot realistically expect that the addition of one type of service will automatically displace another, the availability of the new program provides a climate for more purposeful action toward the desired end. In the case of community care, its very presence creates a social and political climate conducive to pursuing a deliberate policy of controlling institutional supply. The role of community care in this instance is not causal but enabling. It facilitates carrying out a desired policy.

This lesson is important for those planning long-term care in the United States. Unless those who operate the system have control, the system is unlikely to work as promised. We cannot count on effects resulting simply from displacement of one care modality by another. Thus, centralized funding again emerges as a critical component needed to shape the long-term care program.

A major difference between the Canadian experience and that of the American demonstrations is one of scope. The demonstration project is built around services delivered to a defined group (e.g., several hundred people), usually for a circumscribed period. The operational program covering a geopolitical unit, like a province or a county, must contend with the whole context of the area—the suppliers as well as the consumers of service. In such systems, actions taken have effects over the full enterprise. Displacing an individual from a nursing home queue may increase overall utilization if the next person in line uses the service. Conversely, few circumscribed demonstrations have the opportunity to affect supply; they operate by redirection. In contrast, the province-wide programs offered both the scope and the permanence to change the shape of the system.

Introducing new or expanded programs cannot be achieved by simply reallocating extant resources. New money was added to the system to support new ventures. The inflow of money was controllable, but it is misleading to suggest that long-term care programs can be established in the community without new investment. The critical question is whether such expenditure will lead to subsequent savings. At the broad population level, as noted above, such a result is more a question of political resolve than automatic substitution.

Long-Term Care as a Social Program

Long-term care is, by definition, a hybrid between health and social services. This is inevitable because long-term care is an undifferentiated mixture of what is needed to improve functioning or to compensate for functional impairments. In the United States, current long-term care arrangements are criticized both because they are *too* medically oriented (i.e., the benefits are nested in expensive and sometimes inhumane medical programs while obvious social needs remain unmet) and also because they are *insufficiently* medically oriented. Timely and appropriate medical diagnosis and treatment are often lacking, with social services and residential placements used to compensate for functional disabilities without earlier medical efforts to improve that functioning. Although the benefits for long-term care were more generous and accessible in the provinces studied than in the United States, these polar problems of too much or too little medical or social involvement remained.

Organizationally, it is possible to handle long-term care in several ways: (1) it may be considered a health program and placed in a health organization; (2) it may be considered a social service program and placed in a social service department; (3) components of long-term care can be divided and assigned to either health or social service departments, leading to dual responsibility; or (4) a new department of long-term care can be created either as a freestanding unit or a unit in the health or social services department. If a long-term care program is placed entirely or largely in the department of health, an additional question arises about whether the program should be administered as a distinct entity or as a part of an integrated health program where dollars are moved about flexibly. Proponents of integrating acute and long-term care services have proposed an extension of Medicare benefits to cover long-term care under a "Title XXI" of the Social Security Act (Somers 1982).

The placement of long-term care within the health aegis was a politically logical progression in Canada, but is not necessarily the only or the best placement. Despite health sponsorship, there remains a clear and regrettable separation of long-term care and acute care. The regularity of this finding leads us to question the organizational wisdom of that sponsorship. If health sponsorship is not sufficient to bring long-term care into the mainstream of medicine, perhaps it is because long-term care does not belong in medical care (Gillick 1984).

Long-term care could be approached as a social service. This term is used in its generic form to apply to societal concerns. It is not intended to connote any form of welfare or charity. In fact, if the choice of sponsorship or management lies between public welfare as is known in the United States today and health, we believe the latter is a better choice. The National Study Group on State Medicaid Strategies (1983) has, in essence, taken this position in recommending a division of the Medicaid program into two distinct components: a federally financed and administered National Primary Health Care Program and a state-administered Continuing Care System.

Purely medical models of long-term care are rare. A close approximation is represented by the British geriatric medicine service, although it, too, must interact with an independent social services system for much of community and residential care. Even though the medical specialty of geriatrics is well developed in England, it has yet to gain wide acceptance as an intergrated part of acute medicine. At the same time, the long-stay hospitals managed by the geriatric specialists tend to be rigid and sterile, addressing care from a technical aspect rather than providing an alternative lifestyle. Visitors to England are usually ushered to the "old people's homes," which are operated as social service programs and where the home-like atmosphere impresses the viewers.

A socially based system of long-term care has much to commend it. Long-term care as a health program leads to second-class health care. By contrast, provision of long-term care under social auspices does not imply any loss of benefits for medical care or hospital care under universal health entitlements. Long-term care clients would continue to receive health care on the basis of their medical needs, but the overall coordination of the services related to their functional dependency would rest elsewhere. The long-term care client would have an additional set of advocates to urge more intensive medical attention to appropriate problem areas. Organized coordinating mechanisms, like Manitoba's paneling process, may further facilitate coordination between health and social care. It is important to distinguish between general management and medical care. The program would be directed at maximizing functioning by combining medical treatment with environmental manipulation. In the hands of case managers without prejudices toward one mode over another, it would permit creative solutions.

In Canada, as in the United States, long-term care was initially viewed as a logical extension of acute hospital care—a sort of infirmary overflow to reduce the "unnecessary" use of expensive hospital beds. With the growth of the elderly segment and the recognition that long-term care has an intrinsic time frame, not merely one relative to hospital time, the issue of hospital displacement was itself displaced. The imposition of Diagnosis-Related Groups (DRGs) has once again raised interest in long-term care as a means of reducing acute hospital use. The Canadian data offer some encouragement in this regard. Aggregate data suggest an increase in long-term care use correlated with a reduction in acute care, but the critical intervening variable seems to be supply.

The Canadian system wherein the extended care, or chronic hospital, component of institutional care remains within the acute care sector is very similar to the original intentions of the Medicare program in the United States. If long-term care were to emerge as a social program, some comparable arrangement would be necessary. The result might closely resemble the proposal offered by Bruce Vladeck (1980) after his review of the American nursing home scene. Under the current pressure from the new prospective payment arrangements based on DRGs there is already movement toward vertical intergration of acute hospitals and nursing homes (as has occurred in rural Manitoba). The opportunities for cross-subsidization seem greatest in this arena.

How then do we avoid recreating the second-class care system of the Medicaid era? The more attractive solution seems to lie in developing a first-class social program rather than a second-class medical approach. The critical difference is the imposition of universal coverage in place of a welfare model. The universal entitlement element does not. automatically imply that the program need be funded exclusively from tax revenues. Various forms of premiums can be collected using different strategies. The result should be a centralized resource pool, which can then be used to support an organized effort to provide care for the disabled elderly. Decisions can be made about how to distribute the resources. These decisions may vary geographically and temporally to allow program flexibility to meet local situations.

Social operation is not inconsistent with health sponsorship. Long-term care funds are most likely to be successfully obtained from a reallocation of health dollars. The critical element is to make the allocation decision at a policy level rather than leave it to practitioners who face constant demands for service. The several provinces illustrate mechanisms by which this reallocation can be accomplished by program budgeting, but such budgeting requires an ability to set bounds to spending. The open-ended health-budgeting approach is not consistent with allocation strategies.

Health funds are the most likely source of long-term care dollars for several reasons. The health budget is large. Investment in long-term care does seem to yield savings in acute care, especially hospital care. Precedents already exist in areas like acute home care. However, these resource allocation decisions must be recognized as very different from the decisions that can be made on the firing line. Aaron and Schwartz (1984) point to health care rationing decisions in the United Kingdom that work only because those closest to the actual sources of care are protected from having to deny that care.

The social long-term care program would cover the costs of providing a mix of services to those elderly needing assistance in maintaining independence. If, as we hope, community-based care is viewed as the preferred modality of service, institutional care would then be treated as a secondary choice when the preferred modality was not feasible. The housing component of institutional care could then be addressed as a housing cost. Personal funds should support this component to the same extent that these funds could have paid for noninstitutional housing. Where subsidies are financially required, they should be provided in the same manner that rent subsidies are offered.

Separating extended hospital care and social long-term care creates a new need for communication between systems. At some point, some individuals will move from chronic medical care to long-term care and vice versa. However, the shift is not necessarily any greater than that faced by an individual entering the medical system from the general population.

Developing a socially based program with universal entitlement in the United States would mean taking a giant stride. The United States does not yet have in place a program of universal health insurance, and now we are proposing a universal program for long-term care. But the concept is not without precedent. For most of this century, indeed, we have had a universal benefit for education and at least a basic universal benefit for almost all elderly Americans through Social Security.

Need for Decentralization

Another major lesson from Canada concerns program scale. Although Canada is geographically larger than the United States, its total population is analogous to that of California. Some Canadian provinces have populations more akin to many United States counties. In Canada, long-term care is largely a provincial issue and even then it is administered at more local levels. As is the case in Europe, although policies can be made centrally, the program's operation requires active local control (Kane and Kane 1976).

Extrapolating to the United States, we see the need for programs built around manageable geopolitical units generally smaller than a state. The federal role would be heavily weighted toward financing—probably in some sharing arrangement with the states— and the assurance of minimal program guidelines and standards that provide at least a floor of equity for the program. This pattern has been established in the United States with other programs such as Medicaid.

Community Care

The Canadian experience offers further solace to advocates of community care. Providing such a benefit with broad coverage of homemaker services as well as nursing did not lead to runaway utilization. The use of such services is controllable by relatively simple case management, and control becomes easier as the shape of the program and concomitant public expectations become established.

Community care emerges as a flexible component of long-term care, sometimes to its detriment. When budget restrictions are imposed, it is easier to cut back on community care by limiting resources to each case management unit than to close beds. (Ironically, when service dollars are thus reduced, the case management agencies sometimes reduce case management activities such as reassessments, thereby vitiating their assertions about its efficacy.) But more optimistically, community services can be created more easily than some have suggested. The short lag time between the introduction of a community care program in British Columbia and the response of community agencies ready to provide services suggests that such programs can be mounted with little delay where potential foci of organization exist already.

The heart of the community care programs is homemaking services. A small number of people needed hands-on nursing, but the overwhelming majority needed only assistance with basic tasks. Nursing and other therapist needs, if present, are more likely to be episodic. In all three provinces, homemaking programs were operated as social agencies rather than health programs and maintained separately from the home nursing services. In many instances, the amount of care needed weekly was quite modest, sometimes only a few hours. These small aliquots of service, often provided to supplement informal care, were viewed as critical to an individual's remaining at home. Although scientifically sound data to support these contentions are lacking, the strength of conviction of both providers and recipients is impressive. At the very least, such observations raise an important note of caution for those who urge more active restriction of services toward clients who have great gaps between service needs and extant resources.

The Rise of Corporate Medicine

Starr (1983) has identified the last quarter of this century as the era of corporate medicine in America. Within both the proprietary and nonprofit sectors, there is a clear pattern of consolidation. As already noted, prospective reimbursement of hospitals has stimulated their interest in acquiring control of long-term care resources to alleviate inpatient utilization. But this tendency to vertical integration had already begun before the introduction of DRGs. Firms had recognized the advantages of controlling various levels of care to diversify investments.

At the same time, there has been a horizontal integration for reasons of economy. Chains of facilities have come under single management with joint purchasing and common procedures. As a few of these corporations grow to vast size, the long-term care industry becomes consolidated in the hands of a few powerful giants with great leverage.

Certainly the image of corporate care conjures up impersonal, inflexible, cookie-cutter care. Regulatory efforts are more likely to confront powerful political and economic opposition. The balance between system control and provider control will favor the latter.

The existing providers already represent an active and often effective lobby. At the individual professional level, they often represent forces to maintain the status quo. Any efforts to modify the system will have to contend with these influences. Moreover, the greater the extent of change proposed, the more intense is the opposition to be expected. The coalescence of large corporations will thus produce a politically potent force opposed to any increased role for government, especially one that threatens to systematize care.

The above formulations discourage those wishing to reform nursing home care. A resigned sense that present conditions are inevitable seems to permeate policy discussions. However, the longer action is delayed, the harder it will be to take action. Government has several strong cards: its position of major purchaser and, just as important, the instinctive and natural alliance of large segments of the general public. The level of public discontent with the state of public support for long-term care should not be underestimated as a force toward change, if channeled appropriately.

Proprietary vs. Nonprofit

The controversy around the role of proprietary organizations in long-term care was not resolved by our look at Canada. Each province had a mixed portfolio of proprietary and nonprofit providers, although the proportions varied. Despite the concerns about the excess costs of nonprofit care, there is also an appreciation that it represents a different form of care. On the basis of national character, one would expect Canada to be more inclined toward nonprofit sponsorship than is the United States. Hospital care there is certainly much less proprietary than in the United States, but medical care remains predominantly in the private practice mode.

The extrapolation from our experience favors a mixed long-term care economy that encourages productive competition between proprietary and nonprofit agencies. But the competition requires that both types of agencies be paid on the same basis. This prerequisite threatens to place the nonprofit programs at substantial risk, especially when there is some question about whether the two sponsors provide the same product to the same groups. To offset this danger, the government may want to assure the balance by setting minimum proportions of representation by nonprofits or considering some other form of subsidy that would not encourage inefficient management.

In the United States, the issue is how to stimulate the growth, or survival, of nonprofit agencies. The future of proprietary agencies in the United States is uncertain. As long-term care has become the fastest growing segment of the health care industry, it has attracted

a great deal of interest from business. There is something discon-
certing about reading, in the business section of newspapers, that
long-term care is a good place for investing venture capital.

There is no a *priori* reason to suppose that nonprofit agencies cannot compete effectively with proprietary ones, if they compete on
the same terms. Left unfettered, the Canadian nonprofits, which
were paid on a cost-reimbursement basis, tended to eschew concerns about costs. There is clearly slack to be taken up in management practices. In some instances the nonprofits seem more willing
to take the difficult cases and subsidize the necessary, but unpaid,
costs associated with them. However, even this is not universal.
The opposite experience of high selectivity of admission policies in
nonprofit homes was noted in Vancouver.

Although there is no clear evidence of any demonstrable difference in quality of care between proprietary and nonprofit nursing
homes, the studies performed to date are not very good. In part we
lack sensitive measures of quality, certainly ones that can be derived
from easily retrievable data sources. Nonetheless, it is difficult to
believe that a board of directors responsible for returning a profit to
its stockholders will not behave differently from one in which the
only benefit board members receive is the pride of association with
the enterprise.

Role of Competition

America's entrepreneurial ethic has led to a strong faith in competition and the free marketplace as a means of assuring quality and
reducing cost. This confidence may well be misdirected in the case
of long-term care. Competition in medical and social services is
more likely to produce duplication and gaps in service as various
providers compete for the most lucrative markets and leave others
uncovered. With a product as unspecific as long-term care, it is
particularly unrealistic to expect the consumers to fend for themselves. When decisions are made in times of crisis, the likelihood of
careful shopping is even more remote.

The contention that a simplistic reliance on competition is
unworkable does not mean there is no role for the concept. Quite
to the contrary, competition can be used effectively to achieve

desired social ends, but there must be some general system in place to define that direction. The Vancouver Long-Term Care Program's use of the bidding procedure for home-care agencies is a good example of how a program can use competitive bidding to move the system in a desired direction. By contrast, the absence of overall direction in Ontario has produced redundancy and competition for cases, with resultant excess capacity in some places and not enough in others.

The United States lacks the guidance system to effectively direct competition in long-term care. The critical missing link in using competition productively in the United States is organizations that can assume both authority and responsibility for defined populations. These populations are best defined in terms of geopolitical areas to assure coverage and to avoid selection bias. Within this framework, various competitive strategies can be employed. Some will feature competition among different providers of the same service. Others will foster competition among various modalities of care to serve the same problems or clients.

Case Management

As long as we spend public dollars—and a basic message of this book is that we need to spend more public funds on long-term care—we will need some mechanism to control those expenditures and exercise responsibility for the most effective use of available resources. Two of the provinces studied developed extensive case management programs, and the third is moving to do so. Their experience confirms that case management *is* a desirable programmatic direction. Case management is also a mainstay of long-term-care demonstrations in the United States (Capitman et al. 1983; Greenberg, Doth, and Austin 1981; Baxter et al. 1983), and several states have introduced or proposed a case-management function for Medicaid clients and users of in-home supportive services (Toff 1981; Kane 1984). Our Canadian study reinforces the importance of case management and suggests some characteristics to be cultivated and others to be avoided.

Certain criteria can be proposed for a case management system. Not all of these are necessarily represented by any one of the programs encountered. Rather they form a composite of the best of several.

Independence from Providers. If the program also provides care, it will encounter conflicts of interest. One of the prime characteristics of case management is objectivity. The more decisions are left to professional judgment, the more critical is the capacity for objective decisions.

Coverage of a Defined Population. To meet this criterion, the program should be designed to cover a defined geopolitical region. First, this provides a visible program with a mechanism for accountability. Second, this minimizes the capacity for selection bias and provides a stronger relationship with the various provider agencies in an area. Target groups must also be defined. The British Columbia and Manitoba programs rather easily incorporated almost all adults with functional needs in the same case-managed financing system. British Columbia's program has recognized, however, that skills and resources for assisting the mentally disabled and the mentally ill qualitatively differ from those needed for the frail elders and physically disabled. The program has changed several times in an effort to determine the best way to provide case management and program responsibility for those populations but, in general, specialized personnel have carried the responsibility in British Columbia and Manitoba. Similarly, some Ontario home care programs have developed specialized care coordination (e.g., for hospice). The key seems to be clearly defined target groups and making sure that nobody in need falls through the cracks.

Control over Resources. The so-called "broker" model, whereby the case manager can only suggest care, is impotent. To succeed, case management needs responsibility and authority.

Sensitivity to Client Preferences. The recommendations for care should be based on client needs and preferences. The decisionmaking should separately ascertain the level of care needed, the type of care needed, and the best source for that care. Client preferences are especially germane for the latter.

Minimizing Hospital-Based Decisions. Hospitalization is an inopportune context in which to make decisions about how much long-term care is needed and where it should be delivered. The assessment of functioning tends to be inaccurate, and the patient's own chance for decisionmaking is minimized. Hospital personnel are often under pressure to facilitate discharge as expeditiously as possible. In any event, they are rarely well-positioned to make community arrangements. The two case-managed systems we studied tried to minimize decisions being made from the hospital and by hospital personnel. The Canadian case managers tried to give some priority for facility admission to persons at home over and above persons in hospitals, so that there would be no disincentive to "go home and try it." Powerful as the hospital is, it should not hold all the cards in long-term care planning. We are tempted to propose a redrafting of the Medicare requirement for a maximum hospital stay of three days, before nursing home care is covered, to require that the patient go home for three days before a nursing home is considered.

Case management is a popular concept in the United States today. Indeed, it has assumed a "trendy" legitimacy as the mechanism of choice to manage Medicaid long-term care expenditures. It is important to distinguish, however, between a case management program for a universal public benefit as opposed to a residual means-tested benefit like Medicaid. If case managers must keep "hands off" until people have exhausted their resources in the private market, the impact of case management on the overall system is blunted. It becomes too little too late.

In advocating case management, we are not necessarily recommending a complex system. Inevitably, case managers will use professional judgment in their planning process. Because of the concern in the United States over the potential for litigation, there has been a tendency to rely on complex forms and elaborate decision models; completing the form is more arduous than working on the decision. What is much more desirable is a format that emphasizes common language and definitions but avoids pseudoscientific decision algorithms. Case management, as it evolved in Canada, is inevitably an inexact science that must rely on common sense, good will, and a responsive stance on the part of the case manager.

Creative Tinkering

Various pundits on the American long-term care scene have described its evolution as "creative tinkering." This term refers to development of various segments individually, responding to particular deficiencies or crises of the moment. The result is a disjointed program in which each action is associated with an effort to exploit the new opportunity and often a need for countermeasures to stem that zeal. An occasional by-product of this approach is the spawning of yet another interest group determined to expand its holdings in long-term care.

These observations give us pause in suggesting modest next steps for improving the current situation. Surely, many would agree that long-term care in the Canadian provinces we studied has enviable features: It is more balanced between community and institutional care; costs are subsumed as part of health costs that remain lower than those in the United States; and the real risk of catastrophic financial disaster for individuals and families faced with long-term care needs is incurred by the social collectivity rather than the individual.

How are we in the United States to proceed from where we are now to a state closer to the ideal? Suggestions like expanding Medicare benefits to include long-term care, or conducting more active experimentation with programs like Social Health Maintenance organizations, represent tinkering in the right direction, but they are not likely to bring about the necessary reforms.

We advocate a system which at first appears paradoxical. Long-term care should be run as a social program, but funded out of health dollars. The necessary condition for a meaningful and workable long-term care program is universal entitlement for people of all ages for hospital and medical care as well as long-term care. Without this broad base of coverage in an entrepreneurial environment, we will encounter segmented development of covered services or covered populations. The burdens of financing will be disproportionately distributed while the capacity to control costs will be severely threatened.

Long-term care is a test of national character. The way we provide for our disabled elderly reveals a great deal about our social values. What is required is an expression of national will. The Canadian experience has shown the way.

REFERENCES

Aaron, H. J. and W. B. Schwartz. 1984. *The Painful Prescription: Rationing Hospital Care.* Washington, D.C.: The Brookings Institution.

Baxter, R. J., R. Applebaum, J. J. Callahan, Jr., J. B. Christianson, and S. L. Day. 1983. *The Planning and Implementation of Channeling: Early Experiences of the National Long Term Care Demonstrations.* Mathematica Policy Research.

Capitman, J. et al. 1983. *Preliminary Report on Work in Progress: Evaluation of Coordinated Community-Oriented Long-Term Care Demonstration Projects.* Berkeley, Calif.: Berkeley Planning Associates.

Evans, J. G. 1982. "Anglo-American differences in cure for the elderly: Reflections on a visiting professorship." *Journal of the American Geriatrics Society,* 30:348–351.

Gillick, M. R. 1984. "Is the Care of the Chronically Ill a Medical Prerogative?" *New England Journal of Medicine,* 310:190–193.

Greenberg, J. N., D. Doth, and C. Austin. 1981. *Comparative Study of Long-Term Care Demonstration Projects: Lessons for Future Inquiry,* Minneapolis: University of Minnesota Center for Health Services Research.

Kane, R. A. In press. "Testimony on Reauthorization of the Older Americans Act Presented to the Subcommittee on Aging of the Senate Committee on Labor and Human Resources." Government Printing Office, Washington, D.C.: GPO.

Kane, R. L. and R. A. Kane. 1976. *Long-Term Care in Six Countries: Implications for the United States,* DHEW Publ. NIH 76–878. Government Printing Office, Washington, D.C.: GPO.

National Study Group on State Medicaid Strategies. 1983. *Restructuring Medicaid: An Agenda for Change.* Washington, D.C.: Center for the Study of Social Policy.

Somers, A. R. 1982. "Long-Term Care for the Elderly and Disabled: A New Health Priority," *New England Journal of Medicine,* 307:221–226.

Starr, P. 1983. *Social Transformation of American Medicine.* New York: Basic Books.

Toff, G. E. 1981. *Alternatives to Institutional Care for the Elderly: An Analysis of State Initiatives.* Intergovernmental Health Policy Project, Washington, D.C.

Vladeck, B. G. 1980. *Unloving Care: The Nursing Home Tragedy.* New York: Basic Books.

APPENDIX A

Income Maintenance Programs in Canada

BEGINNING with the 1927 Old Age Pensions Act, Canadian provinces had offered income supplements to the elderly on a means-tested basis, with federal cost-sharing to help finance the program. But the Old Age Security Act of 1951 created a uniform federal system of old-age pensions financed by federal taxes and administered through a network of regional, district, and local offices of the Income Security Program Branch of Health and Welfare Canada, and provided regardless of income. Originally limited to persons over 70, this payment is currently provided to all persons over 65 who have lived in Canada for forty years after attaining the age of 18. Partial payments are made on a prorated basis to those who fail to meet the full residency requirement. OAS payments are made at a flat amount, regardless of income, with the benefits increasing annually according to the Consumer Price Index. In January 1984, the OAS payment for an individual who met the full residency requirement was $263.78 per month. OAS income is taxable.

Guaranteed Income Supplement (GIS)

The GIS was established in 1967 to bring to a minimum level the incomes of pensioners who relied largely on the OAS for income. The payment is based on the person's income in the preceding year, with the maximum GIS being reduced $1 a month for every $2 of income. For married couples, each spouse is considered to earn half the family income. In January 1984, the maximum GIS payment was $265.60 for a single person or a person whose spouse was not on OAS, and $204.86 for each partner of a married couple. Therefore, if OAS and GIS were the only source of income, an individual would have been guaranteed $529.38, and a couple $937.28, in monthly income.

Spouse's Allowance

In 1975, the federal government established a Spouse's Allowance for the pensioner's spouse aged 60 to 64. The maximum Spouse's Allowance was set at the OAS payment plus the maximum GIS married rate. Like the OAS, the Spouse's Allowance is subjected to a prorated residency requirement. It is also income-tested for the portion that exceeds the OAS maximum. The maximum Spouse's Allowance was $468.64 in January 1984. Unlike the OAS, the GIS and Spouse's Allowance benefits are not taxable.

Canada Pension Plan/Quebec Pension Plan

The Canada Pension Plan, introduced in January 1966, applies to all provinces except Quebec, which has exercised its constitutional prerogative to establish a similar plan for people working in Quebec in lieu of the CPP. Employees contribute 1.8 percent of their earnings up to a "maximum pensionable" ceiling in a compulsory plan, and these contributions are matched by the employer. In 1984, the first $2,000 of earnings was exempt from this payroll tax, and the maximum pensionable amount was $20,800. (The upper limit rises by an established formula, and the lower limit is set at 10 percent of the upper limit.)

Benefits under the plan include a retirement pension calculated at 25 percent of the person's average adjusted contributory career earnings; a disability pension calculated with a flat-rate portion, and an earnings-related portion that equals 75 percent of the imputed retirement pension; a survivor's pension calculated by a flat rate and 37.5 percent of the spouse's imputed retirement benefit (payable to spouses between 45 and 64 years of age, or with dependent children, or a disability). There is a pro-rated reduction in this benefit when the spouse is between 35 and 45, is not disabled, and has no children (a spouse under age 35 is ineligible until reaching 65 unless she has children or is disabled); and a death benefit to the estate, which is a lump sum equal to six months of a retirement pension to a maximum of 10 percent of the maximum pensionable earnings in the year of death (e.g., $1,600 in 1982). There is also a disabled contributor's child benefit and an orphan's benefit, each consisting of a fixed monthly amount payable on behalf of a dependent child of a recipient of a disability or survivor's pension.

In 1984, the maximum benefit for the monthly retirement pension was $387.50. The Quebec Plan is similar to the CPP with only slight variations in its contribution and benefit structure. Benefits under these two pension plans are taxable. Table 2.7 summarizes the coverage of the various federal income programs.

Provincial Income Supplements

Six provinces, the Northwest Territories, and the Yukon have chosen to supplement the OAS/GIS standard of guaranteed income (CYB 1981). These programs are generally available to GIS (and/or Spouse's Allowance) recipients and thus income-tested on that basis. For the most part, those supplements are not cost-shared by the federal government. In 1980, for example, Ontario provided a single pensioner a monthly supplement of $48.88, and a married pensioner $74.95. This Guaranteed Annual Income System (GAINS) cost Ontario almost $90 million in 1982–83. British Columbia had a similar GAIN program, which, in addition, guaranteed an income to persons age 60 to 64. In 1979, British Columbia's monthly maximum supplement for OAS pensioners was $38.88 ($49.83 for couples with both spouses eligible). The guaranteed income for persons 60 to 64 not covered by the federal spouse's allowance program was $305 (or $580 for a couple with both eligible). Manitoba's supplement for low-income elderly persons amounted to $46.82 for a single person and $50.58 (each) for a couple per quarter in 1982–83. Saskatchewan, Alberta, and Nova Scotia also had provincial supplemental income programs for the elderly in place by 1980, but the programs vary from province to province and are not easily compared.

REFERENCE

CYB (*Canada Year Book, 1980–81*) 1981. Statistics Canada, Minister of Supply and Services, Ottawa.

APPENDIX B

Homemaker Services in the Vancouver Long-Term Care Program

Excerpts from *Information and Proposal Documents for Agencies Wishing To Provide Homemaker Services on Behalf of the Vancouver Long-Term Care Program, Effective April 1, 1984.* Vancouver Long-Term Care Program, Vancouver Health Department, September 1, 1983, Tender No. 28–83–13.

THIS appendix contains the questionnaire to be completed by applicants, pp. 14–57 of the original, modified to fit a standardized format. For information, contact Michael Sorochan, Administrator, the Vancouver Long-Term Care Program, Vancouver Health Department.

PROPOSAL SUBMISSION FOR THE PROVISION OF HOMEMAKER SERVICES ON BEHALF OF THE VANCOUVER LONG-TERM CARE PROGRAM

I. GENERAL INFORMATION

1. Name of Agency:
   (a) If a company, attach a copy of the company charter following this page.
   (b) If a nonprofit society, attach a copy of the society's constitution and registration under the Societies Act following this page.

2. Location of Agency:
   (a) Local address _____
   (b) Head Office address _____
   (c) To which office should correspondence regarding this RFP be addressed? _____

3. Local telephone number of Agency _____

4. Geographic boundaries of area served by Agency:
   (a) Indicate on attached map areas presently serviced within the City of Vancouver (Map One).
   (b) Indicate on attached map areas your agency would prefer to serve within the City of Vancouver (Map Two).

5. Name the designated contact person(s) with regard to this proposal: _____

6. Was any resource person(s) excluding those within your own *local* agency asked to assist in the preparation of this document?

   Yes _____ No _____ If Yes, identify outside resource.

II. ORGANIZATION/MANAGEMENT

Organization and Senior Management

1. Identify the *principals* of your organization. If a corporation, identify owners, partners, and members of the board. If a nonprofit society, identify members of the board and executive director/administrator.

Name	Position/Tenure	Occupation

2. If any of the previously listed individuals have specific operational duties with respect to the agency, complete the following:

Individual's Name	Duties

3. If your agency has a head office not located in Vancouver, what administrative responsibilities, duties, or functions are handled outside your local Vancouver office (e.g., billing, payroll, policy, etc.)?

4. Outline your agency's history, goals, objectives, philosophy, experience, and any other pertinent information.

5. Describe methods used by your agency to evaluate your administrative and operational practices. Give examples of changes which resulted from such an evaluation.

6. Does your agency have an established mechanism for on-going review and evaluation of the quality of your homemaker service? If YES, please describe mechanism and any changes which have resulted from such reviews.

7. (a) Does your agency have a field policy and procedures manual?

   Yes _____ No _____

   (b) How do you make it available to staff?

   (c) Enclose one copy of your agency's policy and procedure manual and state how long it has been in existence.

8. (a) Is your agency presently providing homemaker service to the Vancouver Long-Term Care Program?

   Yes _____ No _____ Starting Date _____

(b)   Number of clients actively served at this time.

(c)   Percentage of clients by care level and purchased in June 1983:

	PC	IC1	IC2	IC3	Ex.Care
LTC	____	____	____	____	____
MHR	____	____	____	____	____
Home Nursing Care Pgm. (hospital replacement)	____	____	____	____	____
Other	____	____	____	____	____

(d)   Name the organizations which have been a source of referral or have purchased homemaker service from your agency over the last three years. Include the following information for each organization:

- Name of organization
- Name of manager/supervisor
- His/her address and telephone number
- Area where service provided and for what period
- Description of clienteles served
- Average number of clients actively served per month
- Average hours of homemaker service per month billed to the organization

9. Attach or outline your agency's organizational chart below. Include the structure of the organization and all levels of management, including supervisory staff.

(a)   For each organizational position, provide the following information:

- Position title
- Incumbent's name(s)
- Qualifications/educational level

(b)   If any of the above positions are not full time, indicate why, hours per week, and what coverage there is for the position when this employee is not working.

_____

_____

(c)   Describe what references you require and how you check these references.

_____

_____

(d) Attach a copy of your existing or proposed policy on hiring procedures. State how long existing written policy has been in effect.

10. It will be a requirement of the Long Term Care Program that agencies ensure their employees are medically, emotionally and physically able to perform all homemaker tasks.

(a) Briefly describe the medical information you require.

(b) Attach a copy of your existing or proposed policy on this procedure. State how long existing written policy has been in effect.

(c) If your agency has a medical form for prospective employees, attach a copy.

11. It will be a requirement of the Vancouver Long Term Care Program that agencies hire persons who can communicate effectively with their clients and with agency staff. (a) Briefly describe your criteria and method of determining whether a prospective employee meets them. (b) Attach a copy of your existing or proposed policy in this regard. State how long existing written policy has been in effect.

12. Does your agency have a probationary period for new employees? If YES, attach a copy of your existing or proposed policy in this regard. State how long existing written policy has been in effect.

Personnel Practices

13. It will be a requirement of the Vancouver Long-Term Care Program that agencies ensure their staff are appropriately dressed, groomed, and identified.

(a) Attach a copy of your staff policy on this issue and describe how each staff member is advised of this policy. State how long existing written policy has been in effect.

(b) Describe the steps taken in the event of noncompliance.

14. It will be a requirement of the Vancouver Long Term Care Program that agencies ensure their homemakers do not smoke while providing service.

(a) Attach a copy of your staff directive on this policy and describe briefly how each staff member is advised of it. State how long existing written policy has been in effect.

(b) Describe the steps taken in the event of noncompliance.

15. It will be a requirement of the Vancouver Long-Term Care Program that agencies have a policy regarding agency staff nonacceptance of gifts/gratuities from Long Term Care clients and/or significant others.

   (a) Attach a copy of your existing or proposed staff policy on this issue. State how long existing written policy has been in effect.

   (b) Describe the steps taken in the event of noncompliance.

16. It will be a requirement of the Vancouver Long-Term Care Program that agencies have a policy regarding confidentiality of client information.

   (a) Attach a copy of your existing written or proposed policy on this issue. State how long existing written policy has been in effect.

   (b) Describe the steps taken in the event of noncompliance.

17. It will be a requirement of the Vancouver Long-Term Care Program that homemaker agencies provide only services authorized by LTC staff (e.g., as outlined in the LTC Home Support Plan Form).

   (a) Briefly describe the method(s) used by your agency to ensure that the services provided by the homemaker are, in fact, the services ordered by Long Term Care.

   (b) Attach a copy of any existing or proposed staff policy dealing with this issue. State how long existing policy has been in use by your agency.

18. Homemakers may be requested to handle client's personal funds.

   (a) Attach a copy of your agency's existing written or proposed policy regarding this matter. State how long existing written policy has been in effect.

   (b) Indicate what protective mechanisms are implemented to safeguard rights of client and homemaker when this service has been requested by Long-Term Care.

19. Indicate how your agency supervisors ensure that homemakers are adhering to the above personnel practices (Items 15–20).

20. Briefly describe the method(s) used by your agency to validate the homemaker's time spent in providing service to a Long-Term Care patient. Attach a copy of any existing or proposed

forms used to verify that the hours of service recorded are accurate. State how long existing forms have been in use by your agency.

III. TECHNICAL ASPECTS OF STAFFING AND SERVICE DELIVERY

General Information

1. How many homemakers do you have on staff?
   Full Time _____ Half Time _____ Less than Half Time _____

2. How many male homemakers do you have on staff?
   Full Time _____ Half Time _____ Less than Half Time _____

3. What percentage of your present homemakers have been with your agency for:
   Less than 1 year   _____
   1–2 years   _____
   2–4 years   _____
   More than 4 years   _____

Staff Competency

4. (a) What percent of your present homemakers have completed a community college homemaking training course?
   (b) What percent are presently enrolled in such a course?
   (c) What incentives, if any, do you offer homemakers to complete the course?

5. How many of your present homemakers have relevant training other than the community college homemaker training course? Give details.

6. It will be a requirement of the Vancouver Long Term Care Program that all homemakers assigned to clients requiring assistance with activities of daily living will be trained to perform the Personal Assistance tasks as defined in Attachment I(A). Attach a copy of your existing or proposed staff policy on this issue. State how long existing written policy has been in effect.

7. The Vancouver Long Term Care Program will require that, in the event an untrained/inexperienced homemaker is called upon to provide personal assistance to a Long Term Care client, such homemaker must be instructed by a qualified

professional. What is your agency's procedure when there is no qualified homemaker available to provide personal services? Attach a copy of your existing written or proposed policy on this issue. State how long existing written policy has been in existence.

8. Indicate the number of homemakers in your agency who speak a second language.

9. It will be a requirement of the Vancouver Long Term Care Program that agencies provide pre-employment orientation for new staff, which will include the contents of "Homemaker Job Orientation" (Attachment #3) in addition to relevant Long-Term Care policies and procedures. Attach your existing written or proposed orientation procedure for the following staff: homemakers, supervisors. State how long existing written procedure has been in effect.

   (a) For homemakers ————————————————————————
   (b) For supervisors ————————————————————————

10. It will be a requirement of the Vancouver Long Term Care Program that agencies have regular in-service education programs.

   (a) Attach existing written or proposed policy concerning staff in-service education. State how long existing written policy has been in effect.
   (b) State frequency of in-service education programs.
   (c) State what incentives are used to motivate staff to attend in-service programs.
   (d) State approximate levels of attendance at in-service programs.
   (e) Describe your in-service programs for the past year under the following headings:

Instructor	Position	Subject and Date(s) Given
————	————	————————————
————	————	————————————
————	————	————————————

11. (a) Briefly describe your staff evaluation procedures.
    (b) State frequency of formal staff performance evaluation.
    (c) State who is responsible for evaluation of various levels of staff.

Homemakers————————————————————————

Supervisors————————————————————————

Other————————————————————————————

(d) Does your agency have staff evaluation forms currently in use?

Yes _____ No _____

If Yes, attach form(s) to this page.

(e) What steps does your agency take in the event that an employee is found to be unsatisfactory?

Homemaker Supervision

It will be a requirement of the Vancouver Long-Term Care Program that agencies provide supervision to the homemaker.

12. How many field supervisors do you have on staff?

Full Time _____ Part Time _____

(a) Briefly describe what education, training, and experience you require of a field supervisor?

(b) State the number and percent of field supervisors in your agency who speak a second language.

(c) What is the current staffing ratio of supervisors to homemakers?

(d) Describe the basis used to determine the ratio of your field supervisors to homemakers?

13. (a) How often does the field supervisor visit a homemaker who is caring for:

- a client who requires minimal homemaking service?
- a client who requires heavy homemaking service?
- a client who requires personal assistance?
- a client who requires personal assistance and whose condition is fluctuating or unstable?
- a client who requires a live-in homemaker?

(b) Attach a copy of your existing written or proposed policy which outlines how often and on what basis visits by the supervisor are made. State how long the existing written policy has been in effect.

14. What method(s) is used by the field supervisor to keep office staff informed of client's status?

15. It will be a requirement of the Vancouver Long-Term Care Program that agencies encourage independence in clients.
    (a) Describe how your agency and staff reinforce the concept of helping clients maintain maximum independence?
    (b) Attach existing written or proposed agency policy regarding the above and state how long existing written policy has been in effect.

Reporting

16. It will be a requirement of the Vancouver Long-Term Care Program that agencies have procedures for notifying Long-Term Care:
    (a) of their ability to provide requested service;
    (b) the date service will start;
    (c) commencement of service when referred directly to agency from a hospital social worker;
    (d) of changes in a client's condition requiring immediate adjustment in homemaker hours and care plan;
    (e) when reduction of homemaker services seems appropriate;
    (f) of client's admission to hospital;
    (g) of client's temporary or permanent cancellation of service;
    (h) when they wish to terminate service with a specific Long-Term Care client.

    Attach copies of existing written or proposed procedures for each item and state how long the existing procedures have been in effect.

17. It will be a requirement of the Vancouver Long-Term Care Program that agencies provide regular, relevant information about a client's status.
    (a) How often do your supervisors submit a written report to Long-Term Care about the status of:
       • a client who requires minimal homemaking service?
       • a client who requires heavy homemaking service?
       • a client who requires personal assistance?
       • a client who requires personal assistance and
       • a client who requires a live-in homemaker?

(b) Attach an example of an existing or proposed completed report form to this page. State how long the existing form has been in effect.

Scheduling Service

18. (a) In organizing schedules for homemakers, what methods does your agency use to attempt to meet unique requirements of clients (i.e. flexibility of scheduling)?

(b) What are the minimum hours of homemaker service you bill Long Term Care to meet the above needs?

Emergency Coverage

19. It will be a requirement of the Vancouver Long-Term Care Program that agencies establish a system so that emergencies occurring with their LTC clients can be responded to outside of regular office hours. Attach your existing written or proposed procedure for dealing with a client emergency situation. State how long existing written procedure has been in effect.

Client Billing

20. Some clients are required by Long-Term Care to pay a daily fee for homemaker service. It will be a requirement of the Vancouver Long-Term Care Program that the agency collect the fee from the client and deduct that amount from its billing to the Long-Term Care Program.

(a) Briefly describe the method(s) used by your agency to collect any assessed daily fee from clients.

(b) Attach a copy of the form used by your agency to bill clients for a daily fee, or to bill them for hours of service which they purchase privately (purchase from you beyond those ordered by Long Term Care).

(c) What is your billing schedule for client fees?

(d) Do you require payment in advance of the service delivered?

Yes _____ No _____

(e) What is your agency's average time delay in billing clients · for service provided?

Special Services

21. Services are continually changing to meet the needs of Long Term Care clients.

(a) Do you provide or intend to provide the following services:

	Currently Provide	Plan to Provide
• respite (companion) service	Yes__No__	Yes__No__
• bath team	Yes__No__	Yes__No__
• emergency live-in homemaker	Yes__No__	Yes__No__
• contract live-in homemaker	Yes__No__	Yes__No__

(b) If Yes, attach description of service and include relevant terms of agreement for each service (e.g., minimum hours) and how long you have provided these services.

(c) Certain client circumstances require live-in homemaker coverage. What special financial or other benefits do you offer homemakers to encourage acceptance of such a placement?

22. Briefly describe any other services your agency has developed (or would propose developing) to meet the needs of Vancouver Long-Term Care clients.

Perceived Community Needs

23. As providers of service, agencies are in a position to become knowledgeable about a community.

(a) Do you perceive any unique factors or needs in the community which are relevant to LTC clients?

Yes _____ No_____

(b) If Yes, list factors or needs and indicate how you have determined that these factors or needs exist.

IV. FINANCIAL AND COST ASPECTS

Financial and Cost Considerations

1. What are your 1983–84 hourly rates and the number of hours projected to be delivered to the Vancouver Long-Term Care Program in the 1983–84 fiscal year (i.e., April 1, 1983–March 31, 1984)?

2. The number of homemaker hours purchased from successful bidders will be based on several factors, e.g., evaluation of RFP's, number of agencies participating from both profit and nonprofit sectors, total allocation of hours to Vancouver Long-Term Care Program, maximum limits per agency, and desire of agency. When completing the attached "Hourly Homemaker Rate Schedule," several blocks of hours should be completed in the event the total number of hours allocated to any agency is less than they desire and have indicated on the schedule. The hourly rate arrived at is intended to be a "blended" or "average" rate for provision of services listed in 3(b) to (f) on the following page. Also, considering the principle of "economies of scale," it is anticipated that with each increase in blocks of hours there would be a commensurate decrease in the hourly rate. The maximum number of hours contracted from any one agency will not exceed 25% (estimated 350,000 hours for 1984–85) of the total program allocation of hours, and the minimum will be 25,000 hours. Cost breakdown by various categories (e.g., homemaker salaries and benefits, etc.) is required.

    Complete the attached "Hourly Homemaker Rate Schedule for 1984–85 Fiscal Year" as per the attached example (minimum gradation 5,000 hours) and provide the following information:

    (a) Indicate the minimum number of hours your agency would be willing to provide and the "blended" hourly rate (as you have calculated on the attached "Homemaker Hourly Rate Schedule").

    (b) Indicate the maximum number of hours your agency would be willing to provide and the "blended" hourly rate (as you have calculated on the attached "Homemaker Hourly Rate Schedule").

3. The Vancouver Long-Term Care Program also wishes to consider the option of purchasing service at specific rates for

designated services. What would be your hourly rate for the provision of the following services in the 1984–85 fiscal year:

(a) Respite (companion) service _____

(b) Bath team service _____

(c) Emergency live-in service _____

(d) Contract live-in service _____

(e) Personal assistance services only or a combination of personal assistance and other purchased services (see attachment 1A and 1B)_____

(f) Nonpersonal assistance services only (See attachment 1B)
_____

(g) Any other special services _____

4. There are other factors beyond the hourly rate that affect the total cost of purchasing service from a homemaker agency.

(a) What is the minimum number of hours that the Vancouver Long Term Care Program can purchase from your agency per homemaker visit?

(b) Item #19 in General Terms and Conditions outlines the Vancouver Long-Term Care Program policy regarding overtime rates. State the formula used by your agency to establish an overtime rate(s).

(c) On occasion clients are not home for a regularly scheduled visit. What steps are taken to determine whether a client will be available for the next visit and to ensure that the homemaker visit is not unnecessarily repeated?

Attach your existing written or proposed policy on this matter. State how long policy has been in effect.

(d) There are occasions when a homemaker visits a Long-Term Care client who, for some reason, refuses service or who may not be home due to unforeseen circumstances. Under these and similar circumstances, what is your agency's policy in regard to billing the Vancouver Long-Term Care Program? Attach your existing written or proposed policy on this matter. State how long policy has been in effect.

(e) What is your agency's policy in regards to homemaker travel time and the billing of such time to the Vancouver Long-Term Care Program? Attach your existing written or proposed policy on this matter. State how long policy has been in effect.

(f) What is your agency's policy in regards to requiring the Vancouver Long-Term Care Program to pay relief time for homemakers who are working a live-in schedule? Attach your existing written or proposed policy on this matter. State how long policy has been in effect.

(g) The Vancouver Long-Term Care Program will require that homemaker agencies notify Long-Term Care staff as soon as possible when a reduction of homemaker hours to a client appears appropriate. What method(s) does your agency use to accomplish this task?

(h) What procedures or innovative service delivery methods does your agency have that result in more cost-effective use of homemaker hours?

Attach your existing written or proposed policy on this matter. State how long policy has been in effect.

SERVICES PURCHASED BY THE VANCOUVER LONG-TERM CARE PROGRAM FROM HOMEMAKER AGENCIES

The following services describe the homemaker's role in relation to personal assistance activities. The Long-Term Care Program does not purchase nursing services under the home support component. Licensed health professionals, when hired as homemakers by homemaker agencies, must work within the following guidelines as outlined below by the Interdisciplinary Personal Assistance Committee, September 9, 1981:

1. All homemakers assigned to clients requiring assistance with activities of daily living will be trained to perform Personal Assistance tasks, as defined in the Provincial Homemaker Training Program (Basic).

2. The homemaker agency assumes responsibility for assessing the individual skills of homemaker staff, and assigning and supervising homemakers appropriately.

3. The purchaser of service will identify services which it wishes to purchase from the homemaker agency and will identify the involvement of other agencies.

4. The homemaker agency will provide service within its capabilities and policies.

5. The Personal Assistance tasks will be adapted to each client's specific needs.
    (a) Hairwashing: routine wash, set, and dry
    (b) Shaving: by safety or electric razor
    (c) Dressing
    (d) Normal oral hygiene: i.e., brushing teeth, dentures
    (e) Infant care: preparing infant formula from written instructions
    (f) Washing: assisting the client to wash himself

(g) Bathing: i.e., bed bath, tub bath (includes sitting in a tub or shower and using a shower attachment) and sponge bath

(h) Toileting: i.e., bed pans, toilet, commode, or urinal

(i) May assist walking without mechanical aid

(j) Assist walking with mechanical aids (e.g., crutches—axillary and elbow, walking aids, canes, or tripod canes)

(k) Special diet: prepare from written instructions

(l) Assist normal feeding process, including use of eating aids

(m) Take temperature

(n) Assist client to transfer: e.g., bed to chair, chair to bed, chair to toilet or commode, toilet or commode to chair, chair to bathtub, bathtub to chair, floor to chair, chair to floor; in bed: up and down, side to side

(o) Nail care: assist with simple routine nail care

(p) Measure urine output

(q) Make an occupied bed

(r) Assist in maintaining healthy skin

(s) Assist client who is responsible for own medication: e.g., provide glass of water, spoon, open bottle

(t) Assist client who is responsible for his prosthesis

(u) Apply general first aid procedures

(v) Assist client who is experiencing symptoms of common maladies (e.g., vomiting, coughing, diarrhea)

6. Special tasks when service is ordered by the Long-Term Care Program.

(a) Housework: Perform or help clients perform housework to maintain normal standards of health and cleanliness. Examples are sweeping, vacuuming, dusting, mopping, cleaning ovens, defrosting refrigerators, etc.

(b) Laundry· Do, or help clients do their laundry, which includes washing, drying, ironing, and mending clothes used by the client.

(c) Cooking: Prepare or help clients prepare meals, which includes planning meals and cleaning up after meals.

(d) Shopping and Errands: Do essential errands and do essential shopping for clients who are not able, where there are no family or other resources to provide the service.

(e) Escort: Go with clients who cannot travel alone to get essential services such as medical appointments or banking, where there are no family or other resources to provide the service.

(f) Communications: Assist client with necessary communications by helping with telephoning.

(g) Household heavy cleaning: Perform or help client perform heavy cleaning tasks such as wall washing and washing of outside windows.

(h) Remediation of Safety Hazards*: Perform, or help clients perform, limited repairs to household and/or grounds needed for safety reasons, and not requiring the skills of a qualified tradesman. This is an exceptional service which must be pre-authorized by Long-Term Care and only for specific reasons, and then only after all family, financial and community resources have been exhausted. (This service excludes grass cutting.)

---

*It is not required that all agencies have staff for the provision of these services. It is required that those agencies not wanting to provide these services directly make arrangements through other agencies or individuals (with prior written approval of the Contracting Officer or delegate) so that their clients may receive these services if authorized by Long-Term Care. The Vancouver Long-Term Care is willing to assist any agency in working out such arrangements.

VANCOUVER LONG-TERM CARE PROGRAM
REQUIREMENTS OF HOMEMAKER AGENCIES

The Vancouver Long-Term Care Program circulated "Expectations of Homemaker Agencies" in December 1981. At that time it was recognized some of the expectations were being met and others were being actively worked on. April 1, 1982, was the date by which all expectations should have been met.

The Vancouver Long-Term Care Program is now redefining these expectations as requirements effective April 1, 1984. The requirements are substantially similar to the December 1981 expectations, with a few minor revisions.

I. HIRING AND PERSONNEL PRACTICES

All agencies will be required to:

1. Screen prospective employees through personal interviews, checking business and personal references following generally accepted personnel practices.

2. Obtain medical certificates confirming a person's medical, emotional and physical ability to perform all homemaker tasks.

3. Hire persons who can communicate effectively with their clients and with agency staff.

4. Be bonded and all employees eligible for bonding.

5. Ensure their staff are appropriately dressed, groomed and identified.

6. Ensure their homemakers do not smoke on the premises of non-smoking clients or while providing service to any client.

7. Assume responsibility for assessing the individual skills of the homemaker and assigning homemaker appropriately.

8. Have a policy of non-acceptance of gifts and gratuities for agency staff.

9. Have a policy regarding confidentiality of client information.

II. ORIENTATION

Each agency will include in its pre-employment orientation for new staff the contents of "Homemaker Job Orientation" (Attachment #3) and relevant Long-Term Care policies and procedures. For previously trained persons, an agency may omit specific areas of established homemaker orientation.

III. IN-SERVICE EDUCATION

It will be required that each agency have regular ongoing in-service education programs with sessions conducted at least once a month aimed at upgrading skills and knowledge. In-service programs should cover a wide range of subjects, including information on various diseases and conditions homemakers are likely to encounter.

IV. SUPERVISION

The Vancouver Long-Term Care Program will require that each agency provide supervision to the homemaker in the provision of care to the client, recognizing the often delicate and difficult task the homemaker has in providing only for those needed functions while encouraging the person to be independent.

The emphasis of this supervision should be to direct and support the homemaker:

1. on initial placement with a new client to establish or reinforce a work plan and the location of equipment and supplies.

2. on a continuing basis, depending upon the skills of the homemaker and the complexity of the situation.

3. on request of Long-Term Care or Home Care.

The overall coordination, provision and supervision of home support services is the joint responsibility of the Long-Term Care staff and agency providing service. Input by the supervisors and homemakers into the home support plan is essential for its continued success.

V. INSURANCE

It will be required that each homemaker agency have at least one million dollars of public liability insurance.

VI. REPORTING

1. Copies of supervisors reports recommending or noting any significant changes in the care plan or care needs must be forwarded to Long-Term Care. All supervisors reports must be filed at the agency and available to Long-Term Care on request.

2. As Long-Term Care purchases homemaking sercices on behalf of the client, agency concerns regarding provision of this service should be directed to Long-Term Care. Any adjustments in the homemaker hours must be approved by Long-Term Care staff.

3. Long-Term Care will not pay for unauthorized nonemergency increase in service hours (this does not apply in case of emergency). In case of emergency, Long-Term Care expects to be contacted as soon as possible.

4. If an agency is unable to provide the Long-Term Care Program authorized services to a client, Long-Term Care requires immediate notification.

5. The agency is required to inform Long-Term Care:
    (a) of the date homemaker service will start;
    (b) of commencement of service referred directly to an agency from a hospital social worker;
    (c) of changes in a client's condition requiring immediate adjustment in homemaker hours and care plan;

(d) when reduction of homemaker service to a client seems appropriate;

(e) of a client's admission to hospital;

(f) of a client's temporary or permanent cancellation of service.

6. Long-Term Care requires that homemakers provide services as requested and authorized by Long-Term Care Program staff.

7. If an agency wishes to terminate service with a client, Long-Term Care must be notified. If termination is due to the difficulty in providing service to the client, Long-Term Care requires adequate notice and a written summary outlining the problems in service provision.

8. Long-Term Care requires homemaker agencies to recognize and adopt the philosophy of encouraging independence and recommend to Long-Term Care as soon as possible a reduction of homemaker service where appropriate.

VII. LONG-TERM CARE POLICIES AND PROCEDURES

1. It is required that agencies conform with Long-Term Care policy and procedures.

2. All homemakers assigned to clients requiring assistance with activities of daily living will be trained to perform the Personal Assistance tasks, as defined in the Provincial Homemaker Training Program (Revised Guidelines to Homemakers in Providing Personal Assistance to Individuals, December 15, 1981). In the event that an untrained/inexperienced homemaker is called upon to provide personal assistance to a Long-Term Care client, the Vancouver Long-Term Care Program requires that such homemaker be instructed by a qualified professional. The professional must be satisfied that the homemaker is competent to provide the required service to a specific client.

3. It is required that agencies provide the full range of services outlined in Attachment I(A) and (B).

VIII. EMERGENCY COVERAGE

It is required that homemaker agencies establish a system so that emergencies occurring with Long-Term Care clients can be responded to outside of regular office hours.

Index

Selected Rand Books

Armor, David J., J. Michael Polich, and Harriet B. Stambul. *Alcoholism and Treatment.* New York: John Wiley & Sons, Inc., 1978.

Brelsford, William M., and Daniel A. Relles. *STATLIB: A Statistical Computing Library.* Englewood Cliffs, N.J.: Prentice-Hall, Inc., 1981.

Brewer, Garry D., and James S. Kakalik. *Handicapped Children: Strategies for Improving Services.* New York: McGraw-Hill Book Company, Inc., 1979.

Comstock, George, Steven Chaffee, Natan Katzman, Maxwell McCombs, and Donald Roberts. *Television and Human Behavior.* New York: Columbia University Press, 1978.

Crain, Robert L., Rita E. Mahard, and Ruth E. Narot. *Making Desegregation Work: How Schools Create Social Climates.* Cambridge, Mass.: Ballinger Publishing Company, 1982.

Curry, Jane L. (trans. and ed.). *The Black Book of Polish Censorship.* New York: Random House, Inc., 1984.

Downs, Anthony. *Inside Bureaucracy.* Boston, Mass.: Little, Brown and Company, 1967.

Greenwood, Peter W., Jan M. Chaiken, and Joan Petersilia. *The Criminal Investigation Process.* Lexington, Mass.: Lexington Books, D. C. Heath and Company, 1977.

Kane, Robert L., David H. Solomon, John C. Beck, Emmett B. Keeler, and Rosalie A. Kane. *Geriatrics in the United States: Manpower Projections and Training Considerations.* Lexington, Mass.: Lexington Books, D. C. Heath and Company, 1981.

Kane, Rosalie A., and Robert L. Kane. *Assessing the Elderly: A Practical Guide to Measurement.* Lexington, Mass.: Lexington Books, D. C. Heath and Company, 1981.

Lowry, Ira S. (ed.). *Experimenting with Housing Allowances: The Final Report of the Housing Assistance Supply Experiment.* Cambridge, Mass.: Oelgeschlager, Gunn & Hain, Publishers, 1983.

Meyer, J. R., J. F. Kain, and M. Wohl. *The Urban Transportation Problem.* Cambridge, Mass.: Harvard University Press, 1965.

Morris, Carl N., and John E. Rolph. *Introduction to Data Analysis and Statistical Inference.* Englewood Cliffs, N.J.: Prentice-Hall, Inc., 1901.

Park, Rolla Edward (ed). *The Role of Analysis in Regulatory Decisionmaking: The Case of Cable Television.* Lexington, Mass.: Lexington Books, D. C. Heath and Company, 1973.

Quade, Edward S. *Analysis for Public Decisions.* New York: American Elsevier Publishing Company, Inc., 1975. Second Edition, 1982.

Sharpe, William F. *The Economics of Computers*. New York: Columbia University Press, 1969.

Smith, James P. (ed.). *Female Labor Supply: Theory and Estimation*. Princeton, N.J.: Princeton University Press, 1980.

Timpane, Michael (ed.). *The Federal Interest in Financing Schooling*. Cambridge, Mass.: Ballinger Publishing Company, 1978.

Turn, Rein. *Computers in the 1980s*. New York: Columbia University Press, 1974.

Walker, Warren E., Jan M. Chaiken, and Edward J. Ignall (eds.). *Fire Department Deployment Analysis, A Public Policy Analysis Case Study: The Rand Fire Project*. New York: Elsevier North-Holland, Inc., 1979.